M

Law of Trusts

MACMILLAN LAW MASTERS

Series Editor: Marise Cremona

Law of Trusts

Patrick McLoughlin
Solicitor, Theodore Goddard

and

Catherine Rendell
*Senior Lecturer in Law
at the University of Hertfordshire*

Law series editor:
Marise Cremona

*Senior Fellow
Centre for Commerical Law Studies
Queen Mary and Westfield College
University of London*

MACMILLAN

First published 1992 by
THE MACMILLAN PRESS LTD
Houndmills, Basingstoke, Hampshire RG21 2XS
and London
Companies and representatives
throughout the world

ISBN 0–333–54232–0

A catalogue record for this book is available
from the British Library.

10 9 8 7 6 5
00 99 98

Printed in Hong Kong

Contents

**PART III   THE EXPRESS TRUST AS A MECHANISM FOR
PROTECTING PRIVATE WEALTH**

Table of Cases

Table of Statutes

Part I

Nature of Trusts

1 Nature of Trusts

1.1 What is a Trust?

Description

On the surface the trust is a simple idea. Fundamentally, one person (a settlor) entrusts property to another (a trustee) to look after it for the benefit of a third person (a beneficiary).

The concept has, however, caused commentators much difficulty and there are dozens (see Hart (1899) 15 LQR 294 and Scott (1955) 71 LQR 39) of suggested definitions or descriptions of the trust. The difficulty in description of the trust is caused mainly by the complication which arises from attempting to analyse who owns the property which is the subject matter of the trust. The control and management of the property is vested in the trustee whilst the beneficiary is intended to receive the profits and benefit from the property. In some legal systems the beneficiary has been regarded as the owner of the property, but in England the courts of common law initially regarded the trustee as the owner. By regarding the trustee as the owner of the property the courts of common law created a difficulty. They considered ownership to be an absolute concept. Consequently the trustee was considered to be the absolute owner of the property. If the trustee was the absolute owner, it followed that the beneficiary could have no interest. If the beneficiary had no interest the trustee could not be subject to an obligation in respect of the property in favour of the beneficiary. Thus the courts of common law refused to recognise the obligation of trust in respect of property (see Figure 1.1).

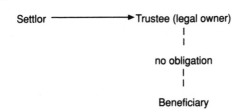

Figure 1.1 The trust and the common law

This was of course a nonsense and unjustly made the trustee the absolute owner of the property even though this was not the intention of the settlor and had never been agreed between the settlor and the trustee. What was really intended was that some attributes of ownership (management and control) should be vested in the trustee, and others (the rights to benefit and profit) should be vested in the beneficiary. In other words, it was intended that there should be a division of the attributes of ownership but that neither the trustee nor the beneficiary should be absolute owner.

The manifest absurdity in the position at common law led to intervention by the King. The King was regarded as the supreme fountain of justice and persons aggrieved by decisions of the courts could petition the King for a remedy. The jurisdiction came to be delegated by the King to the Chancellor and his department of Chancery. The Chancery department eventually developed a court of Chancery doing equity in the name of the King. The Chancery recognised that in justice the obligation of entrustment should be enforced and it thus did so enforce it. It did not directly challenge the courts of common law in its analysis that the trustee was the owner of the property, but it did enforce the obligation in favour of the beneficiary, with the inevitable consequence that the trustee's ownership could no longer be regarded as absolute. The end result is a device whereby technically the trustee is the legal owner but the beneficiary is the owner in equity. The ownership of each is, however, limited and not absolute, since neither of them has all of the rights and powers which would accompany absolute ownership (see Figure 1.2).

Other factors which create difficulty for a definition of the trust include the fact that a trust may be created expressly or arise by implication; the fact that the trustee and beneficiary are sometimes one and the same person; and the fact that trusts are sometimes used for the furtherance of public purposes rather than private persons. The most favoured definition is that given by Underhill, that the trust is 'an equitable obligation binding a person (who is called a trustee) to deal with property over which he has control (which is called trust property) for the benefit of persons (who are called beneficiaries or cestuis que trust) of whom he

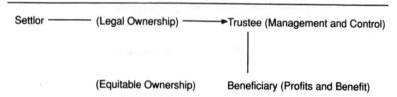

Figure 1.2 **The trust and the effect of equity**

may himself be one and any one of whom can enforce the obligation'. Even this favoured definition has been criticised as it does not cover charitable trusts or unenforceable purpose trusts (see Keeton and Sheridan, *Law of Trusts*, 10th edn, p.4).

Trusts in the 'higher' and 'lower' senses

The word 'trust' is often used in various contexts where no trust in the legal sense is intended. If one person trusts another but there is no legal obligation, a trust in the 'higher' sense of a moral obligation may arise but not in the 'lower' sense of a legal obligation. Ministers and public officials, for example, are often entrusted with possession and control of property without being given legal title. Similarly, the Crown may be trustee for members of the public without the public having any legal right or cause of action against the Crown. The distinction was emphasised by Megarry VC in the case of *Tito* v. *Waddell (No. 2)* [1977] Ch 106. Phosphate was discovered on Ocean Island in the Pacific Ocean at the beginning of the twentieth century. The mining rights were acquired by the governments of the United Kingdom, New Zealand and Australia, and royalties were paid to the islanders, the Banabans. Subsequently the Banabans felt that they had been exploited and claimed that the royalties paid were below 'proper' rates and argued that the Crown was subject to a trust or fiduciary duty to pay larger sums. The islanders relied to some extent upon the use of the word 'trust' in an ordinance of 1928. The Vice-Chancellor decided that the use of the term trust in respect of the Crown did not create a trust in the 'lower' legal sense enforceable in the courts but only a trust in the 'higher' sense of a governmental obligation. Such a trust was a moral obligation which might be 'enforced' through international pressure, but not by an action in the courts.

Trusts and powers

Sometimes a donor of property gives it to a donee and informs the donee of his or her wishes in respect of the property, but without intending to impose an obligation of trust upon the donee. One example would be where one family member gives property to another asking that the property should be used for the benefit of the family generally, but not wishing to create any legal relationship. In *Lambe* v. *Eames* (1871) 6 Ch App 597, a husband on his death gave his estate to his widow 'to be at her disposal in any way she may think best for the benefit of herself and family'. In these circumstances it was held that the widow was not a trustee but had a mere power to divide the property as her husband had indicated (see further section 3.1 on formal trusts). The donee of the property in these circumstances may retain the property for his or her own use.

Mere powers and trust powers

The power is a device very similar to a trust and the distinction is often a source of difficulty for students. The main cause for confusion is the difference between a 'mere power' to dispose of property of the type in *Lambe* v. *Eames* (above), where the donee of property has a power to dispose of it to others but is not under any duty to exercise it; and a 'trust power', where the transferee of property is a trustee and under the terms of the trust the trustee has a power to dispose of property. In the latter case the trustee is under a fiduciary duty to act in good faith and in a fiduciary manner and, if the trustee does not exercise the power a court probably will, particularly if the beneficiaries have given consideration for their beneficial interest: for instance, where the trust is a trust of pension funds (*Mettoy Pension Trustees Ltd* v. *Evans* [1990] 1 WLR 1587).

To add to the confusion there are other variants of powers, and since trusts also come in different forms it is difficult to identify differences between them which would apply to all situations, but below is an attempt to summarise the main differences between the two.

TRUST	**POWER**
A trust imposes an obligation upon the trustee. Whether there is a clear and certain intention to create a trust normally depends upon the words used by the settlor (see section 3.1).	A power gives an authority to the donee without creating an obligation.
Under a trust a beneficiary normally has a well defined interest in the trust property. Even if there is a discretionary trust (cf. section 7.4) where the trustees can decide whether and which beneficiaries should receive benefits, the beneficiaries can require the trustees to exercise their discretion fairly.	Under a power the objects have a mere hope that an interest will be appointed to them. They cannot normally require that the donee exercises the power either fairly or at all.
If trustees fail to distribute trust property the court can make an order for division.	If the donee of a power fails to exercise it the court cannot divide the property amongst the objects.
With a trust to appoint property amongst a class of persons there can be no gift over to other persons in default of an appointment in favour of the first class.	With a power to appoint property there may be a gift over in default of appointment.

The above summary should be referred to for guidance only, as the relationship between trusts and powers is a complex one, and the above distinctions would not necessarily apply to all cases (see further Hayton and Marshall, *Cases and Commentary on the Law of Trusts*, 8th edn, pp.126–31). The distinction will become clearer once the reader has a better understanding of the trust, and powers are considered further in Chapter 3.

1.2 Development of the Express Private Trust: The Use

The use

No person can pinpoint the moment of conception of the trust, and evidence of the early development of the trust is scarce. There is some record of the existence of its forerunner, the use, before the Norman Conquest (see Pollock and Maitland, *History of English Law*, 2nd edn, II, pp.229, 234), and further record of its being used as a temporary expedient to make provision for families and dependants whilst settlors went on crusades during the period 1066 to 1225 (Pollock and Maitland, II, p.231). Even in these early times the 'use' which was the predecessor of the trust was used as a device to avoid disadvantages which attached to particular situations. In the early thirteenth century Franciscan friars harnessed the use to circumvent their rule that prevented them from owning property. By ecclesiastical interpretation there was held to be no objection to land being conveyed to some town to the use of the friars (Pollock and Maitland, II, p.237–8).

Other chapters from the development of the trust tell the story of its being utilised for avoidance of rules. It was often used as an early tax avoidance device. During the thirteenth century land was held under the feudal system whereby persons held land from lords of manors. The lords were entitled to profitable feudal dues in certain circumstances. For example, when a tenant died and left an under-age heir the lord was entitled to the benefit of the land until the heir reached full age. If land was held by a corporation, such as a monastery, the lord of the manor lost these rights since the land was held by a tenant who was not under age and who never died. For this reason statute, principally the statutes of Mortmain, prevented the conveyance of land to religious bodies without licence from the King. This rule was evaded for some time by conveying land to feoffees (the early equivalent of trustees) to the use of a religious body. But just as Parliament today often passes legislation to close similar loopholes in the law, this particular method of avoidance was later prohibited by a statute of 1391 (15 Ric 2 c5).

The use was again seen in its avoidance role during the fourteenth and fifteenth centuries. During the fourteenth century there was a rule that land could not be passed on death by will. The reason for the prohibition was that it was presumed that the heir should inherit and that the land should not otherwise be disposed of. The prohibition could be avoided by the creation of a use during lifetime, to ensure that the beneficial interest passed on death to the intended donee. A further device used during the same period was the avoidance of feudal dues normally paid on inheritance of land by vesting the land in two joint feoffees so that if one died the other remained owner by survivorship, but not by inheritance.

The Statute of Uses: execution of the use

Although the use was popular amongst those persons who had to pay feudal dues, it was correspondingly disliked by the persons to whom dues should be paid. For this reason, the sixteenth century saw a strong attack on the use. The attack was initiated by the King by the introduction of the Statute of Uses in 1535. Megarry and Wade (*The Law of Real Property*, 5th edn, p.1166) explain: 'The King . . . was the one person who had all to gain and nothing to lose by the abolition of uses'; 'It was he alone who was always lord and never tenant.' '[T]he Statute of Uses was forced upon an extremely unwilling parliament by an extremely strong-willed King. It was very unpopular and was one of the excuses, if not one of the causes, of the great Catholic Rebellion known as the Pilgrimage of Grace' (Maitland, *Equity*, p.34). The main object of the statute was to turn uses into legal estates which would be subject to all the usual feudal incidents. It achieved this by 'executing' the use, converting the equitable interest of the cestui que use into a corresponding legal estate. For instance, if freehold land was conveyed 'to A and his heirs to the use of B and his heirs', A was divested of the title and B became the full legal owner.

The Statute of Uses was successful in many cases in preventing the evasion of feudal dues. In some cases, however, it was not so successful. If the use was an active use (i.e., the feoffees had duties to perform) the use was not executed by the Statute; otherwise the feoffee would have been unable to carry out his duties. So an active use (e.g., for the management of family wealth by the feoffee sub-letting lands and collecting the rents) was not affected by the Statute and remained valid. The Statute also abolished the power of devising a use. This aspect of the Statute caused some confusion, and it was generally thought that there was no power to make any testamentary disposition of land or a use. This was one of the factors which led to the rebellion, the Pilgrimage of Grace in 1536. As a concession the Statute of Wills was passed in 1540 allowing land, with exceptions, to be devised.

Evolution of the trust from the use upon a use

The limitations on the use imposed by the Statute of Uses was to lead to the modern-day trust. The trust developed from the use upon a use: that is, where there was a conveyance to A and his heirs to the use of B and his heirs, to the use of C and his heirs. It had been held in 1532 (*Bro Abr Feff al Uses* 40) that the use upon a use was void and gave no interest to C, because the use in favour of C was repugnant to the use in favour of B. It was argued after the Statute of Uses that the use in favour of C was executed by the Statute and therefore valid, but in *Tyrrel's Case* (1557) 2 Dy 155a it was confirmed that the use upon a use was void and was not validated by the Statute. Notwithstanding these authorities, over the period from 1535 to 1635 the use upon a use began to be enforced. The formula adopted by the middle of the seventeenth century was 'to A and his heirs to the use of B and his heirs in trust for C and his heirs'. The court of Chancery held that the second use or trust was enforceable in equity despite the earlier decisions to the contrary. The Statute executed the use in favour of B but then the property was held upon trust for the intended beneficiary, C. So trusts began to be used as freely as uses had been previously.

From the seventeenth to nineteenth centuries inclusive the device used was the use, executed by the Statute, coupled with the trust, which was enforced by the courts. The Statute was repealed in 1925 so that today it is not necessary to have the combined device of use and trust, and a straight trust whereby property is vested in a trustee for the benefit of a beneficiary is sufficient.

1.3 Modern Functions of the Express Trust

During the time of the use's early development it was largely utilised to maximise the benefit of land by avoidance of feudal dues. It also came to be used in a more elaborate manner for the allocation of land amongst members of families, sometimes giving life interests to one family member with gifts of remainders to others. The trust reacted besides to the changes in the nature of society that occurred over the seventeenth, eighteenth and nineteenth centuries. During this time England evolved from being an agricultural society into a society where industry and commerce had major roles to play. Foreign trade and the industrial revolution contributed to a society where company stocks and shares became a major form of wealth. The change in the nature of society was accompanied by a change in the function of the trust. Although it continued to be a tool for the management of landed wealth it became additionally a utensil for the management of the new forms of wealth. Landed property remained important for most aristocratic families, often because of the desire to keep particular land within the family, but sometimes land was as much of a burden as a benefit, through the liability, normally of the life tenant, to maintain it. The new forms of wealth were not accompanied by such burdens. It was not normally intended that particular shares should remain in the family. The life tenant would not have the same obligations in respect of them, and family trustees could easily buy and sell stocks and shares through the stock market with little restraint. It is these historical changes which have largely fashioned the trust into the flexible friend with which we are familiar today, although the flexibility of the trust mechanism has inevitably led to its acquiring other functions, too.

Preservation of family wealth
As explained above, the trust developed as a mechanism for avoiding feudal dues and controlling family property. Initially this meant preserving landed estate in a relatively passive manner but, with the advent of the new forms of wealth, it became a more active machine not just for the preservation of existing property but also (where possible) for increasing the value of the trust estate through investment. Today the trust continues to be used for the avoidance of fiscal liability, such as income tax, capital gains tax and inheritance tax. At the same time family wealth is managed so as to make provision in various ways for spouses, children and other family members, including the making of future gifts. These functions are explored in more depth in Chapter 7. Simultaneously, whilst a trust fund is being held for the assorted beneficiaries the funds are optimised by careful management and investment by the trustees; these subjects will be surveyed in Chapter 9.

Pension funds, unit trusts, employee share ownership trusts
The trust has proved so successful as an investment mechanism that it has been adopted in the commercial sphere for this purpose. One of its principal commercial uses is for facilitating collective investment. The unit trust is a device whereby small investors can contribute to a large fund held by trustees who, because of the size of the fund, can invest the fund over a very wide range of investments and apportion the benefits amongst the various investors according to the amounts of their respective investments. In the field of employment it is used to provide pensions for employees by the combination of trust and contract whereby the employer and employee normally have contractual obligations to contribute money to be held by trustees who will manage the funds and make payment of pensions to employees and dependants. Another modern application of the trust is its use to encourage employee share ownership. These techniques are considered at more length in Chapter 7.

Private provision for dependants and others

An inter-vivos trust (i.e. a trust created by a settlor during his or her lifetime), like a contract, is essentially a private matter and is not subject to public scrutiny or registration, unlike a will which has to undergo probate. It is therefore an ideal vehicle for making dispositions of property, including the making of future gifts, in private. For this reason it is sometimes used to make provision for unmarried sexual partners or illegitimate offspring. Whereas the provisions of a will would be known by other heirs, an inter-vivos trust may be used secretly to give interests which will fall into possession on the death of the settlor. These so-called 'secret trusts' are explained in section 4.2.

To assist causes

Sometimes it is intended that property should be dedicated to a purpose rather than to a person. In such cases the property relationship becomes complex since a purpose, such as relief of poverty, cannot of itself be the donee of property. There must normally be a legal entity, whether an individual or a corporation, who will have rights of ownership in the property and who will have the right and ability to pursue legal process in respect of the property, and the usual rule is that an attempted trust for a purpose is ineffective (see Chapter 12). An exception is made, however, in the case of charitable purposes. Because charity is regarded as being for the benefit of the public, trusts for charitable purposes are valid and enforceable by the Attorney-General on behalf of the public (see Chapter 14).

Trusts and co-ownership of land

The trust has often produced advantages beyond those for which it was originally designed. A particular characteristic which has proved useful is the division between legal and equitable ownership. This can assist transactions if the parties to the transaction can concern themselves with a relatively simple legal title without examining the position in equity. In the conveying of land this can be invaluable. Where, for example, there is a trust of land with separate legal and equitable title, a prospective purchaser of the land needs only to inspect the legal title. He or she does not need to investigate the equitable interests, since after a sale the interests become interests in the proceeds of sale in the hands of the trustees and the purchaser takes the land freed from such interests. By this means the conveyancing process is speeded up. This technique, called overreaching, is so expenditious that it has been adopted in other cases where conveyancing would be complicated.

Where for instance, there is joint ownership of land the title can become very involved, with many different persons having differing interests. To simplify the sale of such land legislation has imposed a statutory trust whereby there are not more than four trustees, who hold one undivided legal title upon trust for themselves and the other co-owners according to their agreed shares. The use of the trust means that the purchaser need inspect only one legal title held by a maximum of four persons and does not need to examine all the different equitable interests of the beneficiaries, which are 'overreached' on a sale, being converted from interests in the land to interests in the proceeds of sale.

Holding land for minors

Land is a very valuable resource in society and principally for this reason Parliament has provided (s.1 Law of Property Act 1925) that persons under the age of majority cannot have full legal control of land. Title to land may, however, be vested in trustees for the benefit of minor beneficiaries, and if desired the land may then be transferred to the beneficiary upon attaining majority or some greater age.

International aspects of the trust

The English trust has been used extensively in jurisdictions which have their law based upon English law. The trust is often used in these places primarily for the tax-savings that may be made, particularly since many such places have low rates of tax. In other jurisdictions, such as other European countries, the concept of trusteeship succumbs to a very different analysis, and in order to further international understanding of the trust concept a number of countries have made themselves parties to the Hague Convention on the Law Applicable to Trusts and on their Recognition, which was given effect in the United Kingdom by the Recognition of Trusts Act 1987.

Article 2 of the Hague Convention states: 'For the purposes of this Convention, the term "trust" refers to the legal relationships created inter-vivos or on death by a person, the settlor, when assets have been placed under the control of a trustee for the benefit of a beneficiary or for a specified purpose. A trust has the following characteristics:

(a)   the assets constitute a separate fund and are not a part of the trustee's own estate;

(b)   title to the trust assets stands in the name of the trustee or in the name of another person on behalf of the trustee;

(c)   the trustee has the power and the duty in respect of which he is accountable, to manage, employ or dispose of the assets in accordance with the terms of the trust and the special duties imposed upon him by law.'

The words used in Article 2 are adequate to describe the English trust and other legal forms of trusteeship in some, but not all, other jurisdictions. The convention may facilitate the adoption of the English concept in other jurisdictions for specific transactions. To what extent this might occur remains to be seen, and it is possible that in some cases there will be resistance to this where the effect of using the English trust would be to circumvent tax liability in the particular jurisdiction, although any such problem might be met by the jurisdiction in question passing appropriate tax laws, since the Convention expressly preserves a signatory's fiscal freedom in this respect.

1.4 The Nature of the Beneficiary's Right

The trust has often been the centre of controversy and no aspect of it has given rise to as much sustained academic controversy as the question of what is the nature of the beneficiary's right under a trust. The extremes in view are: that the beneficiary's right is a right *in personam* (i.e., it is a right against the person of the trustee); the other view is that the right is proprietary in nature and enforceable in the property and against any person who interferes with it. The reader should not think that the debate is purely academic. A good deal of practical importance can depend upon the proper analysis of the nature of the beneficiary's interest: for instance, if it is a proprietary interest it will give the beneficiary stronger rights in the bankrupcty of the trustee than it would if only personal.

The academic debate

The early debate was probably hampered by too absolutist a view of proprietary rights and the assumption that a right was either purely personal or, alternatively, an absolute proprietary right. The answer is, it is submitted, now fairly clear: the beneficiary's interest has some but not all of the characteristics of a proprietary right, but the beneficiary is not 'the' sole owner of the property because, of course, some of the qualities of ownership are vested in the trustee for the duration of the trust. The discussion has been hampered by the same 'absolutist' thinking that prevented the common law courts from recognising the trust. More flexible thinking has allowed commentators to conclude that the beneficiary's right is an intermediate one, having characteristics both of a personal and proprietary nature. Hanbury (1929) 45 LQR 198 said that the right was not a full-blown proprietary interest because it is liable to defeat by a bona fide purchaser of the legal title from the trustee, but he conceded that it was more than personal because in some circumstances rights could be enforced against other persons (such as purchasers of property with notice of the interests of beneficiaries) in addition to the trustee. Latham (1954) 32 Can BR 520, whilst preferring the 'personal' camp, had to concede that there are exceptions when he concluded that the 'cestui que trust has no interest in specific items of the trust fund but merely a right to its due administration, enforceable against the trustees and situated where they may be sued ... where, however, problems of social and economic importance are involved, the courts often attach the interest to specific trust assets'.

Waters added to the debate (1967) 45 Can BR 219, arguing by reference to the case of *Commissioners of Stamp Duties (Queensland)* v. *Livingston* [1965] AC 694 that in some cases a beneficiary has a proprietary interest but not in others. He suggested that the test should be whether on the facts of a particular case a beneficiary's rights are 'direct and exclusive'. *Commissioners of Stamp Duties (Queensland)* v. *Livingston* was a slightly unusual case concerning the question for tax purposes of whether the potential interest of a family member of the intestacy of a deceased proprietor is 'ownership'. The court held that a person entitled on intestacy, but before the administration of the estate, was not 'the owner' of the property and was not liable to estate duty on it on her own death. Waters explained that this was because the beneficiary's rights were not direct and exclusive. The test propounded by Waters might be useful in such uncommon cases but it still does not answer the question as to what is the precise extent of the proprietary interest in the usual case of a simple trust.

The practical issues

Proprietary characteristics of beneficial interests
A beneficiary's interest behind a simple trust certainly has many of the characteristics of a proprietary interest. It can be bought, sold, mortgaged, devised and bequeathed. It has been held that a beneficiary is the owner of trust income for the purposes of income tax. In *Baker* v. *Archer-Shee* [1927] AC 844, Lady Archer-Shee was a US citizen resident in the UK. She was also the beneficiary of a New York trust whereby the income was received by the trustee in New York and retained there. The question in the case was whether Lady Archer-Shee was liable to income tax on sums retained in New York. The answer depended upon whether she was to be regarded as the 'owner' of the income. By a bare majority the House of Lords held that she was.

A beneficiary's right has also been held to be sufficient to entitle the beneficiary to call for a transfer of the property to him or her. In *Saunders* v. *Vautier* (1841) 4 Beav 115, a testator bequeathed his stock on trust to accumulate the dividends until the beneficiary should reach the age of 25 and then to transfer the principal sum together with the accumulated dividends. The beneficiary reached the age of 21 and claimed to have the whole fund transferred to him. It was argued on his behalf that he had 'a vested interest, and that as the accumulation and postponement was for his benefit alone, he might waive it and call for an immediate transfer of the fund'. Lord Langdale MR held that the beneficiary was entitled to the property.

The proprietary nature of the beneficiary's interest has further been regarded as sufficient to give priority in cases of insolvency. In *Re Kayford* [1975] 1 WLR 279, a company conducted a mail-order business. Customers either paid the full price in advance or paid a deposit. The company's suppliers experienced financial difficulties and its accountants advised the company to open a separate customers' 'trust deposit account' and pay into it all moneys paid by customers in advance of receiving goods. The purpose of this was to allow the company fully to refund payments to customers if the company should go into liquidation. When the company did go into liquidation it was held that the moneys in the account were being held on trust for customers and that they, and not the company, were the owners of the account. The moneys were not therefore available to the liquidator to pay the company's debts. Megarry J said that the obligation in respect of the moneys had been transformed 'from contract to property, from debt to trust', equating the interest under a trust with a proprietary interest.

Limitations on equitable ownership

Other decisions demonstrate the limitations on the extent of the beneficiary's equitable ownership, the general limitation being that the powers of management and control are vested in the trustee and the beneficiary is not empowered to interfere with such. In *Re Brockbank* [1948] Ch 206, for example, it was held that beneficiaries could not interfere with a trustee's power to appoint a new trustee on the retirement of an existing trustee. The trustee could appoint a trustee of his own choice and the beneficiaries could not force their choice upon the trust. Similarly, the rule is that it is the trustee alone who is entitled to sue a third party in respect of loss to the trust. This rule was confirmed recently in *Parker-Tweedale* v. *Dunbar Bank Plc* [1990] 3 WLR 767. In that case a house was in the name of one spouse who held it on trust partly for the other spouse. The house was subject to a mortgage and the lender exercised its power to sell as mortgagee. The non-trustee spouse sought to sue the lender for not obtaining the best possible price. It was held that only the trustee spouse had the right to sue the third party lender and not the beneficiary spouse who was not a trustee. In the course of his judgment Nourse LJ affirmed the general rule that a beneficiary is not entitled to sue a third party in respect of the trust property, and he emphasised that in exceptional cases where the beneficiary is permitted to sue, he does so 'in right of the trust and in room of the trustee'.

1.5 Categories of Trust

So far the trust has been considered as an obligation intentionally created and with such intention expressed by the creator of the trust, but the trust is more varied than that. It may arise where no intention has been expressed but where it is appropriate to infer an intention to create a trust or it may be imposed by law irrespective of intention. Additionally trusts are sometimes imposed by statute. It follows therefore that there are three main categories of trust: express, implied and statutory (see Figure 1.3).

Express trusts
Usually little difficulty is encountered in identifying an express trust. If the settlor has expressed an intention in clear terms and has satisfied the other requirements for its formation (see Chapters 3, 4 and 5) an express trust is created. If the intention which has been expressed is equivocal then there will be no trust, but only a mere power.

Implied trusts
Whilst express trusts evolved through the intentions of settlors to avoid fiscal liabilities and to manage family wealth, implied trusts do not share a similar coherent ancestry. The flexibility of the trust concept has made it ideal for filling in gaps in the law in novel cases. In this more haphazard tradition implied trusts have acquired great import in English legal thought and there is hardly any area of law which has not been flavoured by the essence of implied trusts. The main circumstances in which trusts are implied are considered in the next chapter.

Statutory trusts
Trusts are imposed by statute in a number of circumstances where their presence serves a function useful for the management of property. One instance mentioned earlier in this chapter is that whenever there is co-ownership of land, a statutory trust for sale is imposed for the purpose

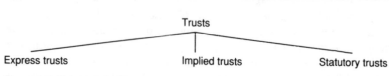

Figure 1.3 Categories of trust

of facilitating conveyancing (see also section 15.2). Another example is the statutory trust imposed in respect of the property of a person who dies without having made a will; his personal representatives must hold his property on trust for his next of kin. Another case is that where land is given to a minor. A minor is not permitted to own a legal estate in land under English law (s.1(6) Law of Property Act 1925) and statute (s.1 Settled Land Act 1925) provides instead that the land is held upon trust for the minor.

Trusts for persons and purposes

Another feature which makes the trust such a flexible and convenient tool is that it may be used to benefit not just persons but also purposes. The typical case of a trust is 'one in which the legal owner of property is constrained by a court of equity so as to deal with it as to give effect to the equitable right of another' (Roxburgh J in *Re Astor's Settlement Trusts* [1952] Ch 534); and the normal rule is that an attempted trust which is not in favour of identifiable persons is ineffective (see Chapter 12). The major exception to the normal rule is that the law does allow the creation of trusts for charitable purposes in the interests of the public (see Chapter 14).

Fixed trusts and discretionary trusts

An expressly created trust will usually take the form of a fixed trust or a discretionary trust. A fixed trust is one where the beneficial interest of each beneficiary is clearly defined: there may be a single individual entitled to the whole beneficial interest, or there may be several named individuals entitled to a defined share, such as a quarter of the trust fund or a fixed sum of, say, £5000. In a discretionary trust, on the other hand, the trustees may have discretions as to which beneficiaries will benefit or as to the extent of the benefit (see further section 7.4).

Summary

1 A trust is an equitable obligation binding on a person(s) known as the trustee(s) to deal with property for the benefit of the beneficiary (beneficiaries) who is (are) normally a person(s), but which in some cases may be an object or a cause. The precise nature of a beneficiary's interest is unclear; it is not purely a personal right but at the same time it does not have all the characteristics of an absolute proprietary right.
2 The trust developed out of the 'use' which was primarily a device used to avoid disadvantageous situations (e.g., the payment of feudal dues). Like its forerunner, an important function of the trust today is avoidance (e.g., of fiscal liability). However, the function of the trust is now much wider and it

has, among other things, taken on a significant role in the commercial sphere as an investment mechanism. Furthermore, the concept of a trust is not confined to the situation where the mechanism is expressly created; it can arise by implication of the law or by statute.

3 Whereas a trust is an obligation to deal with property in a particular way, a power is a right to deal with property in a particular way with no corresponding duty. The objects of a power, in contrast to the beneficiaries under a trust, have no interest in the whole or any part of the property which is the subject matter of the power; they have a mere hope that an interest will be appointed to them.

Exercises

1 Look at Underhill's definition of a trust (p.4–5 at the end of paragraph 1.1).
(a) Explain, with reference to the historical development, how the trust came to be an *equitable* obligation; and
(b) In what respect(s) do you consider Underhill's definition to be unsatisfactory?

2 What do you understand by the notion of a trust in the 'higher' sense as compared to a trust in the 'lower' sense?

3 Distinguish between a trust and a power. What do you understand by a trust power?

4 What do you understand by the concept of a 'use'? How and why did the trust develop from a 'use'?

5 (a) In what respects may the interests of a beneficiary under a trust be said to be (i) of a proprietary nature and (ii) of a personal nature?
(b) Why may it be of practical importance to establish that the right of a beneficiary under a trust is more than a purely personal right?

2 Implied Trusts

2.1 Introduction

An express trust arises where the settlor transfers property to trustees (or exceptionally where the settlor declares himself trustee) and also sets down the terms of the trust. These features are not present in an implied trust. In addition to this difference in the method of creation between express trusts and implied trusts, there is in most cases a difference in function between the two forms of trust. The former are generally intended to continue for some time, whereas the latter, once recognised, are often terminated shortly afterwards. Frequently, once it is established that the legal owner holds on either of the two forms of implied trust, resulting or constructive, the legal owner is then obliged to transfer the property to those persons entitled to the beneficial interest. For instance, where a trustee acquires property in breach of his duty not to profit from his position as trustee, a constructive trust will be imposed in respect of the property acquired and an obligation is placed upon the trustee to transfer the legal title to the beneficiaries, thus bringing the trust to an end shortly after it has arisen. Likewise, where an intended express trust fails (because, say, the beneficiaries are not defined with sufficient certainty), a resulting trust arises and the trustees must return the legal title to the settlor or his estate, again ending the trust soon after its inception.

Less often an implied trust confirms the existence of a trust which was intended but which was not expressly declared, in which case the trust will usually be more permanent. One example is that where a person has made a contribution to the acquisition of property; for instance, by providing part of the purchase price of a house which is purchased in the name of a partner. In this type of case a resulting trust comes about to give effect to the inferred intention of the parties that the contributing party should have a corresponding beneficial interest in the house, but it is not usual for there to be an immediate obligation to transfer the legal title to the contributing party since the purpose of the trust will probably be the retention of the house for some substantial period of time.

The meaning of the term 'implied trust' has been the subject of much debate. Some writers use the term to mean a trust which gives effect to

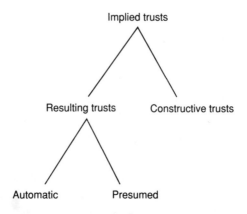

Figure 2.1

---

an inferred intention of a settlor as opposed to a trust which is imposed by equity irrespective of intention; but in this chapter the term is used in the broader sense to describe all trusts which do not arise expressly or by statute.

As the implied trust developed, it has branched out to create the subdivisions shown in Figure 2.1. Given the wide variety of circumstances and the frequency with which implied trusts now arise, it is important to appreciate that implied trusts are not merely a subsidiary aspect of the law of trusts. A study of trust law is just as much about implied trusts as express trusts. However, the purpose of this chapter is to provide only an overview of the concept of an implied trust. As there is no one unifying factor which determines the circumstances in which an implied trust arises, details of the individual situations in which implied trusts operate are dealt with in their relevant context in later chapters.

2.2 Resulting Trusts

A resulting trust is a trust implied in favour of the settlor or, if the settlor is dead, in favour of his or her estate. The term 'resulting' comes from the Latin *resultare* and from the same root as 'resilient'. In this context it means 'springing back' and thus where a resulting trust arises the beneficial interest 'springs back' to the settlor or to the testator's estate. As it is difficult to describe a resulting trust there is a tendency to explain this concept by describing the situations in which such a trust arises. Figure 2.2 sets out the three recognised categories.

Outright failure of an express trust

There may be an outright failure of an express trust for a variety of

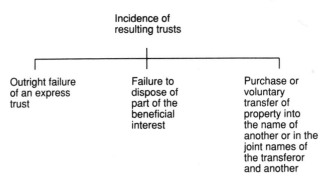

Figure 2.2

reasons: for example, if a settlor attempts to create a trust but there are no beneficiaries or there is no certainty of property or of the trust objects (see Chapter 3). Likewise, if the gift to the beneficiaries is void for perpetuity (see section 12.1) or because a necessary formality has not been complied with (see Chapter 4), the trust will fail to take effect and there will be a resulting trust.

Failure to dispose of part of the beneficial interest

Failure to dispose of part of the beneficial interest may also lead to a resulting trust in a variety of circumstances. For example, bad drafting may lead to there being a gap in the beneficial interest. A simple illustration of this occurs in *Re Cochrane* [1955] Ch 309. Property was settled by a marriage settlement on a wife for her life so long as she resided with her husband. On the termination of her interest, the income was to be paid to her husband for life. There was then a power of appointment in favour of the children of the marriage, but in default of appointment the children took on the death of the last surviving parent. A gap in the beneficial interest leading to a resulting trust occurred because the wife ceased to reside with her husband then later the husband died, and the power of appointment was not exercised in favour of the children who could not therefore take as both parents were not dead. For other illustrations of a resulting trust arising where there is a failure to dispose of part of the beneficial interest see section 6.5.

Purchase or voluntary transfer of property into the name of another or the joint names of the transferor and transferee

Where the beneficial interests in real or personal property are not clearly stated, the court determines the equitable ownership of property by reference to equitable presumptions of intention. One such presumption is the presumption of a resulting trust. This operates in two defined situations: a purchase of property in the name of another or in the joint names of the purchaser and another; and a voluntary conveyance or transfer into the name of another or the joint names of the grantor and another.

A purchase of property in the name of another or in the joint names of the purchaser and another

The presumption that there is a resulting trust when one person purchases property in the name of another or in the joint names of the purchaser and another was clearly stated by Eyre CB in *Dyer* v. *Dyer* (1788) 2 Cox Eq Cas 92 where he said: 'the trust of a legal estate . . . whether taken in the name of the purchasers jointly or in the name of others without that of the purchaser; whether in one name or several; whether jointly or successive, results to the man who advances the purchase-money'.

In other words, if X provides a purchase price of £90 000 for freehold land and the property is conveyed into the name of Y, it is assumed that X did not intend to make a gift of the land to Y, and consequently Y holds on resulting trust for X (see Figure 2.3).

Similarly, if X provides a purchase price of £90 000 for freehold land and the property is conveyed into the names of X and Y, equity again presumes no gift in favour of Y with the consequence that Y holds on resulting trust for X (see Figure 2.4).

However many people provide the purchase money, the person (or persons) to whom the property is conveyed are presumed to hold on resulting trust for the purchasers in proportion to their contributions. Thus if X provides £60 000 and Y provides £30 000 to make up the purchase price of freehold land, and the property is conveyed into the name of Y, there will be a resulting trust for X to the extent of £60 000 (see Figure 2.5). It should be noted that although *Dyer* v. *Dyer* refers only to interests in land, and the above examples all relate to freehold

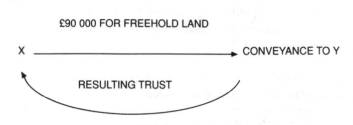

Figure 2.3

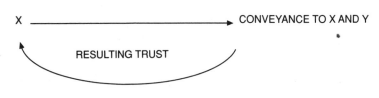

£90 000 FOR FREEHOLD LAND

X ——————————————→ CONVEYANCE TO X AND Y

RESULTING TRUST

Figure 2.4

£90 000 FOR FREEHOLD LAND

X   Y ——————————————→ CONVEYANCE TO Y
(60 000) (30 000)

RESULTING TRUST
to the value of two-thirds
of the property

Figure 2.5

---

land, the principle equally applies to personalty (i.e., all other forms of property).

A voluntary conveyance or transfer into the name of another or the joint names of the grantor and another

A voluntary conveyance or transfer occurs where an *existing owner* of particular property transfers that property into the name of another or the joint names of himself and another. In this instance, in applying the presumption or a resulting trust, a distinction needs to be drawn between real and personal property.

Real property

Before 1926, the effect of the Statute of Uses 1535 was that if a voluntary conveyance was not expressed to be made to the use or benefit of the grantee, there was a resulting trust of the equitable interest in favour of the grantor, and the legal estate was carried back to the grantor by virtue of the statute. The Statute of Uses has now been repealed, and s.60(3) Law of Property Act 1925 now says that in a voluntary conveyance of land a resulting trust shall not be implied *merely* by reason that the property is not expressed to be conveyed for the use or benefit of the grantee. However, it is unlikely that s.60(3) *prevents* a resulting trust from being implied for other reasons, such as the general equitable presumptions. Although s.60(3) was not discussed in *Hodgson* v. *Marks* [1971] Ch 892, the Court of Appeal applied the equitable presumption and presumed a resulting trust in a case where a freehold owner made a voluntary conveyance of land into the name of another.

Personalty

Here it is clear from the decision of the court in *Re Vinogradoff* [1935] WN 68 that the presumption of a resulting trust operates. War loan was transferred by a grandmother into the joint names of herself and her granddaughter (who was aged four at the time). It was held that the granddaughter held on resulting trust for the grandmother.

As there is merely an equitable *presumption* of a resulting trust in the situations outlined above it is quite possible that evidence may be brought to establish that the true intention of the parties to a transaction was otherwise. For example, the presumption could be rebutted by evidence of an intention to make a gift or a loan. Moreover, there are some situations where it would be inappropriate to presume a resulting trust was intended by virtue of the nature of the relationship between the donor and the donee. In these situations the presumption of a resulting trust is displaced by the presumption of advancement under which the presumption is reversed; it is presumed that the donor intended to make a gift of the property transferred. The presumption of advancement arises in two situations: transfers of property by a husband into the name of his wife, and transfers by a person *in loco parentis* to a child.

The presumption of a gift, where a husband transfers property into the name of his wife, developed at a time when women were generally in a far weaker economic position than that experienced by most women today, and it arose out of the legal obligation of a husband to support his wife. Although the presumption still operates, as the social and economic position of women in society is clearly much stronger the presumption is considered to be very weak, and this is especially so in dealings between husband and wife with regard to the matrimonial home (see Lord Diplock *Pettitt* v. *Pettitt* [1970] AC 777).

In *Re Figgis* [1969] 1 Ch 123 the presumption of advancement was applied where a husband was a sole contributor to a joint account. However, this was because both parties were dead at the time of the action and there was no direct evidence as to what the parties intended. In contrast, in *Marshall* v. *Crutwell* (1875) LR 20 Eq 328 the presumption was rebutted as it was established that a husband had put the account into joint names for his convenience, enabling the wife to draw cheques for the payment of housekeeping expenses.

It should be noted that the presumption of advancement has never operated in respect of transfers of property by a wife to her husband; the presumption of a resulting trust operates here. Furthermore, the presumption has never been extended to transfers between male and female co-habiting parties even if they live for all intents and purposes as a married couple.

In the second category, the rule as stated, in *Dyer* v. *Dyer* (above) was that if a *father* purchased or transferred property into the name of his child, he was presumed to have made a gift to the child. The presumption has since been extended to other relationships between a man and a child to whom the man is *in loco parentis* (i.e., where he is in the position of a parent having taken upon himself the duty to provide for the child). Thus an uncle or a grandfather or a stepfather could be *in loco parentis*. However, the relationship of a mother to her child, or a woman to any other child in respect of whom the woman has assumed an obligation to provide, seems not to give rise to the presumption of advancement, as equity does not recognise any obligation on the part of a mother to provide for her child (*Bennet* v. *Bennet* (1879) 10 Ch D 474). Although now the economic position of women is different and statutory obligations are imposed upon mothers to provide for children, there is no case in English Law which has applied the presumption of advancement to a woman and child relationship.

Admissibility of evidence to rebut either the presumption of a resulting trust or the presumption of advancement

It has been stated that where there is a purchase or voluntary transfer of property into the name of another or the joint names of the transferor and transferee, equity presumes the transferee holds on resulting trust for the transferor. In contrast, where a husband transfers property into the name of his wife or a transfer is made by a person *in loco parentis* to a child, equity presumes a gift was intended. As these are only presumptions they may be rebutted by evidence to the contrary, but not all evidence available to rebut the relevant presumption is necessarily admissible. In *Shephard* v. *Cartwright* [1955] AC 431 Viscount Simonds explained in general terms the evidence admissible to rebut the presumption of a resulting trust or the presumption of advancement. Acts and declarations of the parties before, at the time of, or immediately after the transfer are admissible either for or against the party who did the act or made the declaration. However, acts or declarations subsequent to the transfer are only admissible as evidence against the party who made them and not in his favour.

It should also be noted that the evidence which discloses an illegal or unlawful purpose is not admissible to rebut either of the equitable presumptions. This is well illustrated by the decision in *Tinker* v. *Tinker* [1970] 1 All ER 540 CA. There a husband had conveyed property into the name of his wife in order to protect it from the creditors of his business. Being a voluntary transfer from husband to wife the presumption of advancement operated. The husband tried to rebut the presumption by claiming he did not intend to make a gift of the property to his wife, but merely wanted to ensure his creditors did not get their hands on it. This clearly involved placing reliance on an illegal purpose and, as such, the evidence was not admissible to rebut the presumption of advancement. As Lord Denning put it, the husband was 'on the horns of a dilemma . . . As against his wife, he wanted to say the property was his. As against his creditors, that it belonged to her.' The case of *Heseltine* v. *Heseltine* [1971] 1 All ER 952 CA is somewhat difficult to reconcile with *Tinker* v. *Tinker*. Here a wife transferred certain sums of money to her husband in order to equalise their property for estate duty purposes and also to enable him to qualify as an underwriter at Lloyds. As this was a transfer by wife to husband the presumption of a resulting trust operated. The husband, wishing to rebut the presumption that he held on resulting trust, claimed that in order to achieve the purposes of equalising the estates and for him to qualify at Lloyds, the wife must have intended a gift. This therefore rebutted the presumption of a resulting trust and it was then necessary for the wife to rely on unlawful evidence to establish no gift was intended. However, the Court of Appeal, taking into account that the husband had devised the scheme for his own advantages, decided that the husband held the property on a constructive trust for his wife as it was inequitable for him to claim the property beneficially as he had initiated the scheme. Such reasoning is somewhat unconvincing as it is tantamount to suggesting that 'two wrongs make a right'.

2.3 Presumed and Automatic Resulting Trusts

In an attempt to clarify the nature of resulting trusts Megarry J (in *Re Vandervell's Trusts (No 2)* [1973] 3 WLR 744) divided them into two categories, presumed and automatic resulting trusts.

Presumed resulting trusts
Presumed resulting trusts are those which depend upon the presumed intentions of the settlor. Clearly, purchases or transfers of property in to the name of another or joint names of the transferor and transferee fall into this category (see above).

Automatic resulting trusts

Originally it was thought that all resulting trusts were based on the presumed intentions of the settlor. Thus, if the trust which the settlor intended failed (e.g., for lack of certainty of the subject matter of the trust), it was inferred that the settlor would have intended, in the event of the trust failing, that the trustees should hold on trust for himself (or, if he was dead, his estate). However, in the notorious cases of *Vandervell* v. *IRC* [1967] 2 AC 291 and *Re Vandervell's Trust (No 2)* [1974] Ch 269 (CA) there was a change of view, precipitated by the facts of the Vandervell cases themselves. The facts were that Vandervell wanted to make a tax-free gift to the Royal College of Surgeons, so he instructed his bank to transfer to the College certain shares which the bank held as nominee for Vandervell. The transfer to the Royal College of Surgeons was subject to the condition that the trustees of a trust company which Vandervell had established should have an option to purchase the shares from the College, the idea being that Vandervell would declare dividends on the shares to make the gift to the Royal College of Surgeons, and then the shares would pass to the trust company (see Figure 2.6). In *Vandervell* v. *IRC* the Inland Revenue argued that Vandervell was still liable to tax on the income from the shares because (a) he had not complied with the necessary formalities to transfer his equitable interest (see section 4.1) and (b) he had not declared with sufficient certainty in whom the beneficial interest in the option to purchase, held by the trust company, was vested (see section 6.3). Therefore, maintained the Inland Revenue, Vandervell was liable to tax on the basis that he stil' held the equitable interest in the option by means of a resulting trust. One of the arguments put forward by the 'Vandervell camp', based on the assumption that all resulting trusts arise out of the actual or presumed intentions of the settlor, was that as Vandervell was so obviously very anxious to

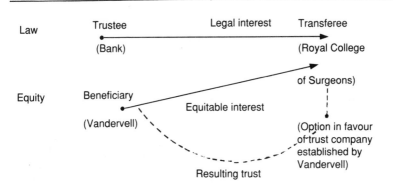

Figure 2.6

divest himself of the equitable interest in the shares, there could be no resulting trust in his favour as this was clearly the last thing he wanted! Consequently in the judgment of Lord Upjohn in *Vandervell* v. *IRC* and elaborated upon by Megarry J in *Vandervell's Trust (No 2) supra* (approved on this point on appeal to the Court of Appeal) the idea emerges that a resulting trust can arise irrespective of intention. On the facts of *Vandervell* v. *IRC*, as there had not been an effective declaration of trust of the option to purchase, despite Vandervell's intentions there was an automatic resulting trust in favour of Vandervell, as it was thought to be impossible for the beneficial interest to remain in the air.

Thus it seems a resulting trust will arise automatically where a person transfers legal title to trustees with the intention also of disposing of the beneficial interest, but for some reason (e.g., lack of certainty, lack of the necessary formalities, the beneficiaries have predeceased the testator) the beneficial interest does not pass.

It is actually unclear whether the situation where there is a failure merely to dispose of part of the beneficial interest falls into the category of an 'automatic' or 'presumed' resulting trust. Neither Lord Upjohn nor Megarry J made reference to the situation. It will be seen in sections 6.5 and 13.3 that the reasoning in such cases depends on the presumed intentions of the settlor, and thus this is an argument for classifying them as 'presumed' resulting trusts. However, in explaining the concept of a 'presumed' resulting trust in the *Vandervell* cases Lord Upjohn and Megarry J confine themselves to the question of whether there is an intention to alienate, rather than there being an intention that the transferee shold hold on trust for the transferor. A completely different situation arises in cases where there is a failure to dispose of part of the beneficial interest where the intention to alienate is assumed, but the question arises as to whether the settlor or donor intended to recover the property if the beneficial interest was not exhausted. Thus, the *Vandervell* cases do not set down a rigid classification for all resulting trusts, but are nevertheless highly significant authorities in their introduction of the notion of an 'automatic' resulting trust.

2.4 Constructive Trusts

Originally all constructive trusts were imposed by law irrespective of the intentions of the parties, and very often despite a clear intention to the contrary. Although this is still true in most cases, in the sphere of establishing an interest in family home (see Chapter 15) it is now clear that intention is highly relevant in proving the existence or otherwise of a constructive trust. The circumstances in which constructive trusts may arise are more diverse than those of a resulting trust. The main areas in which the concept of a constructive trust has been used are explained here, but a more detailed explanation is given where necessary in later chapters, in the relevant context.

Unauthorised profits of fiduciaries
A fiduciary relationship is a relationship of 'trust', in the 'higher sense' as well as possibly in the 'lower sense' (see section 1.1). The categories of fiduciaries are never closed (*English* v. *Dedham Vale Properties Ltd* [1978] 1 WLR 93), but examples include trustees and agents (e.g., company directors and partners). One of the features of a fiduciary relationship is the opportunity to make a personal profit or to take advantage of one's position at the expense of the persons whom one is called to protect or represent. Thus if a party is found to be in a fiduciary relationship, two general principles apply:

(a) the fiduciary must not put himself or herself in a position of conflict between his or her personal interest and his or her duty as a fiduciary;
(b) the fiduciary must not make a profit from his or her position.

These principles were summed up by Lord Herschell in *Bray* v. *Ford* [1896] AC 44 where he said: 'it is an inflexible rule of the court of equity that a person in a fiduciary position . . . is not, unless otherwise expressly provided, entitled to make a profit; he is not allowed to put himself in a position where his interest and duty conflict'. It is important to extract two points from this quotation. First, Lord Herschell made no reference to dishonesty. It is clear that an honest fiduciary can be held liable to account. Second, he recognised that there were exceptions to the rule and that it was, for example, possible for a fiduciary to be expressly authorised to profit from his position.

The liability of a fiduciary to account would appear to have been applied in some cases more strictly than others, and there would further appear to be inconsistencies of approach in the finding of a fiduciary relationship in the first place.

Is there a fiduciary relationship?
As the categories of fiduciary cannot be exhaustively determined, in some cases the courts seem to have taken a wide view of the circumstances in which a fiduciary relationship arises purely to achieve the desired result of making a party disgorge a profit made. For example, in *Reading* v. *Attorney-General* [1951] AC 507 Asquith LJ said that a fiduciary relationship arose 'whenever the plaintiff entrusts to the defendant a job to be performed'. On the facts of the case a sergeant in the British Army stationed in Cairo was held to be accountable to the

Crown for money that he had received from Egyptians for travelling, whilst in uniform, in their civilian lorries carrying contraband goods and thereby enabling the lorries to pass civilian check points without being inspected. The Crown was entitled to the money he had received because he had been able to make the profit by virtue of his uniform and his position in the British Army. In contrast, in *Swain* v. *the Law Society* [1983] AC 598 the House of Lords took a more restrictive view of the circumstances in which a fiduciary relationship arises, with the consequence that the Law Society was not held liable to account to individual solicitors for commission on the compulsory insurance scheme it negotiated on behalf of all solicitors. The scheme was entered into under statutory authority, and the imposition of a statutory duty did not additionally give rise to fiduciary obligations.

What amounts to a breach of duty?
It has been said that, in some cases, the liability of a fiduciary to account would appear to have been applied more strictly than in others.

A strict approach
In a number of cases involving company directors a strict approach has been taken to the two duties of a fiduciary set out above. This is seen, for example, in the decision in *Regal (Hastings) Ltd* v. *Gulliver* [1967] 2 AC 134. Here a company had the opportunity of an advantageous investment by forming a subsidiary company to acquire the leases of two cinemas. However, the freeholder of the cinemas was only prepared to grant the leases if the share capital of the subsidiary company was fully subscribed for. As the company itself did not have sufficient funds to achieve this the directors of the company subscribed for three-fifths of the shares in the subsidiary company. The company was sold to new owners and these directors were held accountable for their profit to the new owners of the company. The approach may be said to be a strict application of the fiduciary principles in that, in circumstances where the directors had acted bona fide, it was thought irrelevant that the new owners in effect obtained a windfall (having paid an agreed amount for the shares in the company they effectively recovered part of the expenditure by requiring the directors to account). Furthermore it was also irrelevant that had the directors not bought the shares in the subsidiary, the company could not have acquired the leases; the directors as controlling shareholders should have passed a resolution at a general meeting to approve the retention of their profit. It is worth noting that arguably, however, there was a conflict of duty and interest, in that it was the directors who decided that the company did not have the financial resources to acquire the shares itself.

Another case concerning a company director in which the fiduciary principle is strictly applied is *Industrial Development Ltd* v. *Cooley* [1972] 1 WLR 443. This is a strict decision in the sense that it establishes that it is not necessary for a breach of duty to occur to show that the benefit has been obtained at the expense of another party. The defendant, an architect, was appointed managing director of the plaintiff company in order to use his contacts in the gas industry to secure contracts for the company. The defendant tried to obtain work from the Eastern Gas Board for the company but the Board was not prepared as a matter of policy to employ development companies; The Board did, however, offer the contract to the defendant personally. The defendant, without informing the plaintiff company of the offer, obtained a release from the plaintiff company by misrepresenting he was ill. Within a few days of terminating his employment with the plaintiffs, he was engaged by the Eastern Gas Board. Admittedly, on the facts, the defendant had not acted in good faith but his arguments that the information came to him in a private capacity (he was a distinguished architect, well known to the Eastern Gas Board before he became director of the plaintiff company) and that the decision whether or not to contract with the plaintiff company lay not with him but with the Eastern Gas Board, were not accepted as negating a breach of fiduciary duty. The court was influenced in deciding that he should be liable to account by the very fact he had obtained the position of director by virtue of his connections.

Perhaps the most often cited example of the courts taking a strict approach to accountability is *Boardman* v. *Phipps* [1967] 2 AC 46. The case concerned the Phipps family trust in respect of which Boardman was solicitor. The trust owned a substantial minority shareholding in a company. Boardman and one of the beneficiaries, Tom Phipps, were dissatisfied with the manner in which the company was run and they suggested that the trust should increase its shareholding to a controlling interest in the company in order to re-organise it and make it more profitable. The trustees and other beneficiaries were approached but expressed no interest in the suggestion, so Boardman and Tom Phipps in their personal capacity purchased shares so as to obtain a controlling interest and carry out the desired re-organisation. This proved very profitable for them, and also benefited the trust through an increase in the value of the shares. Not satisfied with the benefit, one of the other beneficiaries sought to make Boardman liable to account for the personal profit which he had made on the basis that it was acquired by breach of his fiduciary duty. A majority of the House of Lords held that despite the fact that Boardman had acted honestly, had used his own efforts and money in making the company more profitable and had benefited the trust, he was liable to account for the profits which he had made. He had only been able to make the profits by reason of knowledge which he had acquired in his position as solicitor to the trust, and had not taken sufficient steps to obtain the consent with respect to at least one of the trustees. Boardman was, however, allowed fairly generous remuneration for the skill and effort he had put into the venture.

There were strong dissenting judgments from both Viscount Dilhorne and Lord Upjohn. They felt that there was no sensible conflict of duty and interest to justify making Boardman liable to account as the trustees did not wish to buy the shares. The majority had based their finding first on the notion that the information used by Boardman was trust property and confidential, and second on the fact that in the early stages of negotiation with the company Boardman had represented himself as acting as an agent for the trust. However, Viscount Dilhorne and Lord Upjohn thought that the use of information should only be regarded as a breach of fiduciary duty where it would amount to a breach of confidence to disclose the information, and they further pointed out that it was not as though Boardman had been employed to negotiate with the company on behalf of the trust, or that the company was not aware from an early stage that he was contracting in a private capacity.

The majority in *Boardman* v. *Phipps* seemed to take the view that once a fiduciary relationship is established, a fiduciary is automatically liable to account for any profit made. Lord Upjohn in his dissenting judgment expressed disagreement with such a broad proposition; a solicitor can act against his client in a matter for which he is not retained provided that in acting for the client he does not learn information which it would be improper to use against the client. For instance, he said, a solicitor can deal in shares in a company in which the client is a shareholder provided he does not put himself in a position of conflict of duty and interest. The strict view of the majority in *Boardman* v. *Phipps* seems out of line with some earlier cases. For example, in *Aas* v. *Benham* [1891] 2 Ch 244 it was held that a partner may use information obtained in the course of the business for his own use or benefit in matters *outside* the scope of the business.

A less strict approach
In contrast with the strict approach of the cases already discussed, *Queensland Mines* v. *Hudson* (1978) 18 ALR 1, manifests a less strict application of the breach of fiduciary principle and is particularly difficult to reconcile with *Regal (Hastings) Ltd* v. *Gulliver*. Queensland Mines had wanted to develop certain mining operations but although the defendant, the managing director of the company, was successful in obtaining licences on behalf of the company, the company had a liquidity problem which meant the scheme could not proceed. Consequently the

defendant, with the knowledge of the Board of Directors, resigned and successfully developed the mines for himself. The Privy Council held that that the defendant was not liable to account to the company for the profit he had made. This was either because the company had rejected the scheme due to its financial problems which thus took the defendant outside the scope of his fiduciary duty, or because the defendant had acted with the full knowledge of the Board of Directors of the plaintiff company which had consented to his activities. This suggests that the rejection of a commercial opportunity by the Board of Directors of a company protects a director from liability. Arguably, this should not necessarily be the case as there would appear to be a serious conflict of duty and interest in a director rejecting an opportunity on behalf of the company and then taking such opportunity for himself (see further (1979) 42 MLR 711 G R Sullivan). Hanbury and Maudsley (13th edn, p.571) say:

> If the line of reasoning in *Queensland Mines Ltd* v. *Hudson* were to be expanded, it would lead to the development of a line of defences (such as bona fides, illegality, ultra vires, inability, or lack of desire on the part of the company to exploit the opportunity) available to directors charged with breach of duty, a development which the law hither to has not countenanced.

Personal liability to account or constructive trustee
We have considered the liability of a fiduciary to account under the heading of constructive trusts, but it is probably incorrect to say that a breach of fiduciary duty always creates liability as a constructive trustee; there may be only a personal liability to account (see further Jones (1968) 84 LQR 472). Arguably a constructive trust should only arise where the fiduciary has actually used trust property to make an unauthorised profit as one cannot have a trust without trust property. Where, as for example in *Reading* v. *Attorney-General* (see above), the profit is made without trust property there is only a personal liability to account. The cases do not, however, always distinguish between personal liability to account and the imposition of a constructive trust. Some have used the terms (quite incorrectly) interchangeably. The distinction is of great practical importance, as a constructive trust is a proprietary remedy (see Chapter 11). Thus, for example, on bankruptcy the beneficiaries would take priority over general creditors, whereas they would not where there was merely a personal liability to account.

To prevent a criminal profiting from crime
The use of constructive trusts to prevent a criminal profiting from crime

was established in *In the Estate of Crippen* [1911] P.108. In a notorious criminal trial Dr Crippen was found guilty of murdering his wife. By her will she left him all her estate. It was decided that Dr Crippen held her estate on constructive trust for her next-of-kin in order to prevent him from profiting from his crime. It should be noted that the Forfeiture Act 1982 now provides that the court may grant relief from forfeiture of inheritance to persons guilty of unlawful killing, other than murder, where the court is satisfied that the justice of the case so requires.

The vendor under a specifically enforceable contract for the sale of land

A binding contract for the sale of land makes the vendor a constructive trustee of the land for the purchaser. The basis of the trusteeship is that the purchaser is entitled to call for specific performance of the contract and thus, by reason of the equitable maxim 'equity deems done what ought to be done', the purchaser is treated as having an interest in the property. It should be noted, however, that it is a strange type of trusteeship because the vendor retains a beneficial interest (in the proceeds of sale) which entitles him or her to continue to occupy the land and enjoy the rent and profits until completion. The purpose of imposing the trustee status is that the vendor is required to manage and maintain the land with the care of a trustee, thus providing protection for the purchaser.

Mutual wills

Mutual wills arise where two people, by agreement, execute wills in which they both leave their property or part of it in identical ways, agreeing not to revoke the wills. They usually arise between husband and wife. For example, a husband (H) and wife (W) might make an agreement that they will each leave all of their property in their respective wills to the survivor, on the understanding that on the death of the survivor their joint property is to pass to their daughter, Miranda. The problem with this is that it is an established principle that all wills are revocable, and an agreement not to revoke a will does not make it irrevocable. Thus a new will in breach of the agreement takes effect, but equity (in order to prevent a party from reneging on his or her agreement) imposes a constructive trust under which the beneficiary or beneficiaries under the new will hold the property which is subject to the agreement on constructive trust for the person or persons to be benefited by the agreement. There are conflicting views as to precisely what property will be the subject of a constructive trust (see Mitchell (1951) 14 MLR 136). Figure 2.7 illustrates the possible effects of mutual wills.

It is quite clear that the trust will include the property received by H2 from H's estate. Moreover, in *Re Hagger* [1930] 2 Ch 190, the view was taken that as the trust arose at the death of the first to die it would attach also to all the property owned by the survivor (W) at the time of death of H. As to whether it includes property subsequently acquired by W after the death of H, the position is less clear and fraught with problems. The

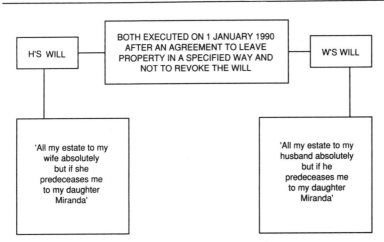

H dies on 11 June 1990. W remarries (to H2) on 24 December 1990. W dies on 1 January 1991 without executing any further will. (W's will of 1 January 1990 will automatically be revoked by her marriage to H2.)

DEVOLUTION OF H AND W'S PROPERTY

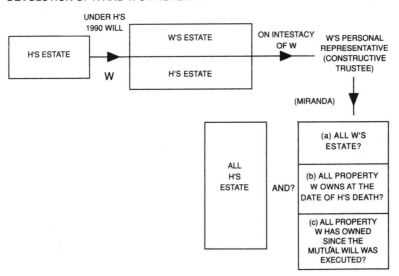

Figure 2.7

view may be taken as regards such property that the agreement to execute mutual wills operates as a covenant to settle the after-acquired property (see Chapter 5), but this would in effect reduce W to the status of a life tenant as she would not be able to dispose of the property inter vivos. If, on the other hand, W's obligation was simply not to dispose of the property *by will* inconsistently with the agreement, and thus she could do as she plased with it during her lifetime, this would seem to pose a problem of lack of certainty in the creation of a trust (see Chapter 3).

Irrevocable licences to occupy land
A licence to occupy land may be defined as a permission to be physically present on land without being there by virtue of a proprietary interest in the land. As such, a licence is a personal right which does not bind third parties. Licences to occupy may arise gratuitously or by contractual agreement. The common law regarded any licence to be revocable by the licensor, even if, in the case of a contractual licence, this involved a breach of contract. Equity, however, has taken a different view, finding that in some circumstances a licence to occupy may be, or become, irrevocable by the licensor, and furthermore in some cases it may be binding and irrevocable as against a third-party purchaser. One way in which an irrevocable contractual licence has been made enforceable against third parties is by means of a constructive trust. In *Binions* v. *Evans* [1972] 2 All ER 70 where a purchaser of land expressly agreed to take subject to a contractual licence to occupy (a purely personal right), the purchaser was held to the agreement by the imposition of a constructive trust. The use of constructive trusts to enforce contractual licences against third parties in appropriate cases was not totally ruled out by the Court of Appeal in the significant authority of *Ashburn Anstalt* v. *Arnold & Co* [1989] Ch 1. Although the court felt unable to accept as a general proposition the view that when a sale of land was made 'subject to' a contractual licence a constructive trust would be imposed on the purchaser to give effect to the licence, Fox LJ stated that the court would impose a constructive trust where the conscience of the estate owner was affected.

To give effect to a declared trust lacking formalities
In some cases the doctrine of constructive trust has been used to give effect to an express trust which would otherwise be unenforceable due to lack of evidence in writing which is normally necessary to make a trust of land enforceable (see Chapter 4). For example, in *Bannister* v. *Bannister* [1948] 2 All ER 133 a woman made an oral agreement to sell the cottage she owned to her nephew on the understanding that she could continue

to live in the cottage for as long as she wished. The price agreed was for this reason less than the full value of the property. The cottage was conveyed to her nephew but there was no mention in the conveyance of her being allowed to live in the cottage. The nephew sought, relying on the absolute title vested in him by the conveyance, to evict his aunt from the cottage. He argued that no trust of the land came into existence as this required writing under s.53(1)(b) of the Law of Property Act 1925. The court held that since it was fraudulent of the nephew in the circumstances to attempt to rely on the absolute character of the conveyance, he held the cottage on constructive trust for his aunt to allow her to remain there for so long as she wished. A constructive trust, it should be noted, requires no formalities (s.53(2) of the Law of Property Act 1925). The basis of imposing a constructive trust was the principle that equity will not allow a statute to be used as an instrument of fraud. It should be noted, however, that in *Rochefoucald* v. *Boustead* [1897] 1 Ch 196, the court (in similar circumstances to those of *Bannister* v. *Bannister*) regarded itself as enforcing the express trust notwithstanding the absence of writing, and therefore found it unnecessary to invoke the doctrine of constructive trusts.

The use of constructive trusts in this area has arguably been extended by the decision in *Lyus* v. *Prowsa Developments* [1982] 1 WLR 1044 where no fraud in the strict sense would seem to have been present. Here a purchaser was bound on the basis of a constructive trust when he agreed to take 'subject to' certain rights which would not otherwise have been binding upon him. This was so even though there was no evidence put to the court that a sum less than the full market value had been paid on account of the agreement to take 'subject to' the rights, and therefore possibly the purchaser had not been unjustifiably enriched in any way.

Intermeddling

'Intermeddling' in trust property can take a wide variety of forms, but it basically occurs where someone who is not a trustee of the property interferes or intermeddles with the trust property or the administration of the trust when he/she knew, or ought to have known, that a breach of fiduciary duty was being committed. This important area of constructive trusts is discussed in detail in sections 11.3 and 11.5. A simple example at this stage will suffice. Supposing S, a solicitor to a trust (without consulting the trustees), invests trust monies which are in his possession in a manner which is in breach of the duty of care owed by trustees in investing trust property, and this causes loss to the trust. S, although not a trustee, having assumed a duty of a trustee will be liable to the beneficiaries of the trust in the same way as an expressly appointed trustee, but on a constructive trust basis.

Establishing an interest in the family home

Where a party claims an interest in the family home but is not named in the conveyance and there is no express declaration of trust in writing (s.53(1)(b) of the Law of Property Act 1925) in his or her favour, he or she will have to rely on resulting or constructive trust principles to establish an interest in the family home (see Chapter 15). Such a person may be able to establish a constructive trust where there is evidence of a common intention that the party was to have an interest in the property and they are able to show they have acted to their detriment in reliance upon such an agreement.

2.5 Overlap between Resulting and Constructive Trusts

Before the *Vandervell* cases (above) and the development of the constructive trust to establish an interest in the family home there appeared to be a fairly clear distinction between the concept of a resulting trust and that of a constructive trust. All resulting trusts were implied trusts in the sense that they arose out of the actual or presumed intentions of the parties, whilst constructive trusts were imposed by law irrespective of intention. It has already been explained that the concept of an 'automatic' resulting trust has developed and no longer requires intention. At the same time more recent cases suggest that, at least in one sphere, namely establishing and interest in the family home, a constructive trust does require intention (see section 15.5). Thus there has been a blurring of the distinction between resulting and constructive trusts and this is particularly so in the sphere of establishing an interest in the family home. This issue is explained more fully in Chapter 15.

2.6 Nature of a Constructive Trust: Is the Trust a Right or a Remedy?

The traditional view is that the constructive trust is a substantive relationship akin to an express trust. In the United States of America, however, the trust has been treated as a remedy given to prevent unjust enrichment. This approach is supported by the *Restatement of Restitution* (#60) which reads: 'Where a person holding title to property is subject to an equitable duty to convey it to another on the ground that he would be unjustly enriched if he were permitted to retain it, a constructive trust arises.' The American view has been adopted to some extent in English authority (an approach foreseen by Scott (1955) 71 LQR 39). Lord Denning MR (in *Hussey* v. *Palmer* [1972] 3 All ER 744) has said that a constructive trust 'is a trust imposed by law whenever justice and good conscience require it. It is an equitable remedy by which the court can enable an aggrieved party to obtain restitution.' In other cases, however, the court has refused to treat the trust as a remedy. Browne-Wilkinson J (in *Re Sharpe* [1980] 1 WLR 219) described Lord Denning MR's approach as 'novel', and added that 'in order to provide a remedy the court must first find a right which has been infringed'. The facts of *Re Sharpe* demonstrate the possible practical importance of the distinction. A nephew had bought a house with the assistance of £12 000 provided by his aunt by way of loan and with the understanding that she could remain in the house as long as the loan was unpaid. Later the nephew became bankrupt and one issue which arose was whether the aunt had an interest in the house which was binding upon the trustee in bankruptcy. Browne-Wilkinson J decided that the aunt had an interest in the house by way of constructive trust. It was argued for the trustee in bankruptcy that the constructive trust was only a remedy awarded by the court and that, since the bankruptcy had occurred before the court order, the bankruptcy took priority over the trust. His lordship rejected the view that the constructive trust was remedial in this sense and held that the constructive trust arose out of a substantive right which was created before the bankruptcy and which was therefore binding upon the trustee in bankruptcy. The imposition of a constructive trust on the facts in *Re Sharpe* has been doubted (in *Ashburn Anstalt* v. *Arnold* [1988] 2 WLR 706), but the decision remains seminal in respect of the extent to which the constructive trust may be remedial.

Professor Birks (*Introduction to the Law of Restitution*, pp.88–93) has argued that neither the traditional view that the constructive trust is a substantive right, nor the more modern view that the trust is a remedy to enable an aggrieved party to obtain restitution, is entirely correct. In respect of the traditional view he says that use of the term 'trust' is misleading as there has been no entrustment of property. Where a plaintiff has a claim *in rem* against a defendant, the defendant by necessity holds the property for the benefit of the plaintiff and hence the word 'trust' is used; but, he states, this is simply a conclusion to describe the outcome of a claim on some other ground, and should not be confused with entrustment. Of the modern view, Birks submits that the trust is sometimes restitutionary to undo an unjust enrichment, but on other occasions it is not. Where, for example, a vendor of land under a contract for sale holds on constructive trust for a purchaser the trust is not being used to reverse any unjust enrichment of the vendor.

Summary

1 There are two types of implied trust, resulting trusts and constructive trusts. Resulting trusts arise where there is an outright failure of an express trust or where there is a failure to dispose of part of the beneficial interest. There is also, subject to exceptions, a presumption of a resulting trust where one person purchases or voluntarily transfers property into the name of another, or into the joint names of the transferor and another. Resulting trusts may be 'presumed', in which case they depend on the presumed intentions of the settlor, or 'automatic', where they arise irrespective of intention. Likewise, a constructive trust may arise out of the intentions of the parties or it may be imposed by law, irrespective of the parties' intentions. As resulting and constructive trusts have common characteristics the distinction between them is not always clear.

2 The circumstances in which a constructive trust arises are many and varied. This is because the boundaries of the concept of a constructive trust are somewhat vague. This has enabled it to be developed to deal with new situations. The generally accepted view is that a constructive trust is not a remedial device but a substantive relationship akin to an express trust.

3 The main areas in which constructive trusts arise have merely been touched upon in this chapter. However, one important area where constructive trusts operate which has been dealt with more fully is the imposition of a constructive trust to prevent an unauthorised profit by a fiduciary. The principle operates whether the profit was made honestly or dishonestly. It is not possible to make an exhaustive list of fiduciary relationships, and there is evidence to suggest that in some cases a fiduciary relationship is found to exist purely to impose a duty on a party to disgorge a profit. The case law on the circumstances in which a fiduciary must account for a profit made is not entirely consistent. Some cases seem to take the view that once it is established that the fiduciary has learned of the opportunity to make the profit by reason of the fiduciary relationship, he or she will automatically be liable to account, whether or not there is an actual conflict of duty and personal interest. Other cases are not so rigid. A further problem is that the case law does not always distinguish between the imposition of a constructive trust and a personal liability to account even though this has important practical consequences.

Exercises

1 Compare and contrast resulting and constructive trusts.

2 Distinguish between 'presumed' and 'automatic' resulting trusts.

3 Discuss the effect of the following transactions:

(a) Anita purchases shares in Fastbuck Plc but the title of the shares is registered in the name of Belinda, a friend;

(b) Charles purchases a house, the title to which is registered in the joint names of Charles and David, a friend;

(c) Eric purchases a house, the title to which is conveyed into the name of Fanny (aged 20), his daughter by adoption;

(d) George opens a bank account with £10 000 he has won on the horses (the account is in the joint names of George and his wife Harriet);

(e) Ivy puts up £80 000 for a house, the legal title to which is conveyed into the name of Jack with whom she is co-habiting, on the advice of Jack that this is the only way of avoiding any claim by her separated husband.

4 'It is an inflexible rule of a Court of Equity that a person in a fiduciary position is not, unless expressly provided, entitled to make a profit; he is not allowed to put himself in a position where his interest and duty conflict' (Lord Herschell, *Bray* v. *Ford*).

(a) Explain the reasons for this principle.

(b) Do you think the principle has been too strictly applied in some cases?

5 'It is not safe to make the attractive over-simplification of saying that a fiduciary must always account for all gains which come to him by reason of his fiduciary position' (Hanbury and Maudsley, 13th edn, p.565). Discuss.

6 Distinguish between a personal liability to account and the imposition of a constructive trust, explaining the practical importance of the distinction.

7 Princeland Mines Ltd was interested in developing mining operations. It appointed Able as a director of the company because of his experience in negotiating the licences necessary for the type of operation contemplated. Able was successful in obtaining seven licences for Princeland Mines Ltd but, due to severe liquidity problems, the company was only able to make use of four of the licences. Subsequently, Able obtained a release from his position as director of Princeland Mines Ltd under the terms of his contract and shortly afterwards he obtained transfers of the remaining three licences from Princeland Mines Ltd to himself with the co-operation of the remaining directors. Able successfully developed the three mines to which the licences related, making substantial profits.

   The shareholders of Princeland Mines Ltd now wish to make Able account for the profits he has made. Advise the shareholders.

Part II

Creation of Express Trusts

Part I

3 Certainty

A properly created trust is a legally binding obligation enforceable in the courts, but before a court will enforce any obligation it must be convinced that the obligation has been defined with sufficient certainty. In the case of a trust it must be certain that the settlor intended that there should be an obligation of trust; that the settlor has clearly indicated what property is subject to the obligation; and that the beneficiaries are plainly defined; or, in the words of Lord Eldon LC (in *Wright* v. *Atkyns* (1823) Turn & R 143, 147), 'First that the words must be imperative . . . secondly that the subject must be certain . . . ; and thirdly, that the object must be as certain as the subject.'

The requirements of certainty are of significant practical importance because uncertainty can cause disputes about the ownership of property both between the person who is the donee (and who is possibly trustee) on the one hand and the beneficiaries on the other hand; and between the beneficiaries and the donor's estate. In addition uncertainty can cause argument with the Inland Revenue which will attempt to levy income tax on the beneficial owner of income-producing assets. A settlor may have attempted to create a trust of property so that he is no longer taxable on the income produced by that property but may find that he has failed to form the trust with sufficient certainty and that this results in him receiving an unexpected tax bill in respect of the property interest which has not been disposed of.

3.1 Certainty of Intention or Words

The settlor must show that he intends a trust. This will normally be demonstrated by the words used by him, but conduct may also be important. Whether oral evidence and conduct is admissible to prove intention depends upon the degree of formality required to prove the particular type of trust (see Chapter 4).

The significance of the requirement is that there must be an adequate degree of certainty to prove to a court that a trust was intended since, if a court erroneously holds that the donee of property is a trustee where this was not intended, it will be unfairly depriving the donee of ownership. Alternatively, if it makes the error of deciding that the donee is absolute owner when this was not in the contemplation of the settlor it will be

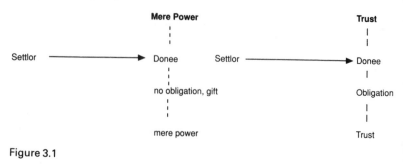

Figure 3.1

unfairly depriving the intended beneficiaries and enabling the donee fraudulently to keep the property for himself.

Mere powers and certainty of intention

When a settlor transfers property to a donee he may intend an obligation of trust. If he does not wish to create an obligation there will be a gift. It is often difficult to ascertain which was intended because, even if there is a gift, the settlor may have requested the donee to deal with the property in some manner but without intending an obligation. In such a case the direction as to how the property is to be dealt with will not create an obligation or trust but will be a mere power (see Figure 3.1).

Powers of appointment and certainty

Sometimes a donee of property is instructed to appoint some person or persons to become beneficiaries of the property. If the donee has been given a general power of appointment allowing any person, including the donee, to be appointed then this indicates that there is no intention to create an obligation in favour of a beneficiary, since the donee could appoint himself and there can be no question of a court ordering him to do otherwise and there is therefore no trust. On the other hand, a specific power to appoint amongst a class of persons excluding the donee may

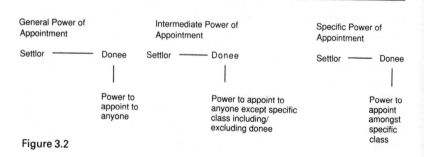

Figure 3.2

create a trust if the words used are imperative. If the words are not mandatory there will, of course, be a mere power (see Figure 3.2).

A third possibility is an intermediate power of appointment. This might be a power to appoint to anyone in the world except specified persons. If the trustee is excluded and the words of the settlor are imperative (see below) a trust will be created.

Formal trusts and precatory words

In the case of a formal document, such as a will or deed inter vivos, whether there is an obligatory direction creating a trust or simply a request giving rise to a mere power will depend primarily upon the words used. Extrinsic evidence will only be admitted by a court in exceptional circumstances. If the words are unequivocally imperative, such as 'on trust', there will normally be a trust. If the words are not compulsory or are precatory – that is, they express hope or desire – then it is highly unlikely that a trust has been created. In early cases (before the mid-nineteenth century) the courts were quite likely to hold that a trust was created by precatory words (for the reason behind this see Parker and Mellows, 5th edn, p.61) but in modern cases the opposite is true.

Lambe v. *Eames* (1871) 6 Ch App 597 is one of the leading cases on the use of precatory words. A testator gave his estate to his widow 'to be at her disposal in any way she may think best for the benefit of herself and family'. The widow subsequently gave part of the property to an illegitimate grandson of the testator. Legitimate members of the family claimed that there was a trust for them. The Court of Appeal held that there was no trust. R. Malins at first instance (1870) LR 10 Eq 267) said that the words 'were rather intended as a hint to her, which was not intended to be obligatory upon her'.

In most cases where the words used are words of hope, desire (see *Re Diggles* (1888) 39 Ch D 253) or confidence there will be no trust. For example, in *Re Adams and Kensington Vestry* (1884) 27 Ch D 394 a testator gave all his property to his widow 'in full confidence that she would do what was right as to the disposal thereof between his children'. It was held that the widow took the property absolutely. There was no trust for the children.

If, however, precatory words are accompanied by other words which indicate an obligation then there will be a trust. Such was the case in the leading House of Lords decision of *Comiskey* v. *Bowring-Hanbury* [1905] AC 84. A testator left his property to his widow 'absolutely in full confidence that she will make such use of it as I should have made myself and that at her death she will devise it to such one or more of my nieces as she may think fit'. This part of the direction, being precatory, would not have been enough to impose a trust; but the will went on to direct that 'in default of any disposition by her thereof by her will or testament I hereby direct that all my estate and property . . . shall at her death be equally divided among the surviving said nieces'. The additional words directing that in any event the property was to be divided between the nieces showed that a trust was intended and the House of Lords (Lord Lindley dissenting) so held. Particular words used in one context may create a trust (such as the use of the term 'confidence' in *Comiskey* v. *Bowring-Hanbury*); whereas the same words in another context may not (such as the use of the same term 'confidence' in *Re Adams and Kensington Vestry*). The question is one of construction of the terms of the particular trust: 'Undoubtedly confidence, if the rest of the context shows that a trust is intended, may make a trust, but what we have to look at is the whole of the will which we have to construe' (see Cotton LJ in *Re Adams and Kensington Vestry*).

Another exceptional example where a trust may be created notwithstanding the presence of precatory words is where the words used by a settlor are identical to words used in some previously decided case where a trust was found. In *Re Steele's Will Trusts* [1948] 2 All ER 193 the precatory word used in a will was 'request' but the wording of the entire bequest was precisely the same as in an earlier trust reported in *Shelley* v. *Shelley* (1868) LR 6 Eq 540 where a trust was established. Wynn Parry J held that, since the draftsman for the settlor had used words matching those in the antecedent case, a trust must have been intended.

Informal declarations

It is not always necessary for a trust to be created by formal will or deed (see Chapter 5). A trust may be created informally by speech or conduct. In the case of an informal declaration the courts will look at the words used together with surrounding circumstances in order to decide whether or not a trust has been created. In *Paul* v. *Constance* [1977] 1 WLR 527 a man had a bank account in his own name but on several occasions he had told a woman friend, 'The money is as much yours as mine', and the account had been operated jointly with them paying in joint bingo winnings and with her being allowed to draw on the account. The Court of Appeal held that even though it was difficult to pinpoint a specific moment in time when a trust was created, there was sufficient certainty that the man intended to create a trust of the account for them both jointly.

It should not be thought, however, that every informal transaction will be considered to be a trust. A trust must have been intended. If another transaction was intended but is not complete then it will not be regarded as a complete trust. Equity will not, for instance, construe an incomplete gift as a perfect trust. In *Richards* v. *Delbridge* (1874) LR 18 Eq 11, J.D.

was the owner of a lease of premises. He endorsed on the lease a memorandum stating that he was giving the lase to E.B.R. and he handed the lease over to E.B.R.'s mother to hold for him. This amounted to an incomplete gift since there was no deed of assignment of the lease to E.B.R. The Court held also that it could not be considered to be a complete trust with J.D. holding on trust for E.B.R. since it was never intended to create a trust, but J.D. instead intended a gift which he had never completed.

Commercial agreements and intention to create trusts

It is common for parties to commercial agreements to make use of the trust, especially since the trust can be particularly useful in providing priority to beneficiaries in the event of insolvency. It will be recalled (see Chapter 1) that in *Re Kayford* [1975] 1 WLR 279, a company conducting a mail-order business experienced financial problems and its accountants advised it to open a separate customers' 'trust deposit account' and to pay into it all money received from customers for goods not yet delivered, withdrawing money only upon delivery of goods, so that if the company should go into liquidation the money could be fully refunded to the customers. The company took the accountants' advice except that initially the account was simply in the company's name. When the company went into liquidation it was held that the money in the account was held on trust for the customers and could not be treated as part of the company's assets in the liquidation.

A comparable problem has sometimes arisen where money has been advanced by way of a loan for a particular purpose, and it is difficult to tell whether a simple loan was intended or whether there should also, or alternatively, be a trust. In *Barclays Bank Ltd* v. *Quistclose Investments Ltd* [1970] AC 567, a company, Rolls Razor, had declared a dividend on its shares which it was unable to pay without a loan. Quistclose Investments agreed to make the loan on condition that it was used to pay the dividend and it was paid into a special bank account on the understanding that it would only be used to meet the dividend due. Before the dividend was paid Rolls Razor went into liquidation. The question which then arose was whether the transaction was simply a loan in which case it was the property of Rolls Razor and could be claimed by its creditors, or whether Rolls Razor held the bank account on trust for Quistclose, in which case Quistclose could recover the money in priority to creditors. The House of Lords held that the intention was not to make a simple loan but instead it was intended that there should be a primary trust for the purpose of paying the dividends with a secondary trust in favour of Quistclose in the event that the primary trust was not carried out. Consequently Quistclose procured repayment of the money (see also section 12.4).

In these commercial circumstances it can be particularly difficult to decide whether a trust has been created. Even if the word 'trust' has been used this is not conclusive since the substance of the transaction may negate the expressed intention for a trust. The conundrum has arisen recently in contracts for the sale of goods on credit in which the seller of goods attempts to retain some proprietary right in the goods pending full payment by the buyer (a so-called 'title retention' clause). The case of *Re Bond Worth* [1980] Ch 228 (see also *Clough Mill* v. *Martin* [1985] 1 WLR 111) is a good example of the difficulty. In that case a contract for the sale of fibre for carpets provided that 'equitable and beneficial ownership' should remain with the seller until the buyer made full payment. Meanwhile the buyer was allowed to use the fibre in carpet manufacture and to sell the carpets. On the insolvency of the buyer the seller claimed that the fibre was held on trust for it. Slade J held that the contract did not create a trust since it was really intended to act as a charge by way of security (so that in the event of failure in payment by the purchaser the seller would be able to sell the fibre to procure payment), and the buyer's right to absolute ownership upon full payment was inconsistent with a trust for the seller. Although the attempt to create a trust failed in *Re Bond Worth* it does not necessarily follow that it would fail in all other cases. The courts will examine each case individually to determine whether a trust has been created.

Certainty of intention and implied trusts

The question of certainty of intention to create a trust may be an issue not only in respect of express trusts but also in the case of implied trusts. Although implied trusts sometimes arise without any intention on the part of the legal owner, on other occasions an implied trust comes about because of some intention, whether express or implied (see Chapter 2). Sometimes the intention of the parties has been clearly expressed and a constructive trust is imposed by equity to give effect to that intention: for example, where a purchaser of land agrees to take subject to an interest of a third party which would be void against the purchaser for lack of formality, a constructive trust arises to give effect to the certain intention of the parties (see Chapter 2).

In cases where no intention is expressed an implied trust may arise because of an inferred intention of the parties. In this case there may be problems of ascertaining what the common intention of the parties is. One instance which occasionally appears in the context of personal relationships (but which is also relevant in the commercial sphere) is where one person lends money to another to enable the other to purchase land. The intention of the parties may be that there is simply to be a gift, or an unsecured loan, or that there is to be a loan secured by a charge over the property in favour of the lender or that the person making the contribution should have a beneficial interest in the land, giving rise to an implied trust in favour of the contributor in proportion to the contribution. These circumstances are examined in detail in Chapter 15.

3.2 Certainty of Property

The settlor must have clearly identified the property which is to be the subject-matter of the trust so that it is clearly separate from the remainder of his estate, otherwise dispute may arise between the intended beneficiaries and those otherwise entitled to the settlor's estate.

Property as a Whole and Beneficial Shares

Glanville Williams (1940) 4 MLR 20 has pointed out that certainty of subject-matter may import two distinct requirements. First, the property which is the subject-matter of the trust must be certain. Second, if there is more than one beneficiary there must be certainty as to the extent of the beneficial share of each. In uncommon cases there might be difficulty over the property as a whole as in *Re London Wine Co (Shippers) Ltd* (1976) 126 NLJ 978. A wine company sold wine to customers on the basis that the customer paid for the wine in advance which was stored by the company and which was to continue to be stored by the company until some future time when delivery would be taken. Meanwhile, the company would issue certificates of title to the customers with a reference to the number of a particular consignment, but there was no actual physical segregation of the wine within the warehouse. A question arose over the ownership of the wine. It was decided that it was not held on trust for the customers since there was no clear property upon which the trust could fix. More often the uncertainty is uncertainty as to the beneficial shares to be taken by various beneficiaries. *Boyce* v. *Boyce* (below), where there was a gift of several houses to be divided between several beneficiaries but it was not clear which beneficiaries would receive which houses, is an example.

Objective or subjective test?

Occasionally a settlor may specify the extent of the subject-matter by use of a variable adjective such as 'reasonable' or 'substantial'. In such a case it has not been authoritatively decided whether the test to be used in deciding the meaning of the word is an objective one decided upon by the courts, or whether the meaning of the word used should be considered to be that intended subjectively by the settlor. An objective test was accepted at first instance in *Re Golay's WT* [1965] 1 WLR 969, where the testator instructed his executors to allow a beneficiary 'to receive a reasonable income from my . . . properties'. Ungoed-Thomas J considered 'reasonable income' to be certain property on the basis that 'the testator intended by "reasonable income" the yardstick which the court could and would apply in quantifying the amount'.

In contrast with this is the analogous decision of *Re Kolb's WT* [1962] Ch 531, which examined the validity of a power to invest the testator's estate in 'Blue Chip' investments. Despite expert evidence on the meaning of the phrase 'Blue Chip', Cross J said that the test to be applied was a subjective one depending upon the standards of the testator. The clause was therefore void for uncertainty because there was no certainty as to the testator's interpretation of the phrase. It is suggested that the approach in *Re Kolb* is an overzealous application of the principle that the courts should seek out the intention of the testator. By trying to find the testator's intention in *Re Kolb* the court was forced to conclude that it was impossible to discover exactly what that intention was, and the result was that the power to invest failed altogether, which was the thing furthest from the testator's intention. It is submitted that the objective approach in *Re Golay* is better since it avoids the failure of the gift, and surely if a testator in a will uses particular terminology he must be taken to know that it is his executors or the courts who will be applying that terminology, and therefore that the meaning will be subject to the interpretation of the trustees or the courts and not that which the testator might subjectively intend.

Discretions given to beneficiaries

Sometimes the trust property is to be ascertained by the trustee or beneficiary exercising a discretion or choice given by the trust instrument. If such a discretion is given to trustees it imposes a duty upon them and, in default of their exercise of the discretion, the court will carry out their functions and there is no problem of uncertainty of subject-matter. If, however, a discretion is given to a beneficiary to choose part of the trust property, no obligation is imposed and there may be problems of uncertainty if the discretion is left unexercised. In *Boyce* v. *Boyce* (1849) 16 Sim 476 a testator directed that his houses should be held upon trust for his widow for life, and after her death to convey one of them to his daughter Maria (whichever she might choose) and to convey any other houses to his daughter Charlotte. Maria died in the testator's lifetime without having expressed a choice and the question arose as to what Charlotte would receive, if anything. The Vice-Chancellor decided that

Charlotte would receive nothing because her beneficial share was uncertain.

This type of case causes substantial difficulties. The beneficiary has the right, but not the duty, to make an election. Apparently the gift will be valid if the election is actually made, but not if the election is not made. Whilst the donee of the power is alive the gift is held in limbo since the donee could make an election at any time during his lifetime (Coke on Littleton) but may become void on his death if he has not by then made the election.

Gifts-over of uncertain amounts

Probably the most common case of uncertainty of beneficial shares is where there is a gift of certain subject-matter to one person for his or her lifetime with a direction that some indefinite part of the property is to be passed to other beneficiaries on the death of the life tenant. *Sprange* v. *Barnard* (1789) 2 Bro CC 585 (see also *Curtis* v. *Rippon* (1820) 5 Madd 434) is one instance of this type of case. A testatrix gave property to her husband 'for his sole use; and, at his death, the remaining part of what is left, that he does not want for his own wants and use, to be divided between' the testatrix's brothers and sisters. Lord Arden MR held that there was no trust for the brothers and sisters since it would be impossible to ascertain to what property they would be entitled. Similarly in *Palmer* v. *Simmonds* (1854) 2 Drew 221, a gift of residue to T.H. for his use, and directing him to leave the 'bulk' of it on his death to other beneficiaries, was held to be an absolute gift to T.H. as it would be impossible to ascertain the beneficial share of the other beneficiaries since the term 'bulk' was uncertain. It may be possible on the facts of some similar cases to find that there is sufficient certainty to hold that there is a valid life interest followed by a remainder interest. In *Re Last* [1958] 1 All ER 316 the testatrix stated in her will that she gave and bequeathed to her brother all property and everything she had, money or otherwise. At her brother's death anything that was left was to go to her late husband's grandchildren. It was held that the brother had a life interest in the income only and the capital was to pass to the grandchildren. *Sprange* v. *Barnard* was not referred to.

Effect of uncertainty of subject-matter

Reflex action on certainty of words

If the subject-matter is uncertain the uncertainty sheds doubt upon the intention of the settlor to create a trust and makes it more likely that the words used by him should not be regarded as mandatory. Sir Arthur Hobhouse in *Mussoorie Bank* v. *Raynor* (1882) 7 App Cas 321, p.331, said: 'the uncertainty of the subject of the gift has a reflex action upon the previous words and throws doubt upon the intention of the testator, and seems to show that he could not possibly have intended his words of confidence, hope or whatever they may be . . . to be imperative words'. This has an important effect since, if there is uncertainty of intention, the property will be taken absolutely by the donee and will not be held upon a resulting trust as would normally occur in the case of uncertainty of subject-matter alone.

Destination of property

As has been seen above uncertainty of subject-matter may arise in a number of ways. If there is uncertainty as to the subject-matter the property may remain with, or there may be a resulting trust of the property for, the settlor, or a donee may be able to keep the property absolutely. The possibilities are considered in depth in Chapter 6.

3.3 Certainty of Beneficiaries

The uninitiated might assume that there should be no difficulty in establishing with certainty the beneficiaries or objects of the trust, and in most cases the uninitiated would be correct. In other cases the question of certainty of objects has proved the most perplexing conundrum. The law requires that there must be persons (either individual or corporate) and that those persons must be sufficiently identifiable.

The requirement of beneficiaries

In the case of a private trust it is not enough that there is a purpose. The purpose must be to benefit persons. The reason for the rule is that a legal obligation needs some person who has the benefit of it and who can make an application to court to enforce it. If there is no such person with a right to sue then there can be no legal obligation and by definition no trust. According to Roxburgh J in *Re Astor's Trust* [1952] Ch 534:

> The typical case of a trust is one in which the legal owner of property is constrained by a court of equity so as to deal with it as to give effect to the equitable right of another . . . a trustee would not be expected to be subject to an equitable obligation unless there was somebody who could enforce a correlative equitable right.

Thus where there is an attempted trust for some purpose (for instance, for the preservation of the independence and integrity of newspapers as in *Re Astor's Trust*), there can be no trust since there is no one who could act to enforce the intended obligation. In the case of charitable trusts society has provided that the trust may be enforced by the Attorney-General at the public expense, but in other cases it is difficult to see how the intended trust might be enforced (but see Chapter 12).

Specification of beneficiaries
The objects of a trust may be identified in different ways with differing degrees of certainty. For example, if a settlor specifies that 'Samson and Delilah' are the beneficiaries then the beneficiaries are readily identified, and there are rarely problems of uncertainty. If a gift is in favour of a class or genus instead of a named person or persons, certainty is not so easily achieved. For example, a trust may be expressed to be in favour of children as a class (rather than in favour of certain named children), so that as children are born or die they become part of the class or cease to be within it. This type of gift can give rise to difficulties if the classification used is tinged with uncertainty. The term 'friends', for instance, may give rise to different interpretations.

There are at least five different techniques which may be adopted by a settlor to specify the beneficiaries under a trust.

Specified beneficiaries
The simplest and most certain method of specifying objects is to have specified beneficiaries, whether in the singular or the plural, as in the example of a trust for 'Samson and Delilah', given above.

Fixed trust in favour of a class
A trust in favour of a class may be a fixed trust, where defined property is to be divided equally amongst the members of a class of beneficiaries: for example, amongst 'children' or 'brothers'.

Discretionary trust
A further technique is a discretionary trust where the settlor directs that property should be distributed amongst members of a class of persons as the trustees in their discretion so choose (see Chapter 7).

Special power of appointment
A special power of appointment is another tool which might be utilised by a settlor. In this case the settlor specifies a class of persons (excluding the trustee) and the trustee is given a power to appoint a person or persons from that class to become the beneficiary or beneficiaries of the trust: for example, the settlor might specify that the trustee should hold property upon a discretionary trust, with the beneficiaries of the discretionary trust being 'such of my relatives as my trustee shall appoint'.

Intermediate power of appointment

An intermediate power of appointment is a further arrangement which might be adopted. This gives the trustee a power to appoint anyone except for certain people or groups of people (e.g., the trustee, the settlor and the settlor's spouse) as beneficiary, or beneficiaries.

Problems of uncertainty

Uncertainty of objects is a problem which has plagued class gifts. The courts have considered at length the degree of certainty which is required for such gifts.

Basic 'is – is not' test for discretionary trusts

The present law is the result of the decision of the House of Lords in *McPhail* v. *Doulton* [1971] AC 424. In that case trustees of a fund established to benefit employees of a company were given a discretion to apply the income 'to or for the benefit of any of the officers and employees or ex-officers or ex-employees of the company or to any relatives or dependants of any such persons . . . as they think fit'. It was argued that the trust was void, applying the test in *IRC* v. *Broadway Cottages Trust* [1955] 1 Ch 20 that it should be possible to make a list of all beneficiaries. The House of Lords held that the trust was valid even though it might not be possible to make such a list. Lord Wilberforce said, 'the trust is valid if it can be said with certainty that any given individual is or is not a member of the class'. The case was then remitted to Brightman J in the High Court for application of the 'is or is not' test. Brightman J (in *Re Baden's Deed Trusts (No 2) [1972] Ch 607*) held that the test was satisfied and the objects were certain (see Figure 3.3).

The decision was appealed against. In respect of 'relatives' it was objected that there might be some people of whom it was not certain whether or not they were in the class, and that the trust was void. The Court of Appeal (at [1973] Ch 9) took the view that the *McPhail* v.

Ask whether it can be said of each postulant whether he is within the class. If the answer for any person is neither 'yes' nor 'no' but it is uncertain then the trust fails:

yes   yes   yes   no   uncertain

As it cannot be said with certainty whether the last postulant is with the class or not there is no trust.

Figure 3.3 Application of 'is – is not' test

Doulton test was satisfied even though there might be some persons of whom it could not be said that they were or were not member of the class. Megaw LJ said:

> To my mind the test is satisfied if as regards at least a substantial number of objects, it can be said with certainty that they fall within the trust; even though, as regards a substantial number of other persons, if they ever for some fanciful reason fell to be considered, the answer would have to be not 'they are outside the trust' but 'it is not proven whether they are in or out'.

As it cannot be proved that this last category of persons is within the class those persons are treated as excluded. The net result of the litigation is to leave the law in a state of uncertainty, since it is not clear that the House of Lords would agree with the Court of Appeal that the 'is – is not' test is satisfied so long as it can be said that a substantial number of persons will satisfy it (see Figure 3.4).

Test for a fixed trust

The litigation in *McPhail* v. *Doulton* and *Re Baden* has left the law in a state of uncertainty. The statement of the test in the House of Lords appears to be stricter than that in the Court of Appeal. In addition it is unclear whether the decision, which was concerned with a discretionary trust, is applicable to fixed trusts. Hanbury and Maudsley (p.97: see also P. Matthews [1984] Conv. 22, Martin [1984] Conv. 304) suggest that a stricter rule is required in the case of a fixed trust requiring equal division. They say in this case it must be possible to make a list of the possible beneficiaries.

Despite these difficulties the Court of Appeal approach has been hailed by Grbich (1974) 37 MLR 643, as the most important modern development in the law of trusts because the approach allows a trust to

So long as it can be said of a substantial number of persons that they are within the trust, the trust is valid. If a person is not clearly within the class he is treated as being excluded:

As it can be said of a substantial number of persons that they are within the class, the trust is valid. The penultimate postulant is clearly outside of the class, whilst the last beneficiary cannot prove membership of the class and is treated as being outside it.

Figure 3.4 Application of 'substantial number' test

be created without a rigid concept of fixed equitable interests.

The uncertainty in the law referred to above is compounded by problems of concept and evidence which exist irrespective of the debate as to the precise effect of the decisions in *McPhail* v. *Doulton* and *Re Baden*. Emery (1982) 98 LQR 551 has explained that problems of certainty of objects may involve conceptual uncertainty, evidential uncertainty, ascertainability and administrative unworkability.

Conceptual certainty

The objects of the trust 'must be so defined that if the trustees surrendered their discretion the court would carry out the purpose', according to Roxburgh J in *Re Astor* [1952] Ch 534. In order to achieve this the object must be defined by a certain concept. For this reason the law does not support trusts for impersonal purposes. *Re Astor* is an example in which an attempted trust for, *inter alia*, 'the preservation of the independence and integrity of newspapers' was ineffective because the concepts of independence and integrity would prove too difficult to define.

Relatives

Even where the trust is for persons there can be conceptual uncertainty. In *Re Baden* the trust was partly for relatives. The court found this term slightly troublesome. Although the majority adopted the widest possible meaning of 'all descendants of a common ancestor' and by this means concluded that the gift was conceptually certain, Stamp LJ would have restricted its meaning to next of kin.

Persons having moral claims

An obviously uncertain concept is that of morality, so if a trust is in favour of such persons who have a moral claim on the settlor the trust will be void for conceptual uncertainty (Sachs LJ in *Re Baden* [1973] 1 Ch 9, p.20, and Harman LJ in *Re Leek* [1969] 1 Ch 563 at 579).

Friends

Perhaps the category of object which causes most confusion is 'friends'. Because of the development in the law effected by *McPhail* v. *Doulton*, the authorities on the validity of a trust for friends are inconclusive (see *Re Coates* [1955] 1 Ch 495; *Re Gibbard* [1966] 1 All ER 273; *Re Barlow's WT* [1979] 1 WLR 278). If it is necessary, following *McPhail* v. *Doulton*, to say of every given person that he is or is not a friend, then a trust for friends is likely to be void. On the other hand if, following *Re Baden*, it is only necessary to say of a substantial number of persons that they are friends it is more likely that such a trust would be valid.

Trustees as judges of concept
One possible way of rendering certain a class of beneficiaries which would otherwise be uncertain is by making the trustees the judges of concept. In *Re Tuck's ST* [1978] Ch 49 (see P. Matthews (1983) NLJ 913, doubting whether conceptual uncertainty can be cured in this way) the settlor made a gift to benefit persons who should be of Jewish blood and Jewish faith. He further provided that 'in case of dispute or doubt the decision of the Chief Rabbi in London . . . shall be conclusive'. The Court of Appeal held that any conceptual uncertainty in the phrase 'Jewish faith' was cured by the Chief Rabbi clause.

Powers to establish the class
An uncertain class may be ascertained by the vesting in the trustees of a hybrid or an intermediate power of appointment. In *Re Manisty* [1974] Ch 17, Clause 4 of the trust deed gave the trustees 'power . . . to declare that any person or persons corporation or corporations or charity or charities (other than a person or corporation who shall for the time being be a member of the excepted class . . .) shall . . . be included in the class of beneficiaries'. The court held that the power was valid and that the trustees were by the power able to ascertain the class by virtue of their own appointment of beneficiaries.

Words of explanation
Another way of circumventing conceptual uncertainty is to disregard the words which give rise to the uncertainty by construing them as being words of explanation only. In *Re Steel* [1978] 2 All ER 1026 the testator directed that the residue of his estate should be divided 'between those beneficiaries who have only received small amounts'. The words 'small amounts' were problematic and difficult to define. Megarry vc said that the words were merely words of explanation rather than technical qualification, and he ordered an equal division of the residue amongst all persons receiving legacies.

Evidential certainty
If there is conceptual certainty the trust is valid; 'it then becomes a question of fact to be determined on evidence whether any postulant has on enquiry been proved to be within [the class]', as Sachs LJ in *Re Baden* explained. Although it may be difficult to find sufficient evidence to prove that a postulant is within a conceptually certain class, such evidential uncertainty never invalidates a trust. For example, a trust for cousins is valid because the concept is certain even though it might be difficult to obtain evidence to prove which persons are cousins.

If there is evidential difficulty and questions of fact to decide upon, the trustees may be made judges of the facts. In *Re Coxen* [1948] Ch 747 the testator devised a house on trust directing the trustees to allow his wife to reside in it but with a gift over 'if in the opinion of my trustees she shall have ceased permanently to reside'. Jenkins J held that the trustees could decide whether residence continued or not.

Ascertainability

A slightly different evidential problem may exist where even though there is sufficient evidence to prove that a person is within the class of beneficiaries it is difficult to establish the physical whereabouts of the person. Emery (1982) 98 LQR 551 stated that 'it may be possible to draw up a complete list of all those persons . . . There may on the other hand be some doubt as to "the whereabouts or continued existence" of such beneficiaries'. This type of evidential difficulty does not invalidate the trust.

Administrative unworkability

Another factor which may have a bearing upon the practicability of the trust is that the class of beneficiaries may be so wide that the trust is administratively unworkable. Lord Wilberforce in *McPhail* v. *Doulton* said: 'the definition of beneficiaries [may be] so hopelessly wide as not to form "anything like a class" so that the trust is administratively unworkable . . . I hesitate to give examples for they may prejudice future cases but perhaps "all the residents of Greater London" will serve'. In this case the trust will be void. McKay (1974) 38 Conv. 269 has criticised Lord Wilberforce's suggestion as 'incapable of solid justification on the basis of either administrative feasibility or judicial execution'. Hardcastle [1990] Conv. 24 suggests that the idea is an extension of the notion of evidential uncertainty, and although the trust is conceptually certain there comes a point when from a practical point of view it is pointless to attempt to administer the trust. The test was applied in *R* v. *District Auditor, ex p. West Yorkshire Metropolitan CC* (see Harpum (1986) 45 CLJ 391), where a proposed trust in favour of the inhabitants of the county of West Yorkshire was considered to be administratively unworkable. It has been suggested that there is a further principle, connected with administrative workability: that is, that a trust may be void as being capricious, because the settlor has not laid down any sensible criteria for benefiting the objects. In the West Yorkshire Metropolitan CC case the trust was not void on this count as the settlor genuinely intended to benefit the specified class.

Duty to survey objects

The trustees have duties to administer the trust property for the benefit of the beneficiaries. Where the beneficiaries are limited in number and there is no problem of uncertainty the trustees will normally experience no substantial obstacles. In the case of a discretionary trust with a large number of objects the trustees should undertake some substantial survey of the range of objects so as to enable them to carry out their duties, although they do not have to consider every possible beneficiary. They do not need to worry their heads and survey every object from China to Peru (Harman J in *Re Gestetner* [1953] Ch 672). Judicial comments on the duty to survey have not made absolutely clear the extent of the duty and it may be necessary for trustees to apply to the court for directions to ascertain how far the duty extends (Hopkins (1973) 32 CLJ 36) and possibly to take out insurance against liability for maladministration (Crane (1970) 34 Conv. (NS) 287).

3.4 **Charity and Certainty**

The rules of certainty do not apply in the same way to trusts for charitable purposes. A charitable trust is valid notwithstanding that it is not in favour of specified individuals, but is instead for a charitable purpose. Further, it is not essential to specify the purpose with the same degree of clarity which would be necessary with a non-charitable trust. As long as it is clear that there is an intention to make a charitable gift on trust the gift will be valid and will be applied for some charitable purpose (see Chapter 14).

Summary

1 In order to create a valid trust three certainties must be present: namely, certainty of intention, certainty of property and certainty of objects.

2 Certainty of intention requires that the settlor shows by his or her words (and/or, possibly, conduct) that an obligation to deal with property in a particular way is intended. Although a settlor need not use the word 'trust' to create a trust it is unlikely that the court will view precatory words as creating a trust. It is, however, a matter of construction of all the terms of the document in issue to decide whether a trust is intended. Where there is no certainty of intention a donee takes absolutely.

3 Certainty of property requires that both the subject-matter of the trust be certain and that it is possible to ascertain the share each beneficiary holds in the trust property. If the trustees have discretion to decide on the beneficial shares there is no uncertainty as the trustees are under an obligation to make a decision. If a beneficiary has discretion as to what share of the trust property he or she is to take, there will be uncertainty if this discretion is not exercised, and consequent failure of the trust. Where there is uncertainty of the subject matter of the trust there will be a resulting trust of the property unless there is also uncertainty of intention, in which case the donee will take the property absolutely.

4 Certainty of objects requires that the beneficiaries be sufficiently certain. This has caused many problems in relation to class gifts. The test of certainty of objects for discretionary trusts requires that it is possible to say of any given postulant that he or she either is or is not a member of the class. It is unclear whether this test or the stricter 'list test' applies to fixed trusts.

5 A trust must not be administratively unworkable.

Exercises

1 Why does the court require an element of certainty in the creation of a trust? Has the court in recent times become stricter or more liberal in its application of the test of certainty?

2 What attitude does the court take to precatory words in determining whether there is an intention to create a trust?

3 In *McPhail* v. *Doulton*, the House of Lords said that the test of certainty of objects for a discretionary trust is that one must be able to say of any given postulant that they either are, or are not, a member of the class. In *Re Baden* the majority of the Court of Appeal decided that this meant if one was unsure whether a given postulant was a member of the class, they were to be treated as not being a member of the class and the test of certainty would thereby be satisfied. Do you think this is what the House of Lords intended or was Stamp LJ in his dissenting opinion in *Re Baden* correct when he took the view that if one was unsure of the status of a particular postulant, the test of certainty of objects had not been complied with? Which view is to be preferred? (See Grbich (1974) 34 MLR 643.)

4 What is the test of certainty of objects for fixed trusts?

5 What do you understand by administrative unworkability?

6 Distinguish between a general power of appointment and a special power of appointment.

7 Discuss the validity and effect of the following clause in the will of Mary Martin who died recently: 'I give ten of my paintings to my husband Claude knowing that he will divide the remainder of my paintings equitably amongst all my friends and colleagues.' Claude has survived Mary Martin.

8 Discuss the validity and effect of the following clauses in the will of Don who died recently:

(a) I give £10 000 to Oxford District Council to distribute in such manner as the council thinks fit, amongst the residents of Oxford.

(b) The residue of my estate I give to my wife, trusting that she will apply a reasonable proportion of it in the care of my aged relatives.

4 Evidential Requirements

In addition to the requirements of certainty explained in Chapter 3 the success of an intended trust depends upon there being sufficient evidence of its existence and terms. As a general rule the settlor of a trust would be wise to commit the details of the trust to writing. The presence of writing signed by the settlor will avoid problems of several types. It will prevent the settlor or trustee from denying the fact of the trust and will minimise disputes about the terms of the trust. In practice most express trusts will be in writing and will give rise to no disputes of this kind.

Apart from the wisdom of recording the trust in permanent form, the law does actually require writing in some cases. Trusts created on death must be in writing to satisfy the Wills Act 1837. In the case of inter-vivos trusts a distinction is drawn between trusts of land which should be evidenced in writing to satisfy statute, and trusts of personalty which are not required to be evidenced in writing (presumably because historically personalty was not as valuable as land). The statutory requirement of writing will ensure that a trust which exists is not denied and will help prevent a person from fraudulently alleging that property is held upon trust for him or her in a case where no such trust has been declared (see further Youdan (1984) 43 CLJ 306).

4.1 Inter-vivos Trusts

Trusts of personalty

There is no legal requirement that writing is necessary to prove a trust of personalty. Most detailed trusts will, however, be in writing in order to provide clear evidence of the terms. In other circumstances the fact that a trust of personalty can be created and proved by adequate oral and other non-written evidence may give rise to obligations in most informal settings. For example, in the case of *Paul* v. *Constance* [1977] 1 WLR 527, the Court of Appeal held that a man was a trustee of a bank account for himself and a woman with whom he had had a close relationship. The evidence which proved the trust was evidence that they had paid joint bingo winnings into the account and the woman's oral evidence that the man had said to her, 'The money is as much yours as mine.' The courts will not, however, be too ready to find a trust of personalty if the evidence is inconclusive. In *Jones* v. *Lock* (1865) LR 1 Ch App 25 evidence that a father had intended to make a gift of a cheque to his infant child was not enough to show that he intended to make himself trustee for the child, where he had retained possession of the cheque.

Trusts of land

It was noted above that a trust of land ought to be evidenced in writing. The rule is contained in s.53(1)(b) of the Law of Property Act 1925, which reads: 'A declaration of trust respecting any land or any interest therein must be manifested and proved by some writing signed by some person who is able to declare such trust or by his will.'

Two preliminary points need to be made about this provision: first, it only requires *evidence* in writing; it does not require that the trust be *declared* in writing. In other words, an oral declaration will suffice provided that there is some signed letter or memorandum as evidence of that declaration; but the writing under s.53 does not have to include all the terms of the trust. Only the fact or the existence of the trust needs to be in writing (*Re Tyler's Fund Trust* [1967] 1 WLR 1269). The second point is that, although the section directs that the trust must be so evidenced, the effect of non-compliance is not that the trust is completely void; it is rendered unenforceable at the instance of the party alleging the trust (see *Gardner* v. *Rowe* (1828) 5 Russ. 258).

Although the requirement of written evidence is designed to prevent fraud a problem arises in some cases where there is no writing, but there is clear parol evidence of the trust, and the failure to enforce the trust would assist a fraudulent denial of the trust, particularly by a person who had bought the land with notice of the trust. The leading authority is *Rochefoucauld* v. *Boustead* [1897] 1 Ch 196, in which case the plaintiff was the mortgagor of land which the mortgagee sold to the defendant who was registered as absolute owner. The plaintiff alleged that the defendant's purchase was subject to her equitable interest. There was no written evidence of such a trust, but the plaintiff's oral allegation was supported by the fact that after the sale the defendant had remitted profits from the land to the plaintiff. The Court of Appeal held that the parol evidence of the trust was admissible in order to prevent the fraud of the defendant. Thus a trust of land may sometimes be enforceable without satisfying the statutory requirement of writing, if enforcement of the requirement would result in the statute being used as an instrument of fraud (see section 2.4 and section 6.6).

Dispositions of equitable interests

Assuming that a valid trust has been created, the beneficiary has a property right which may be transferred to some other person. The Law of Property Act 1925 requires writing in this situation also, in order to prevent fraudulent allegations that the beneficiary has transferred his interest if he has not in fact done so, and to provide clear evidence at any time of where the equitable ownership resides (see Green (1984) 47 MLR 385). Section 53(1)(c) provides: 'A disposition of an equitable interest or trust subsisting at the time of the disposition must be in writing signed by the person disposing of the same, or by his agent thereunto lawfully authorized in writing or by will.'

The section raises several points of interpretation: first, what is meant by 'equitable interest' and, second, what is meant by 'disposition'? It is generally assumed that the section applies equally to equitable interests in personalty as to equitable interests in realty. This is peculiar since no formality is required to create a trust of personalty and it is arguable that the proper interpretation of 'equitable interest' is restricted to interests in land (see Green, ibid.).

Which 'dispositions' fall within the scope of the section is also a matter of dispute. In most of the decided cases the importance of the question has been one of tax saving. Normally stamp duty is payable upon documents transferring equitable interests; if a transaction can be done orally no duty is payable. So it is normally to the advantage of a taxpayer if he can show that the transaction is not a 'disposition' within s.53(1)(c) and does not need to be in writing. The following are also possible.

Assignment of the equitable interest
This is the clearest example of a disposition. If the beneficiary wants to sell or give his or her interest to an assignee the transaction must be in writing (see Figure 4.1).

Direction to trustees to hold on trust for a different party
If instead of directly transferring his interest to a third party the beneficiary directs that the trustee should immediately hold the property upon trust for a third party, the substance of the arrangement is a transfer of the equitable interest from the beneficiary to the third party

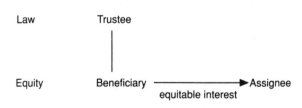

Figure 4.1 Assignment of equitable interest

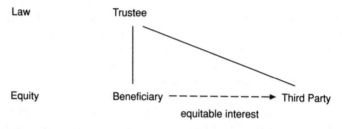

Figure 4.2 Direction to trustees to hold on trust for third party

---

and is therefore a disposition which is ineffective unless in writing (see Figure 4.2).

In *Grey* v. *IRC* [1960] AC 1 there were existing trusts. The settlor later transferred the legal title to shares to the trustees to be held upon trust for himself. He later orally instructed the trustees that the shares were to be held upon the trusts. The trusts of the shares were later confirmed in writing. The issue which arose was whether the vesting of the beneficial interests in the beneficiaries of the trusts amounted to a disposition of the settlor's equitable interest under a pre-existing trust so as to require writing and so that the written disposition would be liable to stamp duty. It was held that there was a disposition by the settlor which required writing and which was subject to stamp duty.

Declaration by equitable owner of self as trustee for third party
Where a beneficiary declares that he holds his equitable interest on trust for a third party the commentators are divided over whether this should be regarded as a declaration of a sub-trust, which in the case of land will require evidence in writing under s.53(1)(b), or whether this should be regarded as an outright disposition of the beneficiary's equitable interest, which must be in writing to satisfy s.53(1)(c) (see Hayton and Marshall, p.65). It has been suggested that the answer depends upon whether the primary beneficiary is to take any active role in managing the property, which will be the case if the primary beneficiary receives income or other benefit from the trustee and then passes it on to the sub-beneficiary; or whether it is intended that the primary beneficiary will drop out of the picture altogether and the trustee will pass any benefits directly to the 'sub-beneficiary' (see Figures 4.3 and 4.4).

It is suggested that, even if the primary beneficiary does act as a sub-trustee by receiving income or other benefit from the primary trustee, there is (in substance) a disposition of the primary beneficiary's beneficial rights which deserves the protection accorded to outright dispositions (Green (1984) 47 MLR 385, p.396).

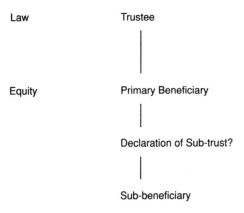

Figure 4.3 Creation of sub-trust where sub-trustee has active duties

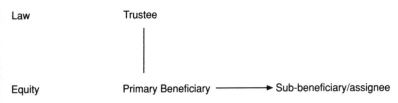

Figure 4.4 Declaration of sub-trust taking effect as assignment of equitable interest

---

Simultaneous transfers of legal and equitable interests

If the equitable interest is transferred at the same time as the legal title to the same transferee the transfer is not a disposition of the equitable interest which needs writing under s.53(1)(c). This was decided in *Vandervell* v. *IRC* [1967] 2 AC 291. It will be remembered (see section 2.3) that Vandervell, wishing to make a tax-free gift to the Royal College of Surgeons, instructed his bank to transfer to the College the legal title to shares of his, the transfer being subject to the condition that trustees of an intended Vandervell family trust should have the option to purchase the shares from the College. Vandervell would then declare dividends on the shares to make the gift to the Royal College of Surgeons and then the shares would pass into the family trust (see Figure 4.5).

Vandervell's equitable interest was intended to pass to the College simultaneously with the transfer by the bank of the legal title. The Inland Revenue argued, *inter alia*, that the transfer of Vandervell's equitable interest was a 'disposition' within s.53(1)(c) which needed to be in writing, with the result that the written transfer would be subject to stamp duty. The House of Lords held that s.53(1)(c) did not apply since

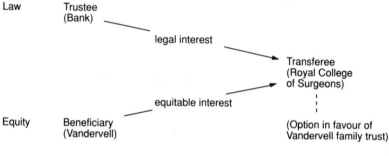

Figure 4.5 *Vandervell* v. *IRC*

it was inapplicable if the legal and beneficial interests pass simultaneously (see Lord Upjohn [1967] 2 AC 291, at 311). Jones (1966) 24 CLJ 19 criticises this, saying, 'the beneficial interest will pass [without the need for writing] only if there is no division of legal and equitable ownership at the time of the transfer' (e.g., in the simple case of a retail sale of goods).

Implied trusts
It is in the nature of implied trusts that they are created informally, often without any expressed intention to create a trust (see Chapters 2 and 3). To require a high degree of formality for their operation would be to contradict their nature, since if they were to be formal they would of course be expressed rather than implied. The special character of implied trusts is acknowledged by s.53(2) of the Law of Property Act 1925 which provides that s.53(1) (see above) does not affect the creation or operation of resulting, implied or constructive trusts.

So no formality is required for the creation of an implied trust, or for the 'operation' of such a trust. It has been held that the term 'operation' includes the termination of a resulting trust, even if the effect of terminating the resulting trust is to perfect an initially imperfect express trust (see *Re Vandervell's Trust No 2* [1974] Ch 269). In *Re Vandervell's Trust No 2* the trust was a trust of personalty which had failed for uncertainty of objects. There had been a resulting trust in favour of the settlor and it was held that the settlor could terminate the resulting trust orally, thereby creating the express trust originally intended. As the trust originally intended was a trust of personalty no formality would have been required for its creation but, in the case of a trust of land which is ineffective for absence of evidence in writing required by s.53(1)(b), it is doubtful that the courts would allow a resulting trust to be terminated orally since a settlor could thereby circumvent s.53(1)(b) by orally purporting to complete an intended trust of land which initially was ineffective for the very reason that it was done orally.

Contract to transfer a proprietary interest

It has been argued that where there is a contract for the transfer of an equitable interest from the transferor to the transferee, the contract gives rise to a constructive trust whereby the vendor holds upon trust for the purchaser who immediately receives the equitable interest, and as a consequence of s.53(2) there is no need for writing in accordance with s.53(1)(c). In *Oughtred* v. *IRC* [1960] AC 206, the House of Lords had to consider the question in order to decide whether stamp duty was payable on the disposition which took place in these circumstances. It was held that duty was payable as it had always in the past been assumed that duty was payable on the documents completing a contract for sale, although the decision fudged the question as to when the equitable interest actually passed.

4.2 Testamentary Dispositions

All dispositions of property on the death of the donor must satisfy the requirements of s.9 of the Wills Act 1837 (as substituted by s.17 of the Administration of Justice Act 1982). There must be a will which is in writing and which is signed by the testator (or someone else at the testator's direction) in such a way as to make it apparent that he intended to give effect to it. The testator's signature must be made or acknowledged by him in the presence of two or more witnesses present at the same time, and each witness must attest and sign the will or acknowledge the signature in the presence of the testator.

Trusts created by will

In the normal course of events, if a person wishes to create a trust on his or her death, he or she will do so by a will conforming with s.9. The terms of the trust must be in the will or some codicil or must be properly incorporated by reference into the will. Any attempted post-mortem disposition or trust which is oral, or which otherwise does not comply with s.9, is ineffective. The purpose of these formalities is to provide a satisfactory way in which the deceased can transfer property on death to persons of his or her choice whilst avoiding possible disputes which might arise if the law allowed informal evidence of the deceased's wishes.

Secret trusts

One disadvantage of the law which requires dispositions on death to be effected by a valid will is that the disposition cannot be kept private since the will is open to public scrutiny. Consequently persons who wish to make a confidential gift on their death sometimes make the gift (publicly) in a will to a legatee on death after first privately procuring a promise

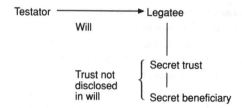

Figure 4.6 Secret trust

---

from the prospective legatee that the property will be held on some secret trust (see Figure 4.6).

If this arrangement is treated strictly it is obvious that the gift to the legatee is valid but he or she is not bound to give effect to the so-called 'secret trust' since it does not comply with s.9 of the Wills Act 1837. The result of taking such a strict approach, however, might be considered unfair if there is strong informal evidence of the trust but the requirement of writing allows the legatee to keep the property for himself. Principally for this reason the courts have shown willingness to allow informal evidence of such trusts in certain circumstances.

This problem may take one of two slightly differing forms which are known as fully-secret trusts and half-secret trusts respectively.

Fully-secret trusts

A fully-secret trust is one of the type described above. There is an absolute gift in a will to a named legatee who has agreed during the lifetime of the testator that after the testator's death the property will be held on trust for a beneficiary whose identity has been communicated in secret to the legatee. For practical purposes it may be said that there are three basic conditions for the enforcement of a secret trust. They were summarised by Brightman J in *Ottaway* v. *Norman* [1972] Ch 698. They are:

(i) the intention of the testator to subject the primary donee to an obligation in favour of the secondary donee;

(ii) communication of that intention to the primary donee; and

(iii) acceptance of that obligation by the primary donee either expressly or by acquiescence.

Intention

The first condition is basically that there must be sufficient certainty of intention, which has been discussed in Chapter 3. The second and third conditions need further examination.

Communication

In relation to the requirement of communication several matters may be mentioned. First, it has been accepted that the communication may be made at any time during the testator's lifetime, before or after the will is made (see Wood vc in *Moss* v. *Cooper* (1861) 1 J & H 352 p.367). But if the legatee learns about the intended trust after the testator's death there is no trust. *Wallgrave* v. *Tebbs* (1855) 2 K & J 313 demonstrates the point. In that case the legatees and intended trustees did not find out about the testator's intention until after the testator's death. It was held that they took the gift absolutely. Another question relating to communication is to what extent the terms of the trust need to be communicated to the intended trustee. The general rule is that both the fact of the trust and the terms of it must be communicated to the intended trustee. It was suggested in *Re Keen* [1937] Ch 236 that it would be sufficient if the testator handed to the intended trustee a sealed letter containing the terms of the trust because, according to Lord Wright MR, 'a ship which sails under sealed orders is sailing under orders although the exact terms are not ascertained by the captain till later'.

Where there are several trustees

If there are several intended secret trustees a problem arises if the obligation has not been communicated to all of them. In such cases the question arises as to whether a trustee who has not accepted the obligation takes the property subject to it. The answer to this question depends upon whether the donees take under the will as joint tenants or tenants in common. They will normally be joint tenants unless the words of the gift to them indicate that they are to take shares, whether equal or otherwise, rather than jointly owning one interest.

If they are tenants in common they are regarded as having severable interests with the result that the tenant in common who accepted the trust is bound by it but the tenant in common who has not accepted is not bound. In the case of joint tenants the law is more complex. A distinction is drawn between the case where a joint tenant has accepted the trust before the making of the will and that where the communication is between the date of the making of the will and death. In the first case (communication prior to the will) all joint tenants are bound. In the second case (communication between the will and death) only the joint tenant who accepted the obligation is bound (see Farwell J in *Re Stead* [1900] 1 Ch 237, p.241). This distinction has been much criticised and Perrins (1972) 88 LQR 225 has argued that the decisive issue should be whether the promise of the joint tenant who accepted the obligation induced the testator to make the gift. If the gift was induced by the promise then it should be held upon trust by both. If the gift would have been made irrespective of the promise then the joint tenant who was unaware of the promise is not bound.

Acceptance

The third condition requires the acceptance of the trust in relation to all property given and normally by all intended trustees. Thus if there is a later addition to the legacy it is only subject to the trust if it has been recognised as trust property by the intended trustees. In *Re Colin Cooper* [1939] Ch 811 the testator had originally asked two persons to hold £5000 on secret trusts. Later, and without their knowledge, he purported to increase the sum to £10 000. It was held that the first sum was subject to the secret trust, but not the second.

Half-secret trust

A half-secret trust occurs when there is a gift in a will which is expressed to be on trusts which have previously been communicated to the legatee but the details of the trust are not contained in the will. The fact of a trust is not a secret but the terms of it are; the trust is therefore only partly secret. The legitimacy of these arrangements was established in 1929 by the House of Lords in *Blackwell* v. *Blackwell* [1929] AC 318. In that case a legacy to several persons was expressed by the testator to be 'for the purposes indicated by me to them'. The terms of the trust had previously been communicated to and accepted by the legatees, who were happy to carry out the trust. The residuary legatees challenged the trust in the hope that they could claim the legacy as residue. The House of Lords confirmed that there was a valid trust. Their Lordships concluded that the Wills Act was not relevant since the terms of the trust were accepted outside the will and were therefore subject to the normal rules for the creation of a trust.

Several distinctions may be made between a half-secret and a fully-secret trust. First, in relation to communication, it has been held that the communication of the trust must occur before or at the time the will is made and not afterwards, whereas in the case of a fully-secret trust the communication may be made at any time during the lifetime of the testator. The distinction was drawn by the Court of Appeal in *Re Keen* [1937] Ch 236, where a testator gave money 'to be held upon trust and disposed of by them among such person, persons, or charities as may be notified by me to them during my lifetime'. The Court held that the provision was void as it 'would involve a power to change a testamentary disposition by an unexecuted codicil and would violate s.9 of the Wills Act'. This decision has been criticised (1937) 53 LQR 501 (W.S. Holdsworth) on the grounds that the time of declaration of trust is irrelevant since the will has no effect until death; also, if the trust operates outside the will, then the date of the will has no significance.

A second problem peculiar to half-secret trusts is that the communication will not be valid if it is in any way inconsistent with the terms written in the will. The point arose in *Re Keen* [1937] Ch 236 where the will referred to a communication which 'may be notified' in the future, but the evidence of the trust was a letter made before the date of the will. It was held that evidence of a past communication was inconsistent with the reference in the will to a future one. The evidence was, therefore, inadmissible.

Theoretical basis for enforcement of secret trusts

Commentators are divided as to what precisely is the theoretical justification for enforcement of the trust. There are three main theories which might apply. The importance of the discussion lies in the fact that different practical results may flow according to which theory is applicable.

Fraud theory

The first idea is that the enforcement of the secret trust represents an extension of the doctrine that 'equity will not allow a statute to be used as an instrument of fraud'. This idea is straightforward and gives rise to little by way of complication. A testamentary disposition is allowed to be proved by parol evidence to prevent a fraudulent legatee from keeping the property for himself. The drawback of this line of reasoning is that it appears to be inapplicable in the case of a half-secret trust, since in that case it is obvious that there can be no fraud on the part of the legatee; if there was no valid trust because of uncertainty of objects there would be a resulting trust to the testator's estate.

Inter-vivos trust dehors *the will*

As a consequence of this drawback a second theory gained favour: namely, that the trust was not a post-mortem one subject to the Wills Act but was instead an inter-vivos one and thus it would be irrelevant that the terms were not contained in the will. Several decisions of the court clearly support this approach. First it was held in *Re Young* [1951] Ch 344 that a person who witnesses a will can take an interest under a secret trust on the basis that the trust takes effect outside, or *dehors*, the will. The normal rule is that a person who takes an interest under a will is not allowed to be a beneficiary of it. The second decision which supports this explanation is that in *Re Gardner* [1923] 2 Ch 230. The normal rule is that if a beneficiary named in a will predeceases the testator then the gift lapses and the deceased beneficiary's estate cannot benefit. It was held, however, that in the case of a secret trust the beneficiary takes a vested interest inter-vivos and thus the fact that the beneficiary predeceases the testator is irrelevant and his estate inherits the gift.

Again, this theory also suffers from defects. The major defect is that it is difficult to conclude that there is an inter-vivos trust since the trust will not be completely constituted until the property passes to the intended trustee. This will occur on the death of the testator by the will and thus will be a post-mortem disposition.

Another difficulty with this approach is that an inter-vivos trust of land is normally required to be evidenced in writing under s.53(1)(b) of the Law of Property Act. A possible answer to this difficulty is to regard the secret trust as a constructive trust which, by s.53(2) of the Law of Property Act 1925, is exempt from the requirement of writing (see below).

Doctrine of incorporation by reference

Not to be perturbed, commentators have recently suggested a third possible justification for the enforcement of secret trust. It has been suggested that they might be an extension of the doctrine of incorporation by reference. This doctrine allows a testator in his will to specify that the terms of some other document should be incorporated into the will. It has been argued, particularly in relation to half-secret trusts, that the testator is simply incorporating by reference into his will some communication which appears outside it. Once more the opinion is fraught with difficulties. First, the idea appears inappropriate to fully-secret trusts since the will does not mention any other communication. Second, the doctrine of incorporation customarily applies only to the incorporation of written documents, whereas the rules of secret trusts allow the incorporation of oral communications. Third, the idea of incorporation results in the written document becoming part of the will and therefore public; the scheme of secret trusts preserves secrecy. Last, if the doctrine of incorporation was applied, the decisions in *Re Young* and *Re Gardner* might have to be overruled.

Are secret trusts express trusts or constructive trusts?

Another theoretical question in respect of secret trusts which remains unanswered is whether such trusts are express trusts or constructive trusts. *Prima facie* a secret trust would appear to be an express one, since it is a trust giving effect to the expressed intention of a settlor; but a constructive trust is also often imposed to give effect to an expressed intention, where the intention would otherwise be ineffective for lack of proper formality.

If the proper basis for the enforcement of the trust is the doctrine of incorporation by reference, the most natural conclusion is that the trust is an express trust incorporated into the will. If the theory that the trust takes effect inter vivos and '*dehors* the will' is adopted it would also be most natural to regard the trust as an express one. The third theory, that equity will not permit a statute to be used as an instrument of fraud, is itself the subject of a debate as to whether the trust enforced is express or constructive (see section 2.4). In this instance, again, the most natural conclusion is that the trust is an express one, particularly as the courts are purporting to override the statutory requirements that the express trust should comply with the requirements of formality.

Due to the formality problem, however, the most convenient course of action would be to categorise the trust as a constructive one so that, by virtue of s.53(2) of the Law of Property Act, it is exempt from the requirement that evidence in writing is required to enforce an inter-vivos trust of land (see section 2.5). Otherwise, if the trust were to be regarded as an express one the trust would only be valid if the property involved was personalty, but not in the case of realty. The issue has still to be fully explored by the judiciary, although such authority as there is indicates that a half-secret trust is an express one and is void if there is insufficient evidence in writing to satisfy s.53(1)(b) (see *Re Baillie* (1886) 2 TLR 660); whereas a fully secret trust is a constructive one and by virtue of s.53(2) does not have to be evidenced by writing (*Ottoway* v. *Norman* [1972] Ch 698). This conclusion is supported by argument of Sheridan (1951) 67 LQR 314, on the basis that as the half-secret trust is mentioned in the will it is express, but the fully-secret trust is not so mentioned and is imposed by the court to prevent fraud, and is therefore constructive. It would be a strange practical conclusion, however, if a half-secret trust was to be void for lack of written evidence, whilst a fully-secret trust would be valid, since in the case of a half-secret trust there is at least some written evidence (in the will), although not sufficient to satisfy the statutory terms.

Summary

1 Where a trust is created on death it must satisfy the formal requirements of s.9 Wills Act 1837 as substituted by s.17 Administration of Justice Act 1982.

2 Whether an inter-vivos trust must be set down in writing depends upon the subject-matter of the trust. No writing is required for trusts of personalty, but a trust of land must be manifested and proved in writing in accordance with s.53(1)(b) Law of Property Act 1925. If such a trust is not evidenced in writing it will be unenforceable unless the requirement would result in a statute being used as an instrument of fraud.

3 A disposition of an equitable interest must be in writing under s.53(1)(c)

Law of Property Act 1925, otherwise such disposition will be void. For this purpose a disposition of an equitable interest includes (a) an assignment of an equitable interest, (b) a direction to the trustees by the equitable owner to hold on trust for a different party, and (c) a self-declaration of trust by an equitable owner in favour of a third party, at least where the original trust and sub-trust are both bare trusts. However, a direction to the trustees by a beneficiary under a bare trust to transfer the legal title to property to a third party, with the intention that the equitable title should pass at the same time, is not a disposition within s.53(1)(c) (*Vandervell* v. *IRC*).

4 In order to avoid the public scrutiny to which a will is subject, the device of either a fully-secret trust or a half-secret trust may be used. A valid fully-secret trust requires (a) a valid will, (b) communication of the terms of the trust either actually or constructively before the testator's death, and (c) express or implied acceptance of the trusteeship by the intended trustee(s). The requirements of a valid half-secret trust differ, arguably anomalously, from those of a fully secret trust in (a) requiring communication of the terms of the trust before or contemporaneously with the execution of the will, and (b) disallowing evidence of the trust which contradicts the terms of the will. Commentators are divided as to the theoretical justification for, and as to the nature of, fully and half-secret trusts. Currently, the most widely accepted theory is that a secret trust arises *dehors* the will, but there is little consensus on whether either or both of fully or half-secret trusts are express trusts or constructive trusts.

Exercises

1 What formalities, if any, have to be followed to establish a trust on death? Are there any exceptions to the rule?

2 Explain precisely the formalities involved in declaring a trust of land.

3 Will either of the following amount to a disposition of an equitable interest?
(a) Ben, the beneficiary under a bare trust, directs Tom and Tim, the trustees of the trust, to hold (henceforward) the property on trust for Catherine absolutely.
(b) Belinda, the beneficiary under a bare trust, directs the trustees Theresa and Tamsin to transfer the property to Charles absolutely, for Charles's own benefit.

4 Explain what formalities if any are required for the following transactions:
(a) Pound declares that he henceforward holds his current account at Barclay's Bank, Cirencester, on trust for his daughter Penny;
(b) Esther declares that she henceforward holds Greenfields Farm on trust for her children;
(c) Tom and Tracy hold shares on trust for Belinda. Belinda assigns her interest in the shares to Sebastian;
(d) Theodore and Tania hold shares on trust for Bruce; Bruce contracts to assign his interest in the shares to Sandra;
(e) Theresa and Tony hold shares on trust for Ben absolutely; Ben declares that he henceforward holds his interest in the shares on trust for Stanley;
(f) Tim and Trish hold a copyright in *Fly Fishing* by Bait and Hook on trust for Brandon. Brandon declares that he henceforward holds the copyright on trust for Stephen for life with remainder to Stephanie.

5 'Secret trusts arise *dehors* the will.' Discuss, and explain the consequences of this view.

6 'The differences between fully and half-secret trusts are anomalous and should be removed.' Discuss.

7 Are fully and half-secret trusts express trusts or constructive trusts? Why does it matter how this issue is determined?

8 By his will made in 1990 Wilberforce left his cottage, 'Sunnynook', to his friends Honest and Reliable jointly, 'on the trusts of which they are aware'. Before the execution of the will Honest agreed to be a trustee of 'Sunnynook' after Wilberforce had shown him a sealed envelope (marked 'not to be opened until after my death') which he said contained the terms of the trust. After the execution of the will, Wilberforce gave the envelope to Reliable who also agreed to act as trustee of 'Sunnynook'. Wilberforce has now died. Reliable has opened the envelope and found that the beneficiary of 'Sunnynook' is to be Simplicity; Simplicity was one of the witnesses of Wilberforce's will.

Advise the executors of Wilberforce's estate as to what should be done with 'Sunnynook'.

5 Constitution of Trusts

The essential act which creates an express trust is the entrustment of the trust property to the trustee by transfer from the settlor (where he himself is not the trustee); it is this entrustment which constitutes the trust. Until the moment of entrustment there is no trust even though the settlor may have had a clear intention to create a trust and even though such intention was expressed with the degree of formality required by law (e.g., in the case of land, by being evidenced in writing: see Chapter 4). One might have thought that constitution of the trust is a straightforward act which should give rise to no problems, and in the majority of cases this is true; but there are exceptions to most rules and the legal authorities, dealt with below, on exceptional problems in relation to constitution of trusts give rise to considerable difficulties.

5.1 Lifetime Creation of Trust

Methods of constitution

If the trust is created during the settlor's lifetime there are two methods of constituting an express trust: the settlor may transfer the legal title of the trust property to other persons to be trustees; or the settlor may declare himself to be trustee of property of which he is presently the legal owner. The methods of constitution of implied trusts are essentially the same; there may be a transfer of property to persons who are then held to be trustees, or a person may already have the legal title to property at the time that a trust is implied or imposed upon him (see Figures 5.1 and 5.2).

The most commonly used method is the transfer of property to other persons to be trustees. If this happens the settlor ceases to have any interest in the property which is then controlled by the trustees for the benefit of the beneficiaries. The settlor cannot seek to control the use of

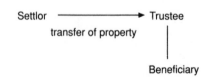

Figure 5.1 Constitution by transfer of property by settlor to trustee

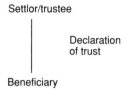

Figure 5.2 Constitution by declaration of settlor of self as trustee

the property or to revoke the trust once it has been constituted. The rule is exemplified by the Court of Appeal decision in *Paul* v. *Paul* (1882) 20 Ch D 742. Under a marriage settlement a wife transferred property to trustees giving life interests to herself and her husband with a remainder to the wife's next of kin who, it was presumed, would be children of the marriage. It later became evident that there would be no children of the marriage and the wife and husband tried to claim the property absolutely, claiming that the next of kin had given no value and had no enforceable right. The court held that there was a complete trust giving the beneficiaries enforceable rights. It was irrelevant that the beneficiaries had given no consideration.

If a person wishes to create a trust with himself as trustee, no actual transfer of property is needed. All the settlor needs to do is to declare the terms of the trust with sufficient certainty (see Chapter 3), and in the case of land to ensure that there is evidence in writing (see Chapter 4).

Method of transfer

If the trust is being set up through trustees rather than by declaration of the settlor then the property must be transferred to the trustees according to the correct rules for transfer of property at law. Goods may be transferred by deed of gift or by the giving of possession to the trustees together with an intention to transfer ownership (see *Re Cole* [1964] Ch 175). A physical transfer is not, however, always necessary. In *Jaffa* v. *Taylor Gallery Ltd*, *The Times*, 21 March 1990, where there was a written trust document (for a painting) and each trustee was given a copy and agreed to act, and one trustee was in Northern Ireland and two in England, it was held that it was not necessary physically to transfer the property to all of the trustees. A chose in action (e.g., a debt), must be transferred by writing of the settlor (s.136 Law of Property Act 1925). Any interest in land must be transferred by deed (s.52 Law of Property Act 1925), and if the title to the land is registered an entry must be made on the Land Register, otherwise the transfer is void at law and the trust will not be constituted.

5.2 Testamentary Creation of Trusts

If the settlor's purpose is the creation of a trust on his/her death it is necessary for the trust to be specified with sufficient certainty in the will. On the death of the settlor legal title will vest in the executors of the will as personal representatives. The executors must carry out their duties in the administration of the estate, which will normally, where the property is land of which they are to be trustees, include the constitution of the trust by the vesting of the property in themselves as trustees by an assent: that is, a statement that the property is to be held by them as trustees. The assent must be in writing and signed by the executor (s.36(4) Administration of Estates Act 1925). For some time it was thought that an assent by an executor in favour of himself did not need to be in writing, but this view was rejected by a decision of Pennycuick J in *Re King's Will Trust* [1964] 1 Ch 542, which disclosed that the previous belief was incorrect and therefore a number of titles were defective (see Walker (1964) 80 LQR 328 and Garner (1964) 28 Conv. 298). Where the property involved is not land there is less of a problem since the assent may be oral or may even be implied from conduct or surrounding circumstances: for example, the fact that a substantial amount of time has passed since the death of the settlor might indicate that the executors are content that the will should have effect with the consequent vesting of the legal title in them as trustees, as in *Attenborough* v. *Solomon* [1913] AC 76.

5.3 Incomplete Transfer

General rule

In the normal case, if it is clear that an attempted transfer of property to trustees is imperfect, no trust is created. Equity will not intervene to perfect an imperfect transfer. In this context it should be emphasised that it is the transfer and entrustment of trust property with the trustees which creates the obligation of trust and a mere intention to create an obligation which is not supported by the necessary action gives rise to no obligation. The foremost manifestation of the principle is the ruling in *Milroy* v. *Lord* (1862) 4 DGF&J 264, where a settlor executed a deed purporting to transfer the legal title to 50 shares in the Bank of Louisiana to an intended trustee for the benefit of beneficiaries. The settlor handed the share certificates to the trustee, but ownership of the shares could only be transferred by registration of a transfer in the books of the bank. Although at the time the trustee had a power of attorney which would have entitled him to apply for registration, this was not done. The Court

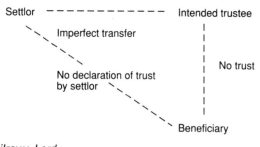

Figure 5.3 *Milroy* v. *Lord*

of Appeal decided that as the transfer of legal title to the trustee was incomplete, there was no trust.

The ruling is important not only for the determination that the intended trustee did not have property on trust but also for rejecting an argument that the settlor himself should be deemed to be holding upon trust for the beneficiaries. It was argued that the settlor intended a trust and that the imperfect transfer to the trustee should be remedied by treating the transaction as a perfect declaration of trust by the settlor of himself as trustee (see Figure 5.3).

The court rejected the argument for, in the words of Turner LJ: 'If it is intended to take effect by transfer the court will not hold the intended transfer to operate as a declaration of trust, for then every imperfect instrument would be made effectual by being converted into a perfect trust.'

So the normal rule is that if the settlor intends to create a trust by transfer to trustees and the transfer is incomplete, the court will not indirectly give effect to the settlor's intention by holding that the settlor himself is a trustee; but there are limited departures from this general rule, as appear below.

Where equity will complete an incomplete transfer
In some less than usual cases an incomplete transfer to an intended trustee may be completed by equity or at least regarded as complete, in which circumstances the trust will be completely constituted. In some cases the trust will be completely constituted by virtue of equity making the settlor hold as trustee where he has not completed an intended transfer.

Where the settlor has made 'every effort'
Although a transfer to trustees may be incomplete, if the settlor has made every effort to complete such transfer equity may regard the transfer as complete, with the result that there will be a fully constituted

trust. This retreat from the basic principle is particularly apt where the proper procedure for transferring the particular type of property includes the registration of the transfer by a third party. Thus it has been held that where registered company shares are to be transferred to a trustee the transfer may be deemed to be complete once the settlor has completed the necessary forms and forwarded them to the company for registration. The trust is complete as soon as the settlor has done everything in his power to transfer the shares, even though at law the transfer is not complete until the moment of registration (*Re Rose* [1952] Ch 312). Similarly the idea is pertinent in the case of land with registered title. If the settlor has completed a transfer form and handed it to the trustee, and all that is left for the trustee to do is to lodge the transfer with the land registry, the transfer to the trustee may be regarded as complete once the settlor has done all that is required of him (*Mascall* v. *Mascall* (1984) 50 P&CR 119).

Although this doctrine of every effort is established at the level of the Court of Appeal it has been the target of serious criticism. McKay [1976] Conv. 139, has criticised *Re Rose* (above). On the reasoning of *Re Rose*, that the transfer is deemed to be complete even though the legal title clearly remains with the settlor, it follows that the settlor is holding the legal title upon trust for the beneficiary. McKay points out that this result is inconsistent with the fundamental reasoning in *Milroy* v. *Lord* (above) that an incomplete transfer should not have the result of making the settlor trustee. The better view of the principle may be that where a settlor has done all in his power to effect a transfer his act is irrevocable and he cannot prevent the completion of the transfer, but the trust should not be regarded as complete until the legal title is actually vested in the trustee.

It should be noted that where there is something remaining to be done the transfer will not be considered to be complete. In *Re Fry* [1946] Ch 312 a settlor wished to transfer shares to his son. He sent the transfers to be registered, but because of defence regulations the transfer could not be registered without the consent of the Treasury. Forms were sent to the settlor for this purpose, which he signed, but he died before consent was obtained. The question was whether the transfer was complete during his lifetime or whether, there being no inter-vivos transfer, the shares formed part of the settlor's residuary estate. It was held that there was no complete gift and the shares belonged to the settlor's residuary estate. He had not strictly made every effort to transfer the shares because he had not obtained a requisite consent to the transfer.

Where the trustee receives the legal title in another capacity

In unusual circumstances, although the settlor may not have transferred the property to the intended trustee for the purpose of setting up the trust, the property may come into the hands of the trustee for some other reason. If this happens then the trustee may hold the property upon the intended trusts. This outcome stems from the rule in *Strong* v. *Bird* (1874) LR 18 Eq 315 that, where a donor has a continuing intention to make an inter-vivos gift to a donee, and on the death of the donor the donee is appointed as personal representative thereby vesting legal ownership in the donee, the vesting of the property in the donee completes what would otherwise be an incomplete gift.

The principle was applied to an incomplete trust in *Re Ralli's Will Trust* [1964] Ch 288. In that case a settlor (A) promised to transfer property upon trust. The property included a beneficial interest which the settlor had under an existing trust, but she had never done anything to transfer her beneficial interest to the trustee. Fortuitously (for the beneficiaries) the intended trustee happened to be the trustee of the existing trust and therefore indirectly had the legal title to the property which the settlor intended to transfer. It was held that the intended trust was completely constituted and the means by which the trustee became legal owner was not significant (see Figures 5.4 and 5.5).

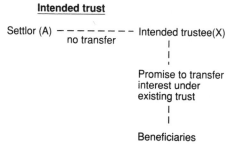

Intended trust

Settlor (A) – – – – – – – – Intended trustee(X)
no transfer

Promise to transfer
interest under
existing trust

Beneficiaries

Figure 5.4 Trust intended but incomplete in *Re Ralli* due to failure of settlor A to transfer beneficial interest to X

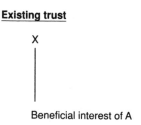

Existing trust

X

Beneficial interest of A

Figure 5.5 Intended trustee X in *Re Ralli* already having legal title to the property intended to be subject to the intended trust

Donatio Mortis Causa

If a person does some inter-vivos act indicating that a transfer should be effective in the event of his/her death the gift may be completed in the event that death occurs. For the principle to apply the transfer must have been clearly in contemplation of death (for instance, because the donor is suffering from an incurable disease), and it must have been made under circumstances indicating that the transfer is conditional upon death. In addition the donor must have delivered the subject-matter of the gift to the donee, or alternatively the means of getting at the subject-matter. If the property is a chattel then control of it should have been given to the transferee. In the case of a chose in action the position is more difficult. It is probably necessary that there should be delivery of an essential title document (this need not be, of course, a transfer to the donee). Last, the property must be capable of transfer by the means used (e.g., delivery). For this reason it had been thought that there could be no *donatio mortis causa* of land. In *Sen* v. *Headley* [1991] 2 WLR 1308 a dying man told a woman who had been living with him for ten years: 'The house is yours, Margaret. You have the keys. They are in your bag. The deeds are in the steel box.' After his death the woman claimed that there had been a *donatio mortis causa* of the house. Mummery J at first instance held that mere delivery of title deeds to land could not effect a transfer. A transfer had to be by deed of transfer or will. But on appeal the Court of Appeal decided that the giving of the keys was a sufficient delivery of the title deeds and that the transfer was complete in equity.

Proprietary estoppel

Equity may regard an incomplete transfer of land as complete where the transferor has made a representation which induces the transferee to act in such a way that it would be unjust for the transferor not to complete the transfer. The transferor will be estopped from reneging upon the promise or representation. The doctrine's modern foundation is the dissenting speech of Lord Kingsdown in *Ramsden* v. *Dyson* (1866) LR 1 HL 129, and will operate to vest a beneficial interest in a donee by way of trust where there is no complete transfer by the donor. *Re Basham* [1986] 1 WLR 1498 is a modern example of the principle. In that case a stepfather promised his stepdaughter that when he died he would leave his house and other property to her. Whilst the stepfather constantly reassured her that she would receive such property she and her husband assisted the stepfather by doing various things, including tending his garden and house, preparing meals for him and dealing with a legal dispute for him. When he died, however, he had not made a will, and the question arose as to whether his property should pass under the rules of intestacy to other persons, or whether the stepdaughter could claim it. It was held that the stepdaughter was entitled to the whole estate. The representations made by the stepfather had been acted upon by the stepdaughter and it would be unfair to deny her the property promised. In order to give effect to the representations it was decided that the personal representatives of the stepfather held the estate upon a constructive trust for the stepdaughter.

Statutory exceptions

There are several statutory exceptions which give rise to a trust even though there is no clear transfer of property to trustees. First, a purported transfer of land to a minor will operate as an agreement for valuable consideration by the transferor to execute a transfer in the minor's favour and in the meantime to hold upon trust for him (s.27 Settled Land Act 1925). Second, where a strict settlement of land is inadequately created for lack of the correct instrument of transfer, the instrument actually used will take effect as an enforceable trust instrument (s.9 Settled Land Act 1925).

5.4 Promises to Create Trusts

Where a settlor has promised to create a trust but has not done so by transferring property to trustees, the question arises as to whether the promise to create the trust is enforceable. In this situation the legal analysis enters a twilight zone between trust and contract. Either concept can give rise to enforceable rights. A promise supported by consideration gives rise to a contract and the person to whom the promise was made can enforce it. An entrustment of property with a trustee gives rise to an enforceable right in favour of the beneficiary without the need for consideration. However, where there is no trust but merely a gratuitous promise to create one, there is neither a trust nor a contract and the beneficiaries have no rights. Nevertheless there is reluctance amongst some commentators and the courts to deny interests to beneficiaries, particularly where a settlor has made the promise to create a trust in a deed. This area of the law has given rise to an almost unparalleled degree of debate, which is outlined below.

Promises given for consideration

If the settlor's promise to settle property upon trust has been made in return for consideration given by the beneficiary, then the beneficiary can enforce the promise. The most common example of this in the field of trusts is where there is a marriage settlement whereby a spouse agrees to settle property upon trusts for the other spouse and the children of the marriage. The other spouse and the children are deemed to have given consideration for the promise to create the trust, which is enforceable (*Attorney-General* v. *Jacobs Smith* [1895] 2 QB 341). Where the marriage settlement is made for persons including children of one spouse from a former marriage the position is not clear, but it would appear that such children cannot normally enforce the promise (*Re Cook's Settlement Trust* [1965] Ch 902) unless their interests are 'interwoven' with those of the children of the marriage (see Kay LJ in *AG* v. *Jacobs Smith* [1895] 2 QB 341).

Other beneficiaries under a marriage settlement are unlikely to have given consideration and, as volunteers, will have no right to enforce the promise of a trust. In *Re Plumptre's Marriage Settlement* [1910] 1 Ch 609, for instance, a wife had promised to settle after acquired property upon the trusts of a marriage settlement, the beneficiaries of which included the wife's next of kin. The next of kin complained that the wife had failed to settle on trust particular property which she had after acquired. It was resolved that the next of kin could not sue because they were volunteers.

If the promise is enforceable the effect is that the relevant property is subject to the trust immediately. If the promise relates to after acquired property the property becomes subject to the trust as soon as it vests in the settlor and neither the settlor nor any other party has a claim to it (*Pullan* v. *Koe* [1913] 1 Ch 9).

It should be noted that if the property which is to be subject to the trust is land the promise to create a trust may be considered to be a contract for an interest in land, in which case the contract will be void if it is not in writing and signed by both parties or, if contracts are to be exchanged in duplicate, one of them must be signed by each party (s.2 Law of Property (Miscellaneous Provisions) Act 1989).

Covenant with beneficiary

Even if the beneficiary has given no consideration the beneficiary will be able to sue at common law if the promise was made in a deed to which the beneficiary is a party, applying the long-standing principle that a promise in a deed does not require consideration. In *Cannon* v. *Hartley* [1949] Ch 213 a father, by deed, had promised to settle after acquired property on his wife and daughter. After the wife's death the daughter succeeded in an action against the father on the promise as she had been expressed to be a party to the deed. The appropriate remedy in this kind of action is damages, since the action lies at common law only and equity will not assist the volunteer with an action for specific performance.

Covenant with trustee
Where the promise has been made in a deed between the settlor and the trustees the position is more difficult. Application of basic principle would invite the conclusion that the beneficiaries who are not parties to the deed cannot enforce the promise; but the trustee who is a party should be able to sue upon it. The authorities have not, however, adhered to these basic principles and the legal position is not at all clear.

Can the trustee sue?
The trustee as party to a deed should be able to sue upon it but there are several court decisions which show that the trustees should not sue upon the deed for the benefit of volunteer beneficiaries. The principle is an extension of the tenet of equity that 'Equity will not assist a volunteer.' If the court permitted a trustee to enforce the promise and constitute a trust his 'would be to give [the beneficiaries] by indirect means relief they cannot obtain by any direct procedure' (see Eve J in *Re Pryce* [1917] 1 Ch 234). In two subsequent cases (*Re Kay's Settlement* [1939] 1 Ch 329 and *Re Cook's Settlement Trust* [1965] Ch 902) trustees were directed not to sue upon covenants to settle after acquired or uncertain property. It is submitted that employment of the maxim that equity will not assist a volunteer does not necessitate the approach in these cases. Equity's assistance was not required since the trustee would be relying upon the right to sue at law, as distinct from equity. The effect of the cases is not simply to refuse equity's assistance to volunteers but to interfere with the trustees' rights to sue at law.

What is the trustee's remedy for breach of covenant?
Even if the trustee has a right to sue at law there is left open a second question as to what is the remedy for breach of convenant. Since the right to sue is a right at law only and equity will not assist because the trustee has given no consideration, if follows that specific performance is not available but only the legal remedy of damages. Assuming that the trustee is entitled to damages the further question must be tackled as to what is the proper measure of damages. It is arguable that the trustee's loss is nominal only since the benefit was intended for the beneficiaries (see Marshall [1950] CLP 43) but some critics say that 'for breach of a covenant to transfer property worth a certain sum [the measure of damages] is the value of the property' (Elliot (1960) 76 LQR 100), and in at least one first instance decision trustees were held entitled to recover

substantial damages (*Re Cavendish Browne* [1916] WN 341). Under the rules of contract it was suggested by Lord Denning in *Jackson* v. *Horizon Holidays Ltd* [1975] 1 WLR 1468 that damages could include loss to third parties, but this suggestion was criticised by the House of Lords in *Woodar Investment Developments Ltd* v. *Wimpey* [1980] 1 WLR 277.

Even if substantial damages are obtained Lee (1969) 85 LQR 213 has contended that such damages would have to be held by the trustee upon resulting trust for the settlor since the trustee is not intended to take beneficially and there can be no trust for the intended beneficiaries, but it is suggested that the argument that the trustee could sue a settlor and then would hold the damages upon trust for the settlor is nonsensical from a practical point of view.

Is there a completely constituted trust of the promise?

The discussion above is based upon the assumption that there is no trust and that it is necessary to look to the law of contract to establish a right to sue. There is, however, an argument that there is a right to sue based upon a fully constituted trust. The argument is based upon the established principle that trust property may include a chose in action such as a right to sue under a contract (see Figure 5.6).

The trust of the chose in action gives the trustee the right to sue a third party for the benefit of the beneficiary. Where the settlor himself has entered into a deed with the trustee it can be argued that the trustee has the right to sue the settlor, which right is held upon trust, so that there is an immediate trust of the chose in action or right to sue the trustee. This appears to be the approach adopted in the case of *Fletcher* v. *Fletcher* (1844) 4 Hare 67, where a settlor covenanted with trustees to settle £60 000 upon trust for his illegitimate son. It was held that there was a trust of the debt for the illegitimate son.

In the course of the judgment Wigram VC said:

> The rule against relief to volunteers cannot . . . be stated higher than this, that a court of equity will not, in favour of a volunteer, give to a

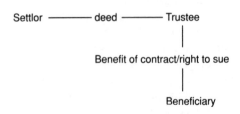

Figure 5.6 Trust of a right to sue

deed any effect beyond what the law will give to it. But if the author of the deed has subjected himself to a liability at law, and the legal liability comes regularly to be enforced in equity . . . the observation that the claimant is a volunteer is of no value in favour of those who represent the author of the deed.

On the basis of the decision Hornby (1962) 78 LQR 228, has submitted that in cases like *Re Pryce* and *Re Kay* the trustees should sue on the ground that there is a completely constituted trust of the promise.

Distinction between ascertained and unascertained property

The submission made by Hornby was put to the court in the case of *Re Cook's Settlement Trust* (above) where there was a promise by a settlor to settle upon trust the proceeds of sale of certain paintings if the settlor sold them during his lifetime. It was held, following *Re Pryce* and *Re Kay*, that the trustees should not sue on the promise. Buckley J distinguished *Fletcher* v. *Fletcher* as a case where the promise related to a specific identifiable sum, whereas the promises in *Re Pryce*, *Re Kay* and *Re Cook* were promises in relation to unidentified future property.

This distinction has been the subject of an enormous amount of debate. The weight of argument appears to be in favour of a trust of the promise even in cases involving after acquired property. Hanbury and Maudsley (p.125) conclude that 'a promise to pay a sum to be ascertained in the future is just as good a chose in action as a promise to pay a specified sum'.

Intention of settlor

It has been said that whether there is or is not a trust of the chose in action or promise depends upon the intention of the settlor. If the settlor intended a trust of tangible property which is not constituted the court should not find a constituted trust of intangible property or a chose in action (see R. Pound (ed.), *Perspectives of Law*, p.248 and Feltham (1982) 98 LQR 17). On this analysis it would be rare to find a trust of the chose in action for it is unlikely that settlors would wish to create trusts where the trustees had a right to sue them.

Conclusion

The technical arguments for and against the enforceability of a promise to create a trust have raged for so long that one is tempted to conclude that they are in themselves inconclusive and the debate is a sterile one. It is suggested (a view propounded by Hanbury and Maudsley, p.131) that the answer depends ultimately upon the policy that society wishes to adopt to such promises, and whether it is thought that a person who has made a gratuitous promise to create a trust should be bound by that promise.

Summary

1 A trust is completely constituted where the settlor has made an effective self-declaration of trust or effectively transferred the legal title to property to trustees and declared the terms of the trust.

2 Once a trust has been completely constituted it is enforceable by the beneficiaries whether or not they are volunteers.

3 If the trust is not completely constituted and the beneficiaries are volunteers, as a general rule the trust will not be enforceable by them. Equity will, however, complete the trust where (a) the 'every effort doctrine' applies or (b) the rule in *Strong* v. *Bird* applies or (c) where there is a *donatio mortis causa* or (d) proprietary estoppel operates. In addition an incompletely constituted trust may become enforceable under a number of statutory provisions.

4 If the trust is not completely constituted but there is a promise to create a trust and the beneficiaries have provided consideration, the trust will be enforceable by them. It should be remembered that valuable consideration includes marriage consideration.

5 Where there is a contract to create a trust and the beneficiaries have not provided consideration, they may not enforce the trust unless (a) they are parties to a contract made by deed (in which case they may receive damages at common law in contract), or (b) they can establish that there is a fully constituted trust consisting of the benefit of the contract (as in *Fletcher* v. *Fletcher*).

6 Where there is a contract with trustees to create a trust and the beneficiaries are volunteers, case law provides that the trustees should not sue on the contract. Even if the trustees do go ahead and sue, the greater weight of authority provides that they will only be entitled to recover nominal damages.

Constitution of Trusts: Summary of issues

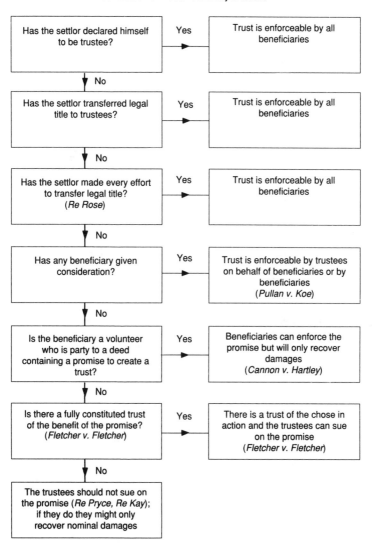

Exercises

1 When may a trust be said to be completely constituted? Outline the circumstances in which equity will perfect an imperfect gift.

2 Explain the concept of marriage consideration.

3 Where a settlor has made a promise by deed with trustees to create a trust:

(a) what reason does case law give for the principle that the trustees should not sue on a contract for the benefit of a beneficiary who is a volunteer? Do you agree with this view?

(b) if the trustees go ahead and sue, do you think they should be entitled to recover substantial rather than merely nominal damages? (See Marshall [1950] CLP 43, Elliot [1960] 76 LQR 100.)

4 Read the case of *Fletcher* v. *Fletcher* [1844] 4 Hare 67). Do you think that the court was correct in finding that there was a fully constituted trust of a promise on the facts of the case? (See Hanbury and Maudsley, *Modern Equity*, 13th edn, pp.127–8.)

5 'Whilst it is possible to have a trust of a promise to settle existing and identifiable property it is not possible to have a trust of a promise to settle unidentified future property.' Explain and discuss (see (1976) 92 LQR 427 (R P Meagher and J R F Lehane); (1965) 24 CLJ 46 (G H Jones); (1969) 85 LQR 213 (W A Lee)).

6 On 1 January 1990 Frail, thinking that he was in imminent danger of dying, told his live-in housekeeper, Robust, that the valuable antique chest in the sitting room was to be removed to Robust's room and added; 'the chest is a gift for the loyal service you have given me'. The chest was removed at Frail's request on 3 January 1990. On 30 December 1990 Frail executed a valid will which, *inter alia*, bequeathed the antique chest in question to his son, Youthful. On 20 June 1991 Frail died. Advise Robust.

7 In 1988 Emily purchased a plot of land, Greenacre. She later told her daughter Fiona that she could use the garden of Greenacre for her dog boarding kennel business. Fiona then built boarding kennels on Greenacre at a cost of £9000. In 1989 Emily executed a will by which she specifically devised Greenacre to her daughter, Gwen, leaving the residuary estate to her husband, Harold. Fiona and Harold were appointed executors of the will. Emily died earlier this year. Advise Fiona.

8 Tom, a married man, entered into a voluntary agreement under seal with Huck and Finn (the trustees of the Huckleberry Trust) by which Tom agreed:

(a) to pay £20 000 to the trustees on trust for Kyp, Tom's son by a previous marriage;

(b) to settle the proceeds of sale of a painting (at the time of the covenant, unsold) on trust for the children of his present marriage;

(c) to transfer 500 of his shares (valued at £3000) in Uncle Tom's Cabin Ltd to Huck.

Tom later executed a document purporting to transfer the 500 shares to Huck but the company refused to register the transfer in exercising its absolute discretion under its Articles of Assocation. The painting was subsequently sold for £30 000 but Tom took no steps either to transfer the proceeds thereof or the £20 000 to the trustees. Tom has now died. Advise Huck and Finn.

6 Consequences of Failure to Satisfy Requirements of Trust

There are several possible effects where the requirements for the creation of a trust described in the preceding chapters have not been satisfied. If there is no transfer of legal title to intended trustees, or if the settlor does not declare himself to be trustee, or if there is insufficient certainty to give rise to an implied trust, the legal and beneficial ownership remains with the settlor or legal owner. In cases where legal title passes to a person taking in the capacity of trustee, but for some other reason the trust fails, there is a resulting trust. And in cases where legal title passes but it is not clear that the transferee is to take as trustee, the transferee takes the property absolutely.

6.1 Uncertainty of Intention

Where legal title has passed to a transferee

If legal title has passed to a transferee but no clear obligation has been imposed upon him/her the basic rule is that the transferee takes the property beneficially, and any direction which may have been given to the transferee in relation to the property operates as a mere power or as a 'hint' to the transferee as to how the property should be dealt with (see *Lambe* v. *Eames* (1871) 6 Ch App 597 as discussed in section 3.1).

Occasionally, however, although there may be insufficient certainty of intention to create a trust, the words used by the transferor may be sufficient to create some other legal or equitable relationship, or an interest greater than a mere power. In section 3.1 the example of *Re Bond Worth* [1980] Ch 228 was given, where it was held that a buyer of goods on credit did not hold the goods on trust for the seller pending payment but that instead the seller had a charge over the goods to secure payment.

Where legal title has not passed to a transferee

In cases where legal title has not passed to a transferee it may be argued that an owner of property has declared himself to be trustee of it, or that it was intended that the property of the owner should be subject to an implied trust. If the facts are not strong enough to prove the argument with certainty, the property simply remains with the owner free from any obligation.

6.2 Uncertainty as to Subject-matter

There are three possible ways in which uncertainty of subject-matter may arise, and the consequences of such uncertainty varies accordingly.

Uncertainty as to the property as a whole

First, in a case where a settlor may have declared himself trustee but it is not clear what property should be taken from his estate for the purpose of the trust, there is no property to which a trust can attach and the property simply remains with the settlor. It will be remembered (see section 3.3) that in the case of *Re London Wine Co. (Shippers) Ltd* (1976) 126 NLJ 978, where customers of a wine company had paid for wine which was stored by the company there was no trust because it was unclear which bottles of wine should be allocated to any particular customer, and therefore the wine remained in the legal and equitable ownership of the company.

Alternatively property of the settlor may have been transferred to trustees but it is unclear what part of the property is to be held upon the particular trust; in this case there will be a resulting trust of any property which the settlor has failed to dispose of.

Trust of certain property but uncertainty as to beneficial shares

Second, if the property as a whole is clear but the settlor has not specified the shares to be taken by various beneficiaries, there will be a resulting trust of the property. In *Boyce* v. *Boyce* (1849) 16 Sim 476 (see section 3.3), a testator directed that his houses should be held upon trusts whereby ultimately they would pass to his two daughters, but he did not provide a clear formula for deciding which house should pass to which daughter; consequently there was a resulting trust to his estate (see Figure 6.1).

There is at least one possible alternative in the case of uncertainty as to beneficial shares, and that is to apply the maxim 'equity is equality' and

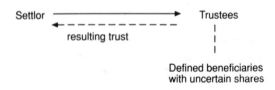

Figure 6.1 Effect of uncertainty of subject-matter

to divide the property equally between the possible beneficiaries where this is not inconsistent with the settlor's intention. In *Doyley* v. *Attorney-General* (1735) 2 Eq Ca Abr 194, a testator made a disposition of personal and real estate to such relations on his mother's side who were most deserving in such manner as the trustees should think fit and for such charitable uses and purposes as they should also think most proper and convenient. The Master of the Rolls directed that the property should be equally divided between the relatives and charity.

Gift to A to hold uncertain amount for B
Third, a gift of certain property may have been made to a person taking beneficially but subject to a beneficial interest of an uncertain part for another beneficiary or beneficiaries. The first beneficiary will take the entire property, as in *Sprange* v. *Barnard* (see section 3.3), since it is clear that the first beneficiary was intended to benefit from the property but there is no trust for the second beneficiary.

6.3 Uncertainty of Object or no Object

The most likely reason for the settlor's failure to create a trust is that he has not defined the objects with sufficient certainty. In this case there is no person to whom the equitable interest can pass. It remains, therefore, with the settlor (see Figure 6.2).

A leading example of this is the case of *Vandervell* v. *IRC*. As was explained above (section 2.3) Vandervell had provided that the legal title to shares should pass to his family trustees by their exercise of an option given to them. However, he had failed to clearly define who the beneficiaries would be. The result was that the beneficial interest remained with Vandervell, who was therefore liable to tax on the income from the shares (see Figure 6.3).

A similar result may occur where a testator attempts to create a trust but there are no objects: for instance, if a testator intends a trust by will in favour of a specified beneficiary, but the beneficiary dies before the testator, the trust cannot normally take effect (there is an exception if the beneficiary is a child of the testator who predeceases him or her leaving

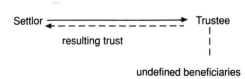

Figure 6.2 Effect of uncertainty of objects

Figure 6.3 *Vandervell* v. *IRC*

issue, in which case the issue take) since there is no beneficiary. The gift lapses and there is a resulting trust in favour of testator's estate.

Similarly there will be a resulting trust where the settlor intended a trust for purposes (see Chapter 12), unless the purposes were charitable, in which case if the property settled cannot be applied as intended it may be applied cy pres for a similar purpose.

6.4 Unfulfilled Condition Precedent

A less usual reason for the failure to create a trust is where the creation was dependent upon some unfulfilled condition precedent. For example, in *Re Ames Settlement* [1946] Ch 217, on the marriage of his son Mr Ames transferred £10 000 to trustees to hold on the trusts of the marriage settlement. When the marriage was declared void the settlement also became void causing a resulting trust of the beneficial interest in favour of the settlor. This type of case bears some relationship to that where there is uncertainty of intention, but is different in as much as there is a certain intention to create a trust which has been frustrated and consequently the transferee cannot take beneficially; there must be a resulting trust for the transferor.

6.5 Failure to Dispose of Part of Beneficial Interest

In some cases the settlor has transferred the legal title of property to trustees, intending that specified objects should take the entire beneficial interest, but unexpectedly only part of the property is needed for the purposes of the gift and the settlor has not fully disposed of the beneficial interest. This most often occurs if the settlor has directed that the income from settled property is to be used for maintenance of a beneficiary, but in the events which happen only part of the income is used, leaving surplus income undisposed of (see Figure 6.4).

In *Re Sanderson's Trusts* (1857) 3 K&J 497, for example, property was left to J by will upon trust 'to pay and apply the whole or any part of the rents . . . of his real and personal estate and effects for and towards his maintenance attendance and comfort'. The Vice-Chancellor held that

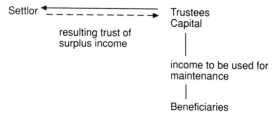

Figure 6.4 Effect of unintended partial disposition

---

there was a resulting trust of any surplus income not used for J's maintenance on the basis that the testator had 'forgotten to deal with the surplus rents accruing during the lifetime of the [beneficiary]'.

More commonly, however, the gift is construed as an absolute gift and any surplus will pass into the estate of the beneficiary. *Re Osoba* [1979] 1 WLR 247 (see also *Re Andrews Trust* [1905] 2 Ch 48) is a modern example of the courts' approach. A testator had left property to be used for the maintenance of his widow and for the training of his daughter until completion of her university education. After the completion of the daughter's education the question arose as to what should be done with the surplus. The Court of Appeal decided that the testator's intention had been to make an absolute gift, the reference to maintenance and education simply being an expression of his motive for the making of the gift. Buckley LJ said:

> If a testator has given the whole of the fund whether of capital or income, to a beneficiary, whether directly or through the medium of a trustee, he is regarded, in the absence of any contraindication as having manifested an intention to benefit that person to the full extent of the subject-matter . . . This must be reconciled with the testator's having specified the purpose for which the gift is made. This reconciliation is achieved by treating the reference to the purpose as merely a statement of the testator's motive in making the gift.

Surplus funds and disaster appeals

It is explained in section 14.10 that a fund set up for the relief of a disaster may be charitable or non-charitable. If the disaster fund is charitable the destination of surplus funds is governed by s.14 Charities Act 1960 (see section 14.2). If the disaster fund is not charitable and there are surplus funds and therefore a failure by the donors to dispose of part of their beneficial interest in the money donated, the position is more complex.

The case of *Re Gillingham Bus Disaster Fund* [1958] Ch 300 involved such a non-charitable disaster appeal. A number of marine cadets were killed and injured when a bus ran into their marching column. An appeal was launched by the Mayor of Gillingham in terms which were not charitable and were also in part uncertain. In addition, legal liability was accepted by the bus company, with the result that more money was contributed than could be used. The funds comprised partly cheques from named donors and partly anonymous donations from collecting boxes. Harman J decided that there was a resulting trust of all the surplus funds. He arrived at the conclusion by asking the question of whether the donors intended to part with their money out and out, or only to give it for the particular purpose specified. The obvious answer in the context of a disaster appeal, he concluded, is that money is given for the particular purpose. As the purpose could not be carried out, there was a resulting trust. Had Goff J decided that the money had been parted with out and out there would have been no resulting trust and the surplus funds would have gone to the Crown as *bona vacantia* (i.e. as ownerless property). This would have been desirable with regard to the anonymous donations as such funds passing *bona vacantia* are generally applied for charitable purposes. However, it would have been disadvantageous for the named donors who would have been prevented from recovering their money. Nevertheless, the resulting trust approach was not entirely satisfactory either. It enabled the named donors to recover their money, but as the anonymous donors could not be found the money was paid into court, theoretically awaiting their collection. The consequence of this is that the money remained in court indefinitely as it is impossible for anonymous donors to prove they have made a donation to the fund.

The approach taken in *Re West Sussex Constabulary's Widows, Children and Benevolent (1930) Fund Trust* [1971] Ch 1 arguably achieves a fairer result even if the reasoning applied in the case is not entirely logical. The case is discussed in section 13.3 as it concerned surplus funds on the dissolution of an unincorporated association rather than a disaster appeal. However, in so far as the funds came from outsiders and not the members of the association themselves, the same principles apply as for surplus funds in the disaster appeal context. The funds come from three sources in the West Sussex Constabulary case: (a) cheques; (b) anonymous donations; and (c) jumble sales and other fund-raising activities. In deciding what should be done with the surplus funds Goff J asked a different question from Harman J in the Gillingham Bus Disaster Fund case: namely, whether the donors would expect, in the event of surplus funds, to get their money back. He decided named donors would so expect (as they can be found) with the happy conclusion of a resulting trust. In contrast anonymous donors would not so expect as they cannot be found. This led to the desirable exclusion of a resulting trust and the funds passing to the Crown as *bona vacantia*. Likewise the money raised from jumble sales and other fund-raising activities passed *bona vacantia* as these involved a contract and the donors had got what they had bargained for and as such were excluded.

6.6 Lack of Formality

Although formality is not required for trusts of personalty an intended trust of land will be unenforceable if there is insufficient evidence in writing to satisfy s.53(1)(b) of the Law of Property Act. Most commentators are of the view that the trust is not entirely void but is only unenforceable (see *Gardner* v. *Rowe* (1828) 5 Russ 258), so that the beneficiary cannot require the trustee to execute the trust, although the trustee could carry out the trust if he or she so wished. This analysis gives rise to substantial difficulties and makes it unclear what the consequences are of not complying with the statute. There appear to be four possibilities, as outlined below.

Settlor retaining beneficial interest?

If the settlor orally declares himself to be trustee it might be argued that although the trust is unenforceable it is nevertheless valid and thus the settlor does not have the beneficial interest, which is therefore vested in the beneficiary. From a practical point of view, however, the settlor will be able to deal with the property as if it was not subject to a trust and will be able to transfer the property to a third party who will take free of the trust. It is submitted, therefore, that in this type of case the settlor retains the beneficial interest. There is no injustice in the settlor retaining the beneficial interest unless the beneficiary has given value for the trust, in which case the trust might be enforced to prevent the statute from being used as an instrument of fraud (see below).

Resulting trust for settlor, or enforcement of the trust?

If there has been a transfer of the legal title to transferees and it is clear from oral evidence that they were to take as trustees, the position is unclear. Assuming that the trust is valid but unenforceable, the beneficiaries cannot require the trust to be carried or any benefit to be allocated to them. The trustees should not be able to keep the benefit for themselves since it is clear that they are trustees. The settlor also should not be entitled to the benefit from the property because the property has been transferred on a valid (but unenforceable) trust and has divested himself of the land. But someone must have the benefit of the land, otherwise it might become sterile and of no use to anyone.

It is suggested that where the beneficiaries have given no consideration or there is no other good reason for them having a benefit they should not have any rights; and, assuming that there is evidence that the transferees took in the capacity of trustees, they too should not benefit from the land. In such cases, for practical purposes the intended trust should be regarded as ineffective and there should be a resulting trust for the settlor.

If the beneficiaries have given consideration it might be thought that they should be able to enforce the trust, but these facts might amount to an attempted contract for an interest in land, and such a contract must be in writing and must be signed by both parties (or each party in a case where duplicates are to be exchanged) in order to be valid (s.2 Law of Property (Miscellaneous Provisions) Act 1989). Nevertheless, if the consideration has already passed from the beneficiaries it may be possible to by-pass the statutory requirement in order to prevent it from being used as an instrument of fraud, and to enforce the trust. This principle is supported by authority, at least in relation to by-passing the requirement of s.53(1)(b), but not yet in relation to the Law of Property (Miscellaneous Provisions) Act 1989.

Bannister v. *Bannister* [1948] 2 All ER 133 is the clearest example of the operation of the principle that equity will not allow the statute to be used as an instrument of fraud. In that case a woman sold two properties to a purchaser after procuring his oral promise that she would be allowed to live in one of them for the remainder of her life. After the sale was completed the purchaser denied the woman's right to remain. It was held that the land was conveyed subject to an oral trust and that it would be unconscionable to permit him to deny that there was a trust. It is not clear, however, whether the trust enforced in this situation is the original express trust, or a constructive trust imposed upon the purchaser (see section 2.4). It may be observed that in a case of this type, where the settlor and the beneficiary are one and the same, the fraud might also be prevented by the resulting trust suggested above.

Trustee having option to execute the trust?

If trust property has passed into the hands of independent trustees, and the trust is valid but unenforceable, it might be argued that the trustees have the option as to whether to execute the trust or not. This alternative would appear to be inappropriate since there is no good reason why the decision to enforce the trust or not should rest with the trustees.

Transferee taking beneficially?

If there has been a transfer of the legal title to transferees and it is not clear from oral evidence that they were to take as trustees, they will of course take beneficially, since there will be no evidence to the contrary.

6.7 Failure to Constitute an Intended Trust

If there is an intention to create a trust but the trust is never constituted due to the fact that trust property has never been transferred to trustees, there is no trust. The effect is simply that the intended settlor retains the property in question and the intended trustees and beneficiaries normally have no right to require the settlor to fulfil his intention by transferring property to trustees, or by holding the property directly upon trust for the beneficiaries himself (see *Milroy* v. *Lord* (1862) 4 DGF&J 264; also see section 5.3). In some cases, however, equity will intervene to complete the otherwise incomplete transfer of property and the trust will be constituted. The jurisdiction of equity to do so is explained fully in Chapter 5.

6.8 Completing Disposition and Terminating Resulting Trust

The failure to dispose of property on trust may be inconvenient but it need not be fatal, at least in some cases. An incomplete disposition may usually be completed if the settlor remedies the defect which caused the disposition to be incomplete. If the reason was failure to define beneficiaries or beneficial shares the settlor can clarify these issues. All that is needed on the part of the settlor is an oral declaration specifying the beneficial interests. No writing is required (see Figure 6.5).

Thus it will be remembered that in *Vandervell* v. *IRC* (see section 2.3) the legal title to shares had been transferred but Vandervell had not defined the beneficiaries and there was therefore a resulting trust of the shares in his favour. In order to complete the trust Vandervell directed that the property should be held on trust for specified beneficiaries. This was an attempted disposition of Vandervell's equitable interest as beneficiary of the resulting trust which had arisen on his failure to define

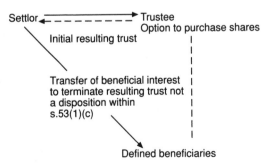

Figure 6.5 Termination of resulting trust

the trusts. In *Re Vandervell's Trusts (No 2)* [1974] Ch 269, the Inland Revenue still sought to make Vandervell liable to tax on the basis that the attempted disposition was unsuccessful since it was not in writing, as required by s.53(1)(c). Also by this time Vandervell had died and his estate wished to claim the shares and therefore also argued that the disposition was ineffective. The court held that the disposition of an interest under a resulting trust is not subject to the formality of s.53(1)(c), which is not applicable to the 'operation of resulting, implied or constructive trusts' according to s.53(2). In rejecting the argument that this was a 'disposition' within s.53(1)(c) Lord Denning MR said:

> There is a complete fallacy in that argument. A resulting trust for the settlor is born and dies without any writing at all. It comes into existence whenever there is a gap in the beneficial ownership. It ceases to exist whenever that gap is filled by someone becoming beneficially entitled. As soon as the gap is filled by the creation or declaration of a valid trust, the resulting trust comes to an end. In this case, before the option was exercised, there was a gap in the beneficial ownership. So there was a resulting trust for Mr. Vandervell. But, as the option was exercised and the shares registered in the trustees' name there was created a valid trust of the shares in favour of the children's settlement. Not being a trust of land, it could be created without any writing.

Green (1984) 47 MLR 385, p.417 (see also Battersby [1979] Conv. 17, pp.34–5) argues that this is wrong and that the disposition of an interest under a resulting trust is just as much a subsisting equitable interest as that under an express trust and is just as deserving of the protection afforded by the formalities required under s.53(1)(c).

Summary

1 Where the legal title to property has passed to a transferee but there is no certainty of intention to create a trust, the transferee generally takes absolutely; the direction to the transferee as to how the property should be dealt with operates as a 'mere power'. Where there is insufficient evidence of a self-declaration of trust the alleged settlor remains absolute owner.

2 Where it is not possible to establish what property is intended to be transferred to trustees, there will be uncertainty of subject-matter and no trust will arise. Similarly, if there is a gift of certain property to a person subject to another taking a beneficial interest in an uncertain part of it, the first beneficiary will take absolutely. In contrast, where the uncertainty of subject-matter relates to the beneficial interest there will be a resulting trust. A resulting trust will also arise where there is uncertainty as to the objects of the trust or where there is no beneficiary to whom the equitable interest may pass.

3 A resulting trust arises where the creation of a trust is dependent upon some condition precedent which is not fulfilled.

4 Where a declaration of trust of land is not evidenced in writing under s.53(1)(b) it will be unenforceable. It is not totally clear whether this may give rise to a resulting trust in at least some circumstances.

5 Where there is a failure to dispose of part of the beneficial interest this generally leads to a resulting trust. In cases where property is held on trust to be applied to the maintenance of a beneficiary but not all the income is needed for this purpose, the courts tend to construe the gift as an absolute one with the effect that there is no resulting trust and the surplus funds pass to the estate of the beneficiary.

6 A disposition of an interest under a resulting trust is not a disposition within s.53(1)(c) (*Vandervell No 2*).

Exercises

1 Explain the effects of each of the following related transactions or events:
(a) On 1 June Bright makes an effective transfer of the legal title to certain shares to Topsy and Tim to be held on trust 'to maintain such of my children as I shall name in due course'; then
(b) on 10 June Bright names Frail and Thin as the beneficiaries of the shares transferred on 1 June; then
(c) on 20 June Frail and Thin die.

2 'A resulting trust for the settlor is born and dies without any writing at all' (see Lord Denning MR *Re Vandervell's Trusts No 2*). Do you agree with this view? (See Green (1984) 47 MLR 385 at 417 and Battersby [1979] Conv. 17, pp.34–5.)

3 During an air display at Farnborough a Second World War fighter plane crashed out of control into a crowd of spectators. The pilot and co-pilot and fifteen spectators were killed, and a further ten were injured. The Mayor of Farnborough launched a non-charitable trust appeal for funds for the families of deceased persons and for the injured survivors. A fund of £10 000 was collected by means of cheques, anonymous donations in collecting boxes and from the holding of a car boot sale. Part of the trust cannot be carried out as the appeal was drafted in such a way that it did not satisfy the requirements of certainty of objects in the creation of a trust. Advise the trustees as to what should be done with the surplus funds.

Part III

The Express Trust as a Mechanism for Protecting Private Wealth

7 Private Trusts

Control of private wealth is the principal function of the express trust. The device has customarily been used to manipulate wealth within families so as to give effect to the wishes of the family member for the time being possessed of the main family assets, usually (at least until recently) the male family 'head'. A settlor might, for example, assign property to trustees to use the income from it to maintain his children during their minority and then to pass the capital to the children upon them attaining majority; or the property could be allocated and controlled in various different ways, some of which are described below.

As the trust has passed from infancy to adulthood it has become an increasingly complex means of not merely controlling the destination of family wealth but also of maintaining and increasing the real value of that wealth. This complexity has developed in parallel with the growing sophistication of financial matters in society. Consequently in creating trusts settlors and their advisers have needed increased awareness of the financial world both in setting up family trusts and in taking the opportunity to use the trust more directly in commerce (e.g., through the utilisation of unit trusts and the use of the trust in pension schemes).

7.1 General Taxation Principles

Lord Tomlin in *IRC* v. *Duke of Westminster* [1936] AC 1, said, 'Every man is entitled if he can to order his affairs so that the tax attaching under the appropriate Act is less than it otherwise would be', and this tenet is at the basis of all tax planning; that whilst evasion of taxes due is illegal, the making of arrangements which reduce the amount of tax due is lawful tax avoidance. The distinction between tax avoidance and tax evasion is neatly illustrated by an example given by J. Tiley (*Revenue Law* (1981), p.19): 'If a person marries in order to reduce his tax burden he is practising tax avoidance; if he tells the Inland Revenue that he is married when he is not, he is guilty of tax evasion and may be prosecuted.'

Tax law and practice often tends to be a cat and mouse game with the Inland Revenue or Parliament as the cat attempting to maximise the number of taxable events, and the taxpayer as the mouse, trying to exploit any opportunities or loopholes left open. The success of the taxpayer in taking full advantage of the principle in *IRC* v. *Duke of*

Westminster reached a high watermark in the decision in *Ramsay* v. *IRC*
[1982] AC 300. In that case the House of Lords had to consider the
efficacy of an off-the-shelf tax avoidance scheme of a type which had at
that time become legion. The nature of the scheme was to turn a
tax-neutral situation into one where there would be an allowable loss for
tax purposes by use of an entirely artificial scheme serving no purpose
other than the avoidance of tax. The House of Lords held that the
scheme should be looked at as a whole and concluded that there was no
real loss to the taxpayer who should therefore not achieve any tax
advantage by it. Lord Wilberforce said that the Westminster principle
was a cardinal principle, but it must not be overstated or extended and it
did not compel the court to look at a document or transaction in blinkers
without considering the context. The Ramsay decision has been held to
be retrospective in effect so that a tax avoidance scheme which had been
sanctioned by the House of Lords in *IRC* v. *Plummer* [1980] AC 896, was
held ineffective in *Moodie* v. *IRC* [1990] 1 WLR 1084, following the
decision in Ramsay.

The effect of the Ramsay decision appears to be that tax cannot be
avoided by adoption of an artificial scheme involving a pre-ordained
series of transactions with the end result being a tax saving. However, if
there are several transactions which do not form part of a pre-ordained
series then any tax saving achieved is lawful. In *Fitzwilliam (Countess)* v.
IRC, The Times, 22 November 1989, an elaborate scheme was devised to
avoid capital transfer tax by taking advantage of exemptions for a
surviving spouse, deeds of family arrangement and other provisions. The
scheme was challenged by the Inland Revenue under the Ramsay
principle. It was held that the scheme was effective because it was not a
pre-ordained series of transactions. Once the first step (an appointment
of £4 000 000) had been taken it did not necessarily follow that the others
would inevitably occur; there was the possibility of change. The result of
Ramsay is substantially limited by this approach.

Principal taxes affecting trusts
The principal taxes affecting trusts are income tax, capital gains tax and
inheritance tax.

Income tax
Income tax is a tax charged upon an individual's income. The general
manner in which income tax affects trusts is that during the term of the
trust the trustees are subject to basic rate tax on all income produced by
the fund. The reason for this is that the trustees are the legal owners of
the income as it arises and it is essential to charge them otherwise there
might be problems, particularly if the income was accumulated by them.

The basic rate is chargeable in most cases but, in the case of trusts where trustees have a duty or power to accumulate the income, there is a surcharge (unless the beneficiary has a vested interest in income as against the trustee). The surcharge may be made even if the beneficiary is entitled to the income and the trustees merely have an ancillary power to accumulate (*IRC* v. *Berrill* [1981] 1 WLR 449). Trustees are liable only if they are resident in the United Kingdom and beneficiaries are not liable if they are not resident in the United Kingdom and if the income arises outside the United Kingdom. This gives liberal scope for tax avoidance schemes and explains the proliferation of off-shore trusts where income is derived from sources outside the United Kingdom and is not remitted to the United Kingdom, so that income tax is avoided (see *Dawson* v. *IRC* [1988] 1 WLR 930).

A beneficiary who is entitled to income as it arises (e.g., a life tenant) is subject to income tax on all income even if none of it is actually remitted to him (*Baker* v. *Archer-Shee* [1927] AC 844). The beneficiary will be taxed at the rate appropriate to him as a person but he will be credited with the amount already paid by the trustees.

If the trust is discretionary then the beneficiary is not taxable on income arising from the trust property, but only on payments actually made. When such payment is made the beneficiary is taxable on the income and receives a credit for tax paid by the trustees. If the surcharge has been paid there is a positive incentive for the trustees to make payments to beneficiaries taxed at basic rate so that the excess may be recovered.

The tax is payable on income. In recent years the revenue have argued that payments made out of capital may be treated as income. This depends upon the nature of the payments. If they are intended to be supplements to the beneficiary's income then they may be treated as such (*Cunards Trustees* v. *IRC* (1946) 174 LT 133). However, the mere fact that payments are recurrent does not make them income. In *Stevenson* v. *Wishart* [1987] 1 WLR 1204 in the exercise of trust powers trustees made payments out of capital in several years to a beneficiary for medical expenses and the costs of a nursing home. The Court of Appeal rejected an argument that these were income payments. Fox LJ said: 'There is nothing in the present case which indicates that the payments were of an income nature except their recurrence. I do not think that is sufficient. The trustees were disposing of capital in exercise of a power over capital. They did not create a recurring interest in property.'

Capital gains tax

Capital gains tax is a tax upon a capital gain realised upon the disposal of an asset. When a trust is created there may be a charge on the disposal of property upon trust, although in some instances the liability may be deferred until some later disposal. Once the trust has been created the trustees will normally be liable on three occasions: (a) when they dispose of assets in the course of administration of the trust (e.g., on switching investments); (b) when a beneficiary becomes absolutely entitled as against the trustees to settled property unless this occurs on the death of a previous beneficiary; (c) on a deemed disposal on the termination of a life interest in possession in property which does not at that time cease to be settled property unless this occurs on death.

Inheritance tax

Inheritance tax is a tax on transfers of value. A transfer of value may be chargeable, exempt or potentially exempt. One of the most important concepts is the principle of the 'potentially exempt transfer': that transfers inter vivos are (with some exception) free from tax provided that the settlor does not die within the following seven years. This may be relevant to a trust, particularly on the transfer of property into trust by the settlor. The tax is normally relevant at two stages of the trust: first, on its creation; and second, whenever property ceases to be 'relevant trust property' by a transfer of value out of trust. A charge on this latter event occurring is normally termed an 'exit charge'.

7.2 Successive Interests

Many family trusts use the technique of a succession of interests in the control of wealth. Often the succession of interests will be that of the settlor's spouse followed by interests of the settlor's children. Where the mechanism is used there will normally be a present interest in possession followed by a future interest or interests. The beneficiaries with present interests will have the benefit of the income from the trust property/ capital, whilst beneficiaries with the ultimate future interests will have a right to the future enjoyment of the trust property/capital (see Figure 7.1).

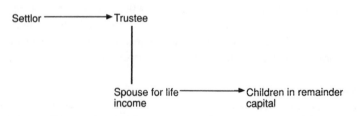

Figure 7.1 Successive interests

The succession of interests may be more complex, with, for example, several persons having successive life interests entitling them to the income for the time being from the trust capital. When a trust adopts a system of successive interests the trustees must perform a careful balancing act whereby they treat both income and capital beneficiaries fairly; this will be explained in more detail later in this chapter.

Taxation
Generally trusts where there are interests in possession are treated moderately by tax legislation. The trustees are taxed at basic rate on the income arising. The life tenant is ultimately liable at whatever rate is appropriate to him; but he is given a credit in respect of amounts already paid by the trustees. If the beneficiary receives the income directly instead of through the trustees then it is the beneficiary and not the trustees who will be assessed. Any payments out of capital are not regarded as income unless they are intended to be so regarded (*Brodie's Will Trustees* v. *IRC* (1933) 17 TC 432), so any payments made under powers of appointment or powers to make advancements of capital will not normally be subject to income tax.

Various events in the history of the trust will give rise to liability to capital gains tax. First, the creation of the settlement is a disposal by the settlor and a chargeable gain or allowable loss will occur. Second, if the trustees dispose of any assets in the administration of the trust a charge will be made on any gain. Third, if any property leaves the settlement – for instance, on the termination of a life interest (otherwise than on death) – causing a beneficiary to become absolutely entitled there is a deemed disposal by the trustees at market value. In the normal case when the life interest ends on the death of the life tenant there is an uplift in value but no charge to tax.

Exposure to inheritance tax must be considered also. If the trust is created on death the tax is chargeable but if created inter vivos there is a potentially exempt transfer; the assets are treated as belonging to the life tenant and on his death tax is charged on the whole of the settled fund at the rate appropriate to his estate.

There are various exemptions and reliefs which may be applicable to the particular circumstances of the case, but it is not the function of this text to deal with the tax position in full.

Rule against remoteness of vesting, inalienability and accumulations
One of the purposes of the successive interest method is to enable the settlor to exercise control over the property far into the future by providing for future interests which will vest in possession at some later date or on some future event. Without the support of the law settlors

would not be able to achieve such control, for after their deaths the living would be able to use what had been the settlors' property in whatever way they wished. In order to ensure a stable and peaceful succession to property the law generally upholds the wishes of a settlor by giving effect to a settlor's instructions as to what is to happen to his property after his death, and for sentimental reasons the law allows the control of the settlor's 'dead hand' to extend a little further into the future. Such future control is limited by the rule against remoteness of vesting which, briefly stated (Gray, *The Rule Against Perpetuities*, 4th edn, p.201) is: 'No interest is good unless it must vest, if at all, not later than twenty-one years after some life in being at the creation of the interest.' The rule basically allows a settlor to make a future gift to his grandchildren on attaining the age of 21 years. Control into the more distant future is not allowed; otherwise the choices of future generations would be too much affected by trusts created by previous generations, and such control could have a stultifying effect upon the economy. It has been suggested, however, that the rule should be abolished and that limitations upon control by a deceased settlor should instead operate through the rules allowing variations of trusts and the rule in *Saunders* v. *Vautier* (1841) Cr & Ph 240, permitting beneficiaries who are of full age and sound mind to bring the trust to an end and receive their beneficial interests (see Moffat and Chesterman, p.294). The current law allows settlors to rely upon the basic period of a lifetime and 21 years; alternatively a settlor can choose to specify a fixed period of 80 years as the perpetuity period for a particular trust, and provide that any future interests must vest within that period.

A related rule is the rule against inalienability, that capital should not be forever tied up and not be transferable. This could occur if there is a trust of income to continue for a long period of time thus leading to inalienability of the capital, which cannot for the duration of the trust be otherwise utilised. In order to limit the extent to which this might occur, the law provides that the period of inalienability must not exceed the perpetuity period. This rule has application to private purpose trusts only, for in the case of a trust for persons the gifts to beneficiaries must satisfy the rule against remoteness of vesting, and will of course have obtained vested interests by the end of the perpetuity period.

Another associated rule is that which restricts the powers of trustees to accumulate income. Whilst the trustees accumulate income under powers given to them under a trust, neither the income nor the capital may be consumed. The rules against accumulations of income ensure that this does not happen for too long. The Law of Property Act 1925 (s.164–5) and the Perpetuities and Accumulations Act 1964 (s.13) provide that income may only be accumulated principally for three possible periods:

for the life of the settlor, 21 years from the death of the settlor or the date of the making of the disposition, or the duration of a person's minority.

Duty to act impartially
Where there are successive interests the trustees have the difficult task of striking a fair balance between the interests of beneficiaries of capital and the interests of beneficiaries of income, which interests are continually liable to conflict. In order to assist the trustees in this task several rules have emerged, and are explained below.

Payment of debts
In the case of a trust by will, if a testator has created successive interests of his residuary estate in favour of A for life with remainder to B and, in accordance with the law, debts have to be paid out of the residue, it would be unfair if the debts were paid out of current income as this would favour the remainderman, B, and prejudice the life tenant, A. Similarly it would be unfair to pay the debts wholly from the capital sum to which B is entitled, without taking something from A.

The rule in *Allhusen* v. *Whittell* (1867) LR 4 Eq 295, requires that both the life interest of A and the remainder interest of B should be used for payment of debts. The trustees must calculate the capital sum which, together with interest over the year following death, would equal the debts, expenses and legacies. This capital sum is taken from B's capital interest and any excess of total expenditure over that sum is taken from A's income interest. In practice, however, some wills exclude this rule, and in the execution of others the rule is ignored by the trustees (see George and George (1946) 10 Conv. 125).

Duty to convert
Sometimes a trust instrument expressly directs the trustees to convert property from one form to another, usually by ordering a sale so that the proceeds may be divided between the beneficiaries. Further, where the trust property is of a kind that it will more naturally benefit either the income beneficiary over the capital beneficiary or vice versa, the trustees may have an implied duty to convert the asset by selling it so that the proceeds of sale may be enjoyed fairly by both income and capital beneficiaries.

The implied duty arises under the authority of *Howe* v. *Lord Dartmouth* (1802) 7 Ves 137. The rule in *Howe* v. *Lord Dartmouth* is that, subject to a contrary provision in the will, there is a duty to convert where residuary personalty is settled by will in favour of persons who are to enjoy it by succession. The trustees must convert any wasting assets (such as leases), reversionary assets (such as future interests under other trusts) and any unauthorised investments into property of a permanent and income-bearing type. It should be emphasised that the rule does not apply to inter-vivos trusts because the assumption made by the courts is that the settlor intended that the particular assets should be enjoyed more by one beneficiary over another.

Apportionment

Where there is a duty to convert there is, in the absence of a contrary intention, a duty upon the trustees to apportion the benefit of the property fairly between the beneficiaries pending its conversion. The rules are quite complex and are often excluded in well-drafted trusts. Briefly, but without dealing with the arithmetic aspects of the rules, they are as follows.

First, wasting assets will generally produce income benefiting the life tenant, but for a limited period of time, during which their capital value will depreciate to the disadvantage of the remainderman. The trustees must make an appointment with the effect that the life tenant receives a fair income but with any surplus being added to the capital. Before 1925 the rules applied to leasehold land but the effect of the Law of Property Act 1925 and the case of *Re Brooker* [1926] WN 93 is probably that there is no longer any duty to apportion.

Second, if the property includes future, reversionary and non-income producing assets (e.g., a future interest under a trust), the property would produce no income pending conversion and this would benefit the remainderman but not the life tenant. An apportionment is made by ascertaining the sum:

> which, put out at 4% per annum . . . and accumulating at compound interest at that rate with yearly rests, and deducting income tax at the standard rate would, with the accumulation of interest have produced at the respective dates of receipt, the amount actually received; and that the aggregate of the sums so ascertained ought to be treated as principal and be applied accordingly, and the residue should be treated as income.

(See Chitty J in *Re Earl of Chesterfield's Trusts* (1883) 24 Ch D 643.)

Reform

The Law Reform Committee (Cmnd 8733, 1982) has recommended that these complex rules should be subsumed to a new statutory duty to act impartially. They considered that the existing rules were outmoded in the light of modern investment practice, particularly where the old rules might require the sale of equity investments which might be necessary to preserve the capital value of the trust.

Advancements of capital

Where the interests of beneficiaries are future interests in capital such beneficiaries are deprived of income for a time, during which time income from it is being used for the life tenant. Circumstances may arise which make it desirable that the future beneficiaries should be able to have part of their capital interest early. Most trusts make provision for such eventuality by the inclusion of an express power for the trustees to make advancements of capital. The express power is often an extended version of the statutory power in s.32 of the Trustee Act 1925, which applies unless a contrary intention appears in the trust instrument. Such a contrary intention might be gleaned from the inclusion in the trust of a duty on the trustees to accumulate income and add it to the capital, since this might show that the settlor wanted to build up a large capital sum which should not be diminished by the making of advancements (*IRC* v. *Bernstein* [1961] Ch 399).

Purpose of advancement

Originally express powers were included to make provision for some substantial preferment in life of the beneficiary (e.g., the setting-up of the beneficiary in business) but today the statutory power and many express powers provide that the trustees may apply monies for the 'advancement or benefit' of the beneficiary. The use of the word 'benefit' makes the power much wider. Viscount Radcliffe, in the leading case of *Pilkington* v. *IRC* [1964] AC 612, has said that the combined phrase 'advancement or benefit' means 'any use of the money which will improve the material situation of the beneficiary'.

The most obvious kind of benefit is a financial benefit (such as the setting-up in business of the beneficiary) or an indirect financial benefit (such as the saving of tax, as in *Pilkington* v. *IRC*). Normally an advancement will not be made to pay off the debts of the beneficiary since payment of the debts is a financial benefit to the creditors rather than the beneficiary (*Re Price* (1887) Ch 603); but if the debts carry heavy interest it may be a financial benefit to have them paid off so as to end the liability for interest (*Lowther* v. *Bentinck* (1875) LR 19 Eq 166).

A non-financial benefit may also be within the ambit of the power. In *Re Clore* [1966] 1 WLR 955 it was held that it was a benefit to a particular beneficiary to make an advancement to him so that he could make a contribution to charity. Because the beneficiary was rich he felt that he was under a moral obligation to make such a contribution. The benefit

may be a social one, such as to maintain a stable home and family as in
Re Kershaw (1868) LR 6 Eq 322, where a beneficiary required a payment
to support her husband's business. There was evidence that if the money
was not available the husband would need to travel abroad for work.
Malins v-c held that it was in the wife's interest to support her husband's
business and an advancement would be properly made. It was irrelevant
that a third party would also benefit. The possibility of third parties
incidentally benefiting was also no bar to an advancement in *Pilkington*
v. *IRC*, where the beneficiary's children might benefit from the advancement if the beneficiary died under the age of 30.

Advancement of land

The statutory power of advancement provides that money, securities or
land held upon trust for sale may be advanced. It might be argued that
the power does not extend to a general power to advance land. It is
likely, however, that the trustees are within their powers to transfer land
to a beneficiary by way of advancement in order to avoid circuitry of
action, since the trustees could advance money to the beneficiary and
then sell him the land (*Re Collards Will Trusts* [1961] Ch 293).

Advancements for maintenance

It is a moot point whether the trustees can make advancements of capital
for the maintenance of a beneficiary. Interpretation of s.32 of the Trustee
Act in conjunction with s.31 would suggest that only income should be
used for maintenance, because s.31 refers to maintenance but s.32 does
not; but there is some authority which suggests that capital may be used,
at least in exceptional circumstances. In *Barlow* v. *Grant* (1684) 1 Vern
255 it was said that the court would generally not allow trustees to break
into the capital for the purpose of maintenance, though this might be
done on rare occasions.

Advancements by way of sub-settlement

After early doubt as to whether an advancement could be made in order
to set up a separate sub-trust the House of Lords has now confirmed that
this may be done (*Pilkington* v. *IRC*, above). But trustees cannot by way
of sub-settlement delegate their discretions except as would normally be
permitted by the terms of the trust instrument or by the general law (see
below, section 9.4). If the terms of the purported sub-trust involve
unauthorised delegation the supposed sub-trust is void, according to
Upjohn J in *Re Wills' Trusts* [1959] Ch 1. So, for example, the sub-trust
should not incorporate a discretionary trust.

It should be noted that the creation of sub-settlement may have the tax
consequence of a capital gains tax charge (and an inheritance tax

charge). Whether this is the case depends upon whether the sub-trust is properly regarded as subsidiary to the main trust or whether it can be regarded for all purposes as separate. If the terms are such that it can operate totally independently of the original trust there is a deemed disposal by the trustees of the main settlement with the trustees of the sub-settlement becoming absolutely entitled (see *Roome* v. *Edwards* (1981) 54 TC 359).

Amount to be advanced

The statutory power permits the adancement of up to one-half of the beneficiary's presumptive share. So, if there are two beneficiaries and capital of £100 000, a beneficiary may have advanced to him up to £25 000, being one-half of the presumptive share of £50 000. The calculation is not, however, always so easy. Most funds appreciate in absolute terms and there may be argument as to whether the value of the presumptive share should be calculated at the date of the advancement or whether a subsequent increase in value may be taken into account. If the power is a power to advance half of the presumptive share at the date of the advancement and this amount is advanced, no further advancement will be allowed, even if the fund increases in value. This analysis was adopted in *Re Abergavenny* [1981] 1 WLR 843.

A related problem is how should the advancement be taken into account when the beneficiary ultimately becomes entitled to the balance of his share. Should the earlier advancement be deducted purely on its cash value, or should it be subtracted on its proportionate value? In *Re Gollins Declaration of Trust* [1969] 1 WLR 1858 A was entitled to five-ninths of a fund. An advancement was made to him of one-third of the fund. The question arose as to whether A was finally entitled to five-ninths minus the cash value of the advancement or five-ninths less the one-third proportionate value. Buckley J decided that the cash value of the advancement should be brought into account. The decision does not rest easily with the decision in *Re Abergavenny* (above), and the Law Commission has recommended that advancements should be taken into account on a fractional rather than a cash basis.

Consents needed

Under the statutory power an advancement cannot be made without the consent of any person entitled to a prior life interest, the reason being that the life tenant has the right to the income from the capital and, if the capital is reduced by the making of an advancement, the amount of the income will be affected, and thus the interest of the life tenant will be prejudiced. The consent of the life tenant cannot be dispensed with even if it is difficult to obtain. This is demonstrated by *Re Forsters Settlement*

[1942] Ch 199, where the life tenant could not be located because she had married a person who on the outbreak of war had become an enemy alien. The court refused to allow an advancement without her consent.

Duty of trustees to exercise care in advancement
In exercising the power of advancement the trustees must exercise their normal duty of care. Normally this does not involve the trustees in exercising any particular control over advancements. They can normally make payments for the stated purpose to the beneficiaries or their parents or guardians and trust the recipient to apply the money for the agreed purpose. Once, however, the recipient shows himself or herself to be untrustworthy the trustees should not make further payments without ensuring that the money will be used as intended. In *Re Pauling's Settlement* [1964] Ch 303 trustees were held to be in breach of duty where a series of advancements were made nominally for the benefit of minor beneficiaries, but which had been used for the benefit of the family generally. One clear misapplication was the purchase of a house for the father of the beneficiaries. Once a misapplication had come to the attention of the trustees they should have ensured that any further advancements were not similarly misapplied. The trustees can take such precautions as making payments directly to some third party for the agreed purpose (e.g., by paying tuition fees direct to a college).

Taxation of advancement
So long as advancements are not being made as supplements to income the advancements will not normally give rise to income tax liability. It was mentioned above, however, that an advancement may give rise to a capital gains tax charge. In the normal case where there is a life tenant and the advancement is to a person entitled in remainder there will also be a charge to inheritance tax, because the life tenant's interest in the capital ends in favour of the person entitled in remainder.

7.3 Accumulation and Maintenance Settlements

The basic structure of an accumulation and maintenance settlement is one where the settlor has given future interests in capital, normally to children upon attaining a specified age, with provision for the beneficiaries to be maintained out of the income but with any surplus income to be accumulated. Although the beneficiaries' capital interests are delayed they may receive some capital early through exercise of a power of advancement. This type of settlement is popular for two main reasons: first, it accords with general parental wish; second, it has been a reasonably tax efficient device (see Figure 7.2).

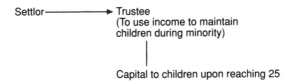

Figure 7.2 Accumulation and maintenance settlement

Taxation

Accumulation and maintenance trusts have tax advantages and disadvantages. The disadvantage is in relation to income tax because such trusts are potentially subject to an income tax surcharge which applies to trusts where there is a power to accumulate income. The surcharge does not, however, apply to income which is treated as belonging to a beneficiary. For example, if he has a contingent interest but is currently entitled to all income arising by virtue of s.31(i)(ii) of the Trustee Act 1925, the trustees cannot accumulate the income and the higher rate does not apply; and income used for the maintenance of a beneficiary is treated as belonging to the beneficiary and the higher rate does not apply. There is one important exception to this last rule, and that is that if the beneficiary is a minor unmarried child of the settlor, any income paid to or applied for his/her maintenance or education is aggregated with the settlor's income for tax purposes.

The capital gains tax position of an accumulation and maintenance trust is largely neutral. There will be a chargeable event on the disposal which creates the settlement and whenever trustees dispose of property for the purposes of investment, and there is a deemed disposal when a beneficiary becomes absolutely entitled (e.g., upon attaining a specified age).

The tax advantage of these trusts is in relation to inheritance tax. The creation of the trust is a potentially exempt transfer and there is no charge unless the settlor dies within the following seven years. There is no periodic charge as there is with discretionary trusts. There is no exit charge upon a beneficiary becoming absolutely entitled. Therefore the creation and operation of these trusts does not generally give rise to any inheritance tax liability, but the trust must satisfy certain conditions: the age contingency must not exceed 25; there must be no interest in possession (i.e., there must be no present interest in capital or income); the trust must not last for more than 25 years or all of the beneficiaries must be of a common grandparent, so that the trust benefits one generation only.

Does the beneficiary's future capital gift include income?
It can be seen from the explanation above that interests under accumulation and maintenance settlements are future interests rather than interests in possession. Where there is a future gift of capital it may be a gift of the specified property or capital only or it may include the income arising upon that property for the intermediate period from the time of the making of the gift until the vesting of it in possession. In most trusts which make future gifts it is quite clear whether or not the future gift includes the intermediate income. If there are successive interests with a future interest following on from a present life interest it is clear that the future gift does not include the intermediate income, since the present life beneficiary is entitled to the income. Where there is no present interest it will normally be clear from the terms of the trust whether the future gift includes income. For instance, its terms may show that income is to be used for the maintenance of the beneficiary, and, of course, this can only be done if there is income available. In rare cases it will not be clear whether the future gift includes the intermediate income, in which cases it is necessary to fall back upon the various judicial and statutory authorities which indicate whether the gift should include income. Whilst some of the rules appear to be logical, it is unfortunate that others do not and a student of these rules must resort to parrot-fashion learning in order to remember them.

Types of gift: personalty, realty, specific, residuary, vested or contingent
Whether a gift of property includes the intermediate income from the property depends to some extent upon the type of gift which has been made. The property given may be specific personalty (such as jewellery or shares) or realty (i.e., land) or may be a pecuniary legacy (i.e., a gift by will of a sum of money). Alternatively the gift might not be specific but might be a residuary gift by will: in other words, anything that is left over after specific gifts have been made and debts and expenses paid.

Whatever the property involved the gift may be present (in possession) or future, and if future may be vested or contingent. A vested gift is one which is bound to take effect at some time; for instance, a gift to A when B dies is vested because B is bound to die at some time. It is irrelevant that A might die before B, in which circumstance A's estate will take the gift. A contingent gift is one which depends upon an uncertain event or contingency; for instance, a gift to A upon attaining the age of 25 is contingent because A might never reach the age of 25. A gift to A if he survives B (in contrast to the example above of a gift to A when B dies) is also contingent, since A might not survive B.

Specific bequest or devise of personalty or realty

The normal presumption, arising from s.175 of the Law of Property Act 1925, is that a gift of specified property includes the intermediate income arising from the property. It has been decided that the presumption raised by s.175 is not rebutted by an express deferral of enjoyment of the gift until some later time. In *Re McGeorge* [1963] Ch 544 a testator devised land to his daughter, but declared that the devise should not take effect until the death of his wife. It was held by Cross J that the devise included the intermediate income by virtue of s.175.

Residuary realty

Again, s.175 of the Law of Property Act 1925 normally results in the gift including the intermediate income from it.

Residuary personalty

A gift of residuary personalty normally includes the intermediate income (*Bective* v. *Hodgson* (1864) 10 HLC 656).

Deferred gifts of residuary personalty

As seen above, the normal presumption is that residuary gifts include the income. But if, apart from the mere fact of the gift being a future one, there is some clear direction that enjoyment of it is to be deferred to some future date, the presumption is rebutted. Cross J in *Re Geering* [1964] 1 Ch 136 stated that 'when a gift of residue is expressly deferred to a future date, then whether it is vested or vested subject to being divested or contingent it does not prima facie carry the intermediate income'. So, for example, in *Re Gillett* [1950] Ch 102 it was held that a future vested gift did not carry the intermediate income where a gift to X was deferred to take effect after the death of A.

Pecuniary legacies

A specific gift of money is known as a pecuniary legacy. A pecuniary legacy does not normally carry intermediate income (*Lord* v. *Lord* (1867) LR 2 Ch App 782) since the sum of money does not form a separate fund or piece of property until it is set aside from the estate at the time when it is to vest in possession. In some exceptional circumstances, however, a pecuniary legacy will include a sum representing interest which might have been earned upon it (as opposed to actual intermediate income which would have been ascertainable if there was separate property which was producing income).

The main exception is that the legacy will carry interest if the gift is made by a parent or someone in the place of a parent who has made no other provision for maintenance and the gift is contingent upon attaining majority. It is assumed that a parent would have intended to maintain the child and the making of the gift contingent upon attaining majority was simply to delay the gift until the child was regarded as mature enough to use it wisely. The clearest statement of the rule is contained in *Re Jones* [1932] 1 Ch 642 where Farwell J said:

> where a contingent legacy is given to an infant, a child of the testator, and no other proper provision made for maintenance, and the legacy contingent on the attaining of [18] or marriage, the infant is entitled to interest, because the court presumes that the testator intended to maintain the child and, as he has made no other provision for it except the interest on the contingent legacy, the Court infers that he must have intended interest to be payable accordingly.

The second exception is that if the testator has shown a clear intention to maintain the beneficiary the gift will carry interest, so that in the case of a gift to children upon attaining some age other than majority (so that the first exception, above, would not apply) the circumstances of the gift may show an intention to maintain. In *Re Jones* (above) there was a gift to the testator's daughters upon reaching the age of 25. Clause 6 of the will specified that the trustees could provide a home for the daughters. From clause 6 the court was able to infer that the settlor intended that the daughters should be maintained and the gift carried interest.

The third and last exception is where the testator directs that the legacy is to be immediately set apart from the rest of his estate. If the property is kept as a separate fund the court will assume that the income arising on the fund is included as part of the gift (*Re Woodin* [1895] 2 Ch 309).

Inter-vivos gifts

The general rule is that inter-vivos gifts include the intermediate income unless there is an express deferral of the gift (*Re Cochrane* [1955] Ch 309), or unless the income has been disposed of elsewhere or it has been directed that it should be accumulated (see Underhill, *Trusts and Trustees*, 14th edn, p.411).

Summary

Table 7.1 below attempts to summarise the rules which determine whether or not a gift of property includes the income upon it.

Table 7.1 When a gift includes intermediate income

	Vested but deferred	*Contingent*
Inter-vivos settlement	No *Re Cochrane* [1955] Ch 309	Yes
Specific gift by will	Yes s.175 LPA	Yes s.175 LPA
Residuary personalty	No *Re Geering* [1964] 1 Ch 136	Yes *Bective* v. *Hodgson* (1864) 10 HLC 656
Residuary realty	Yes s.175 LPA	Yes s.175 LPA
Pecuniary legacies	Interest if: (a) from person *in loco parentis* who has made no other provision for maintenance (*Re Jones* [1932] 1 Ch 642) and the contingency is the attaining of the age of 18; or (b) intention shown to be used for maintenance (*Re Jones* [1932] 1 Ch 642); or (c) clearly set aside from residue *Re Woodin* [1895] 2 Ch 309	

Use of income

If a future gift includes the income (see above) the trustees may have powers to use the income for the maintenance or benefit of the beneficiaries. Most trusts incorporate express powers of maintenance, normally providing that the trustees may ignore the existence of any other available funds in the exercise of the power.

Availability of statutory power

In the absence of an express power the statutory power of maintenance provided by s.31 of the Trustee Act 1925 will be available unless a contrary intention is apparent in the trust instrument. The most usual indication that the power should not be available is where the settlor has directed that the income should be accumulated by the trustees (*Re Turner's Will Trust* [1937] Ch 15), for if they must accumulate the income it is obvious that it cannot be used for maintenance.

Statutory power to maintain during minority

The statutory power given by s.31(1) is a power exercisable during the minority of the beneficiary only. It is a power to use the whole or part of the income for the 'maintenance, education or benefit' of the beneficiary. The power is a power to pay such amount as is reasonable in the circumstances.

Accumulation of surplus during minority

If the trustees do not use the whole of the income, then the remainder must be accumulated by way of compound interest by investing in authorised securities (s.31(2)); but the trustees may in any subsequent year use the accumulations as if they are income arising in the current year (s.31(2)).

Income arising after majority

Once the beneficiary reaches the age of majority he or she will be entitled to all income as it arises under s.31(1)(ii) of the Trustee Act provided that he or she does not have a vested interest in such income. So a beneficiary who has merely a contingent interest is entitled to all income from his or her share of the trust property throughout the period between attaining majority and receipt of the capital. If the interest is vested then any income arising is accumulated with the capital (see section 7.3 below).

Entitlement to accumulations

If a beneficiary reaches majority or marries under that age, the accumulations on his or her share will then be held upon trust for the beneficiary absolutely if either the beneficiary had a vested interest in the income during minority, or if he acquires a vested interest upon attaining majority or marrying under that age (s.31(2)). In other cases the accumulations are held as an addition to the capital of the beneficiary's share and the beneficiary will be entitled to receive the accumulations at the same time as receipt of the capital. For instance, if the beneficiary is entitled to the capital upon reaching the age of 25, that is when he will receive the income which has been accumulated on his share.

Where there are several beneficiaries the trustees must record separately the amount of income accumulated on each share (these may differ if the shares were initially unequal or if one beneficiary has received more income than another) and the accumulations are an accretion to the particular share and not to the fund as a whole (*Re Sharp's ST* [1973] Ch 331).

Use of capital

An express or statutory power of advancement may be used to enable beneficiaries to use capital earlier than would otherwise be permitted (see above, section 7.2), provided that this has not been expressly or impliedly excluded.

7.4 Discretionary Trusts

A discretionary trust is one where there is a class of beneficiaries who do not have any entitlement to capital or income but the trustees have a discretion to allocate income or capital or both to such of the beneficiaries as they think fit. There may be said to be two types of discretionary trust, known as 'exhaustive' and 'non-exhaustive'. If the trustees are required to distribute the whole of the income the trust is exhaustive. Most discretionary trusts, however, include a power to accumulate income and are thus non-exhaustive (see Figure 7.3).

Taxation

The tax treatment of discretionary trusts is unfavourable compared to, say, accumulation and maintenance settlements. Most such discretionary trusts, being non-exhaustive, contain powers to accumulate income. For this reason the trustees are liable to income tax, together with the surcharge which is levied wherever there is such a power. The capital gains tax assessment of discretionary trusts is largely neutral, with tax being payable on the creation of the settlement and on any disposals by trustees in the course of administration of the trust. The inheritance tax analysis is, however, detrimental. The creation of the settlement is a chargeable transfer and is not a potentially exempt transfer. There is also a charge whenever property ceases to be 'relevant property': for example, if the trustees make an appointment of capital to a beneficiary. Further, there is a ten-year anniversary charge on the value of the trust fund at that time including any income which has been accumulated and added to capital.

Although discretionary trusts are hit heavily by tax they continue to

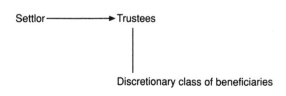

Figure 7.3 Discretionary trust

enjoy some popularity. The reasons are expressed in Whitehouse and Stuart-Buttle (*Revenue Law*, p.433):

> The demise of the discretionary trust has been predicted many times in recent years but, despite an often hostile tax environment, their attractions (notably flexibility) have enabled these trusts to survive. Their exclusion from the PET regime now puts them at a disadvantage when compared to interest in possession settlements and there is no doubt that increased use will be made of accumulation and maintenance trusts and flexible life interest trusts. Nevertheless the complete disappearance of the discretionary trust will not occur.

Nature of beneficiary's interest

The beneficiaries under a discretionary trust have no entitlement to capital or income. They are all merely members of a class of persons and any of them might benefit if the trustees exercise a discretion in their favour. Their right has been described as a 'right to be considered', so that the trustees must consider them but need not allocate any benefit to any particular beneficiary. One leading decision is *Gartside* v. *IRC* [1968] AC 553, in which case the House of Lords held that beneficiaries under a non-exhaustive discretionary trust did not have interests in possession for the purposes of what was then estate duty. Subsequent to this decision it was argued that there would be a difference in the case of an exhaustive discretionary trust in that all the beneficiaries together are entitled to the income and should be regarded as having an interest in such income. Ungoed-Thomas J in *Sainsbury* v. *IRC* [1970] Ch 712, rejected this argument, holding that:

> The only right which any object has in an exhaustive, as in a non-exhaustive trust is to have the trustees exercise their discretion and to be protected by the court in that right. True, the trustees' discretion does not extend in the case of any exhaustive trust, as in a non-exhaustive trust, to deciding whether to make distributions to objects, but only whether the distribution that must be made shall be made to one or more of them and if more than one, in what proportion. But since in an exhaustive as in a non-exhaustive trust, it cannot be said before distribution that an object is entitled to any defined part of the income, this difference between them does not make the right of any individual object quantifiable.

Even if there is currently only one member of the specified class of beneficiaries there is no entitlement to any part of the trust property as long as there is a possibility that another beneficiary will come into existence (*Re Trafford's Settlement* [1985] Ch 32).

In one or two exceptional cases, however, it has been decided that beneficiaries under a discretionary trust do have an interest. In *Re Smith* [1928] Ch 915 there was a trust under which there was a discretion to pay the capital to a mother and subject to that discretion the capital was to be held upon trust for the children. The mother and children purported to assign their interest in the capital by way of mortgage, and the question arose as to whether there was in fact any interest which was capable of being mortgaged. Romer J held that the children and mother together owned the capital and that the mortgage was effective. Some of the reasoning in this case might be taken to indicate that in the case of an exhaustive trust the beneficiaries would be taken together to be the owners of the fund, although it is possible that Romer J was influenced by a desire to prevent the mother and children from reneging on their commitments under the mortgage.

Creditor avoidance

As the cases discussed above demonstrate, a beneficiary under a discretionary trust has no definite interest. It follows from this that if a beneficiary becomes bankrupt there is nothing to pass on to the beneficiary's trustee in bankruptcy or creditors (*Godden* v. *Crowhurst* (1842) 10 Sim 642). Even if the settlor himself is a beneficiary of his own discretionary trust, he has no proprietary right and the interest is not available to the trustee in bankruptcy (*Holmes* v. *Penney* (1856) 3 K&J 90). Until the trustees exercise their discretion in favour of a beneficiary the beneficiary has no interest but:

> If the trustees in the exercise of their discretion, do pay the rents and profits of [the trust property] to the bankrupt to the extent to which sums are paid to the bankrupt in excess of the amount necessary for his mere support, then the trustee in bankruptcy will be able to insist upon the bankrupt accounting to him for the rents and profits so received.

according to Vaughan-Williams J in *Re Ashby* [1892] 1 QB 872.

So the discretionary trust is a very useful means of creditor avoidance. Since a beneficiary does not have a particular entitlement the trustees can ensure on the beneficiary's bankruptcy that they do not pay any more to the beneficiary than is necessary for maintenance, so that there is nothing available to creditors. Once the beneficiary is later discharged from bankruptcy the trustees can safely resume payment to the beneficiary without the fear of the payments being claimed by creditors. Meanwhile the trust fund is safely preserved. The disadvantage of the technique, however, is that the settlor cannot be certain that particular beneficiaries will benefit in any particular way.

It should be noted that a transfer of property upon trust may fall foul of the provisions of the Insolvency Act 1986 if it is made for the purpose of putting assets beyond the reach of persons who are or may make claims against the settlor (s.423) and transactions made within the five years before bankruptcy may also be impeached (s.339–42).

Duty of trustees

Where there is a discretionary trust the trustees have a duty to consider all of the beneficiaries (where possible) and they must exercise their own judgment. They should not act capriciously in the exercise of the discretion (*Klug* v. *Klug* [1918] 2 Ch 67) and they should not blindly follow the instructions of other persons, such as the settlor (*Turner* v. *Turner* [1984] Ch 100). If the trustees appoint capital or income in breach of duty then the appointment may be set aside as a nullity (*Turner* v. *Turner*). If the trustees are in breach of their obligations but are able to remedy the breach the court may allow them to do so. In *Re Locker's Settlement* [1977] 1 WLR 1323:

> Paying too deferential a respect to the settlor's wishes, the trustees omitted to distribute income until [late]. It then seems to have become apparent to them that they might be failing to carry out their trust . . . where the trustees desire to repair their breach of duty and to make restitution by doing late what they ought to have done early, and where they are in no way disabled from doing so, the court should, in my judgment permit and encourage them to take that course. (Goulding J)

7.5 Protective Trusts

The term 'protective trust' is used to describe a form of trust that uses two devices which are effective in some circumstances to protect family property from creditors and the consequences of bankruptcy. The first device is the discretionary trust which, as described above, ensures that trust property cannot be claimed by the creditors of a bankrupt beneficiary. The second device, described below, is the determinable life interest.

Determinable life interest

The determinable life interest is an interest in property which will normally continue for the duration of the beneficiary's life, but which is determinable early on some specified event (such as the beneficiary's bankruptcy) so that the trust property is not available to the creditors of the beneficiary. It is also usual to make the interest determinable upon the life tenant attempting to dispose of his interest. Where, as is usual, the life tenant is the child of the settlor, a gift over of the property to another family member can ensure that the property remains within the family (see Figure 7.4).

The device was upheld in the late nineteenth century (*Billson* v. *Crofts* (1873) LR 15 Eq 314 and *Re Aylwin's Trust* (1873) LR 16 Eq 585), the justification being that the limitation cuts down the extent of the gift which is not absolute but which automatically ends upon bankruptcy. The logic is not applied, however, where a settlor creates a trust settling property upon himself until bankruptcy (*Re Brewer's Settlement* [1896] 2 Ch 503) with a gift over, probably to some member of his family. If a settlor was permitted to do this the bankruptcy laws could be made entirely redundant, since every person would have an incentive to settle their property upon trust for themselves for life or until earlier bankruptcy with some gift over to a spouse or other close associate. The decision to this effect in *Re Brewer* demonstrates that the courts, whilst purporting to apply a linguistic logic, are really making value and policy judgments in upholding or striking down such devices.

It should be noted that great care should be taken in drafting such devices because a distinction is made by the courts between determinable interests and conditional interests. Although a grant to A expressed to be until bankruptcy is valid, a grant to A expressed to be on condition that she does not become bankrupt is void (*Re Dugdale* (1888) 38 Ch D 176). The distinction is a fine one which arises from the precise language used in the gift. The distinction has little to recommend it.

The determinable life interest is an effective mechanism for keeping property from creditors and maintaining wealth within the family. Again, however, like the discretionary trust it has a disadvantage: upon bankruptcy the principal beneficiary loses all interest in the property for all time, even though he might later be discharged from bankruptcy.

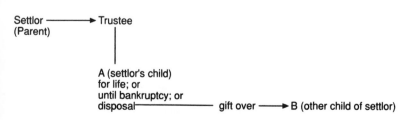

Figure 7.4 Determinable interest

Combination of determinable life interest and discretionary trust: the protective trust

The so-called 'protective trust' is simply a combination of a determinable life interest and a discretionary trust. It seeks to utilise the creditor avoidance potential of the two devices whilst minimising the disadvantages outlined above. In its classic form the settlor creates a life interest for the person whom he wishes principally to benefit (the principal beneficiary). The interest is determinable upon bankruptcy (and possibly other events) so that the property is protected from creditors in the event of bankruptcy. Upon bankruptcy, instead of a gift over to a third party which would deprive the principal beneficiary for all time, there is a gift over of the income into a discretionary trust. The principal beneficiary is a beneficiary of the discretionary trust together with his spouse and children so that during bankruptcy the trustees may pay money to the bankrupt's spouse and children and when the principal beneficiary is discharged from bankruptcy payments may again be made to him (see Figure 7.5).

The discretionary trust lasts for the remainder of the principal beneficiary's life and upon death the main gift over to the remainder beneficiaries will take effect. The device was held effective in *Godden* v. *Crowhurst* (1842) 10 Sim 642 to avoid the creditors of the principal beneficiary.

The trust is normally set out in full in the trust instrument and the form of the trust may be tailored to suit specific requirements of the settlor. Alternatively the settlor may adopt the statutory form of protective trust set out in s.33 of the Trustee Act 1925 by simply stating that the property

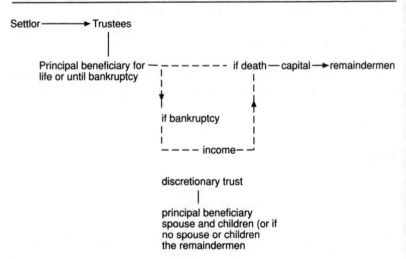

Figure 7.5 Statutory form of protective trust

is to be held upon 'protective trust' for the principal beneficiary and by identifying the persons who are to be entitled in remainder.

Protective trust for settlor

It should be noted that the principle established in *Re Brewer's Settlement* (above) applies so that if the settlor creates a protective trust with himself as principal beneficiary the device is ineffective against the trustee in bankruptcy, who can use the life interest if the settlor becomes bankrupt. The trustee in bankruptcy can either receive the current income as it arises, or can raise capital by selling the life interest to a purchaser, who will then be entitled to the income for the remainder of the principal beneficiary's life (*Re Burroughs-Fowler* [1916] 2 Ch 251).

The protective trust for the settlor is not altogether void. It is only ineffective *vis-à-vis* the trustee in bankruptcy. Thus where a person settles property upon himself and, as is usually the case, the life interest is determinable not only upon bankruptcy but also upon other events which might deprive the principal beneficiary of an absolute entitlement to the income, if another event occurs first the discretionary trust will arise and on a subsequent bankruptcy there will be nothing for the trustee in bankruptcy to claim (*Re Detmold* (1889) 40 Ch D 585). Even if bankruptcy is the first event the trust is not altogether void and, if the trustee in bankruptcy has not sold the life interest, upon discharge of the principal beneficiary from bankruptcy the gift over upon discretionary trust has effect and the principal beneficiary cannot claim sole entitlement to the income (*Re Johnson* [1904] 1 KB 134).

Other determining events

Although the protection of such trusts is primarily designed to have effect upon bankruptcy they are normally drafted more widely so that if any event occurs which might put the trust property at risk the life interest of the principal beneficiary will determine. Whether an event will cause the determination or forfeiture of the life interest depends primarily upon the words used in the trust but, for the purposes of example, it has been held that court orders affecting the life interest may cause forfeiture, such as a sequestration order in *Re Baring's Settlement Trust* [1940] Ch 737; an order of a divorce court creating a charge over the life interest in *Re Richardson's Will Trust* [1958] Ch 504; an order affecting the life interest made under the Trading with Enemy Act 1939 in *Re Gourju's Will Trust* [1943] Ch 24. But, in contrast to the above illustrations, it has been held that an order of the divorce court that a husband pay an annual sum to his wife did not cause a forfeiture in *General Accident, Fire and Life Insurance* v. *IRC* [1963] 1 WLR 1207; on the wording of the trust in *Re Hall* [1944] Ch 46, an order under the Trading with Enemy Act did not cause a forfeiture; and minor events which would affect the principal beneficiary's control of his interest, such as the appointment of a receiver (*Re Oppenheim's Will Trust* [1950] Ch 633) or attorney (*Re Tancred's Settlement* [1903] 1 Ch 715) will probably not cause a forfeiture.

Most importantly, an advancement of capital under a power of advancement will almost certainly not cause a forfeiture. Otherwise the provision of such a power in a trust instrument would be fatal to the interest of the life tenant, who no doubt would refuse his consent to any advancement on the ground that it would cause a forfeiture of his interest.

7.6 Unit Trusts

The versatility of the trust makes it suitable not only for management of family wealth, but also for use in commercial transactions. In particular it is an ideal investment vehicle, and its investment potential has been exploited through the unit trust. The unit trust is a device which enables small investors to invest in a wider range of investments than they would otherwise be able to and thus to spread the risk more than would normally be possible. The investment portfolio of a small investor is normally very limited. To take an example: if an investor had only £1000 to invest in company shares it would not be possible to invest it in more than a few companies because most companies prescribe a minimum shareholding, which in a particular case might be, say, £200. If each company had the same requirement, only five companies could be invested in. In a unit trust a large number of small investors pool their monies so as to create a very large fund, which accordingly can be invested in a much wider range of investments. Each individual investor will receive a return on investment proportionate to his or her share of the investment.

Apart from investment in companies a unit trust may be used to invest in real property through a single property scheme where a large property is developed and the ownership divided into units (often through a vehicle company) and offered to a large number of investors. The Department of Trade and Industry has tried to encourage such schemes by allowing them to be treated favourably for tax purposes.

Structure of the trust and regulation
The structure of the unit trust is that of a trust created by deed between a trustee and a manager. The title to the investments is vested in the trustee or trustees, initially for the manager; but the manager sub-divides the beneficial interest into units which are purchased by individual

investors. If an individual investor wishes to dispose of units the trust makes provision for repurchase by the manager.

The operation of unit trusts, like other investment activities, is subject to regulation under the Financial Services Act 1986. In particular unit trusts are governed by the special rules applicable to collective investment schemes (s.75–93). A unit trust must be authorised by the Secretary of State, who must be satisfied that the trust complies with the requirements of the Act. The most important of these are that the manager and the trustee must be different persons and must each be a body corporate incorporated in the United Kingdom or a state which is a member of the European Economic Community, each of which must have a place of business in the United Kingdom. The manager and trustee corporations must be independent of each other. The trust must also comply with the regulations pursuant to s.81 of the Act governing the issue and redemption of units, the expenses of the scheme, audit, investment and borrowing powers, the keeping of records, preparation of reports and amendment of the scheme. It appears that the Secretary of State has a general discretion to withhold approval of a scheme whether or not the conditions of the section are satisfied (*Allied Investors Trusts Ltd* v. *Board of Trade* [1956] Ch 232).

Nature of the trust

In essence the unit trust is a trust like any other trust. Accordingly it is potentially subject to the rules which usually apply to trusts. One example of this is that the powers of investment under the trust deed might be varied in the usual way. In *Re Municipal and General Securities Company Trust* [1950] Ch 212 it was recognised that s.57 of the Trustee Act 1925 could be applied to a unit trust so as to vary the powers of investment. In nature the unit trust is an absolute trust for the present unit holders. Thus there can be no problem of perpetuity in relation to the beneficial interests or in relation to accumulations of income. In *Re AEG Unit Trust (Managers) Ltd's Deed* [1957] 1 Ch 415, the managers could determine how much of the income should be distributed to the unit holders in a particular year, and the managers were to accumulate any balance and add it to the capital. It was argued that this might involve a trust to accumulate which fell foul of the rules against excessive accumulations. Wynn-Parry J decided that there was no trust for accumulations because:

> if at any time the whole of the certificate holders required the trust to be terminated or altered in a specific request, effect would have to be given to their requirements. Equally if in any given year all the certificate holders required that the balance of the amount available

for distribution should not be added to capital as contemplated, effect would have to be given to their requirement.

Powers of trustees
The trustees have the powers in the trust deed but subject to the limitations of the regulations of the Financial Services Act 1986. The limitations upon the trustees' powers are numerous and include restrictions on amounts which may be invested in other collective investment schemes; limitations on investment in schemes managed by the manager company or any associated company; restrictions on acquiring influential stakes in companies; conditions as to the spread of investments and rules on borrowing; and prohibitions on lending and giving guarantees.

7.7 Pension Fund Trusts

Another common commercial use of the trust is its use in occupational pension schemes. Such schemes arise and operate under a combination of trust and contract, where the beneficiary's entitlement is subject to the making of contributions in accordance with the terms under which the scheme operates.

Nature of the trust
One would suppose that the beneficiary's interest is like any other interest under a trust and is assignable. Generally this is true, and as early as 1847 it was held that an assignment of the emoluments of a fellow of King's College, Cambridge, by way of security for a loan was valid (*Feistel* v. *King's College* (1847) 10 Beav 491). In some cases, however, public policy may result in a pension being non-assignable. In *Davis* v. *Duke of Marlborough* (1818) 1 Swan 74 a pension granted by a statute to the Duke of Marlborough was held inalienable since the object in granting it was that 'it was for a memento and a perpetual memorial of national gratitude for public services'. In line with this decision various statutes provide that pensions given for certain public services are inalienable. Often the scheme itself makes provision for the employee to nominate some other person as beneficiary. Such a provision is analogous to a power of appointment and the beneficial interest passes to the appointee without the need for strict formality such as compliance with the Wills Act 1837 (*Baird* v. *Baird* [1990] 2 WLR 1412.

Pensions funds are generally subject to the normal rules of equity which protect beneficiaries. In particular the trustees must exercise appropriate skill and care and since the beneficiaries have normally paid for their interests, rather than receiving a gift from a settlor, it is all the more important that their interests should be protected. This was emphasised in *Cowan* v. *Scargill* [1985] Ch 270, where the National Coal Board pension fund was managed by trustees which included officials of the National Union of Mineworkers. The union trustees were reluctant to invest the pension fund in oil and gas enterprises and in any overseas companies because of their political convictions. The court held that the trustees must not allow their decisions to be swayed by political motive. Megarry vc said, 'I can see no reason for holding that different principles apply to pension fund trusts from those which apply to other trusts.'

It should be remembered, however, that a pension scheme does not endure within the ambit of the trust alone; the beneficiaries of the trust have given consideration, either through their own contributions or by the provision of their services. Their rights arise then through contract, and the contract is a contract of employment. The scheme will therefore be subject to such rules as would relate to a contract of employment. In *Imperial Group Pension Trust Ltd* v. *Imperial Tobacco Ltd* [1991] 1 WLR 589, the terms of a scheme provided that benefits might be increased in any year by the decision of a committee of management, subject to the consent of the employer company. A question which arose following a change in management of the company was whether the company could arbitrarily refuse consent to a decision of the committee. In every contract of employment there is an implied term that the employer will act in good faith and Sir Nicolas Browne-Wilkinson vc held that this term should be implied in relation to the scheme so that the company could not arbitrarily withhold consent.

Entitlement to surplus funds

An issue which arises time and time again in the operation of pension fund trusts is who is entitled to any surplus monies where the amount of the fund exceeds that necessary to make the required payments to beneficiaries. The question is likely to arise on a transfer of pension rights from one company to another (perhaps on a company takeover or merger) or on the liquidation of a company. The answer depends upon the terms of the scheme. In most cases the fund is built up on terms that the employees pay fixed contributions whilst the employer provides the balance to ensure the contracted benefit. In this type of case any surplus is likely to arise from overfunding by the employer who, for this reason, is entitled to any surplus (*Davis* v. *Richards & Wallington Industries Ltd*, [1990] 1 WLR 1511).

In exceptional cases it may be that even on the strength of the employees' contributions alone there is more money than is needed to pay the contracted pensions. It might be thought that in this instance the surplus should be regarded as belonging to the employees. One recent judgment, however, has indicated that the employees are only entitled to the benefits which they contracted for, and that they have parted with their contributions out and out so that any surplus will pass to the Crown as *bona vacantia* (*Davis* v. *Richards & Wallington Industries Ltd*, above, and see below, section 13.3).

In some schemes, however, there is a discretion given to the employer or trustees or both to use the surplus to pay additional benefits. In these schemes it may be arguable that the beneficiaries rather than the employers (or the Crown) are entitled to surpluses, at least where the trustees of a scheme have power to allocate additional benefits without the employer's consent (see *Mettoy Pension Trustees Ltd* v. *Evans* [1990] 1 WLR 1587).

In the case of a transfer of pension rights from one company to another the transferor employer is normally entitled to the surplus and not the transferee. No portion of the surplus needs to be transferred unless the deed of transfer states otherwise (*Re Imperial Foods Ltd Pension Scheme* [1986] 1 WLR 717), or unless under the terms of the scheme the transferor is not entitled to the surplus. If after the transfer a surplus arises, the transferor cannot claim the surplus since it has parted out and out with its interest. In so far as the surplus may appear to have arisen from the management of a transferor company, the transferee cannot claim it and it will pass as *bona vacantia* to the Crown (*Davis* v. *Richards & Wallington Industries Ltd*, above).

7.8 Employee Share Ownership Trusts

Another modern use of the trust is to facilitate employee share ownership in private companies. Typically the employee share ownership trust is a discretionary trust with trustees appointed by the company, holding shares which may be allocated to beneficiaries who are employees of the company or another company within the same group of companies. The arrangement has tax advantages if it complies with the requirements of the Finance Act 1989, the main requirements being: the majority of the trustees are employee selected, all employees with at least five years' service are beneficiaries; the trust uses funds received to acquire shares or meet expenses promptly; and shares are distributed to individual beneficiaries on similar terms within seven years.

Summary

This chapter has considered the trust as a mechanism for the control of private wealth both in the family and commercial context. The main advantages and disadvantages of the different forms of trust outlined will now be summarised, together with any significant points which need to be remembered in drawing up the terms of the trust.

1 A family trust may take the form of a succession of interests. This has the advantage of enabling the settlor to exercise control over the property for a long time into the future. There are no special tax advantages in creating a trust in this form. Conversely, it may be disadvantageous from the inheritance tax point of view even if the settlement is created inter vivos and as such qualifies as a potentially exempt transfer, as on the death of a life tenant tax is payable on the whole value of the settled fund. In drawing up the terms of the trust care must be taken not to infringe the rules against remoteness of vesting, inalienability and accumulations, and consideration should be given to whether to exclude the rules designed to ensure that the trustees balance the competing interests of successive beneficiaries (*Allhusen* v. *Whittell*, *Howe* v. *Lord Dartmouth*, etc.). It is also necessary to consider whether to exclude the statutory power of advancement, rely upon it, or incorporate a more extensive express power of advancement.

2 Another popular form for a family trust is a maintenance and accumulation settlement. There are tax advantages in creating such trusts, particularly from the inheritance tax point of view if the trusts falls within s.71 Inheritance Tax Act 1984. Such trusts also have the advantage of preventing young, and potentially imprudent, beneficiaries from becoming entitled to large sums of money, but at the same time ensuring that both capital (through the power of advancement) and income (through the power of maintenance, and the entitlement to income provisions of s.31 Trustee Act 1925) are available in the event of need.

3 A discretionary trust is also a popular form for a family trust to take. It enables property to be divided up taking into account circumstances which have not arisen at the time of the creation of the trust, and thus to take into account the needs and behaviour of the beneficiaries. It also allows family wealth to be maximised by taking into account tax planning considerations, and for family property to be protected from creditors of a beneficiary. The main disadvantage of this form of trust is that the tax treatment is unfavourable when compared to, say, maintenance and accumulation settlements.

4 The protective trust was developed to deal with the other main disadvantage of the discretionary trust: namely, the uncertainty caused to the beneficiaries. A protective trust can arise expressly or by reliance on s.33 Trustee Act. It is a combination of the notion of a determinable life interest and a discretionary trust. The beneficiary is in a more certain position than with a discretionary trust in that he/she is entitled to the income from the trust, usually for life, until a 'determining event' occurs. A 'determining event' is broadly one which would deprive the beneficiary of the income from the trust. At this point a discretionary trust comes into being until the death of the life tenant.

5 As the trust is an ideal investment vehicle it has also been of use in commercial transactions, such as unit trusts and occupational pensions schemes. Unit trusts enable the small investor to invest in a wider range of investments than would otherwise be possible and thereby spread risk. Pensions operate under a combination of trust and contract.

6 Check list for deciding whether and how *statutory powers* of maintenance and advancement may be exercised:

Maintenance (s.31 Trustee Act 1925)	Advancement (s.32 Trustee Act 1925)
(a) There must be no contrary intention in the trust instrument to the operation of the section.	(a) There must be no contrary intention in the trust instrument to the operation or the section.
(b) If the beneficiary does not have an interest vested in possession, the gift must carry *intermediate income.*	(b) Consider whether subject matter of the trust is money or personal securities or land held on trust for sale.
(c) The beneficiary must be a minor but it is irrelevant whether his/her interest is vested or contingent. (NB: From 18 years there may be *entitlement* to income under s.31(2) or s.31(1).)	(c) A beneficiary with a prior interest must give consent to the advancement of the *capital* interest and can only do so if of full age and mental capacity.
(d) If the power is exercised, the income (whether the whole or part thereof) must be used for the 'maintenance, education or benefit' of the beneficiary and its application must be reasonable (objective standard).	(d) Although it matters not whether the beneficiary is a minor or otherwise or whether his/her interest is vested or contingent, it is necessary to recall whether any previous advancements have been made and note that in total the trustees may only advance up to one-*half* of a beneficiaries' entitlement.
	(e) The purpose for which the advancement is to be made must be within the ambit of the statutory phrase 'advancement or benefit'.
	(f) It is necessary to consider whether it is reasonable to advance the capital to the beneficiary (or his/her guardian) directly or whether the trustees should apply it for the purpose directly. (This requirement would also apply to an express power.)

Exercises

1 What do you understand by 'conversion' of trust property? Are trustees generally under a duty to convert trust property? How important are the rules relating to conversion and apportionment today?

2 By his will Thomas, who died in 1990, left his residuary estate to Annie and Clarabel to hold on trust for Daisy for life with remainder to Daisy's children in equal shares. His residuary estate comprises (a) a leasehold interest in Blueacre; (b) a freehold interest in Greenacre; (c) a helicopter; (d) shares in a Peruvian tin mine; and (e) a vested interest in the remainder of a trust fund in which his cousin Gordon presently has a life interest. Advise Annie and Clarabel:

(a) whether any of the assets of the residuary estate should be sold;

(b) to whom they should pay any income received from existing assets; and

(c) as to the rights of Daisy with respect to the interest in remainder which has not yet fallen into possession.

3 Would all or any of the following gifts made by will carry 'intermediate income'?:

(a) '£10 000 to my daughter Christina contingent upon her attaining 25 years'?

(b) '£10 000 to my nephew Eric contingent upon attaining 30 years'?

(c) 'All my residuary personalty to Franklin if he becomes a solicitor'?

(d) '"Homeacre" to my son Harold on the death of his mother'?

(e) 'All my stocks and shares to my daughter Jennifer on the death of her father. However, should Jennifer predecease her father leaving issue, her issue should take the stocks and shares on the death of their grandfather'?

4 By her will Tessa left her residuary estate to be held on trust for 'such of my children living at the date of my death who attain 30 years, and if more than one in equal shares'. Tessa died last week, leaving Benedict (aged 14) and Charlotte (aged 22).

(a) Explain the inheritance tax consequences of this gift.

(b) Is any income and/or capital from the fund currently available to either or both of Charlotte and Benedict and, if so, on what basis?

5 A trust fund is held for Godfrey for life with remainder to such of Godfrey's children as shall attain 30 years. One of Godfrey's daughters, Victoria, approaches the trustees of the trust seeking an advancement to enable her to study law on a full-time course. The trustees have already made advancements to Victoria, which have not been applied for the purposes requested. Victoria is aged 27 years and has continuously lived well beyond her means.

Assuming the trustees are satisfied that Victoria intends to study law, may they make an advancement to Victoria for this purpose and, if so, how might they go about it?

6 £30 000 is held by trustees on 'protective trust' for Stanley for life, with remainder to Stanley's sister, Belinda. Last week Stanley was declared bankrupt.

(a) Advise the trustees as to whom they should now pay the income from the trust.

(b) How would it affect your answer, if at all, if Stanley was the settlor of the trust?

8 Variation of Trusts

A settlor as architect of a trust designs it to satisfy objectives which are desirable at the time of creation. He will also try to structure it for the future since the trust is usually intended to endure for a long period of time. After the trust has been created it sometimes becomes desirable to alter the trust in some way, usually as a result of some unforeseen change in circumstances. The law does allow for a variation of a trust if certain conditions are satisfied. The most common reason for novation of the trust is because of change in tax law. In most cases a trust of any substance is devised so as to have tax advantages at the date of creation. If many trusts are so arranged it is not uncommon for the tax laws to respond and be modified to reduce that advantage. In such a case tax advantages can often be reinstated by a well-planned variation of the trust.

The leading procedure for the variation of trusts is that contained in the Variation of Trusts Act 1958 which revolutionised the law and practice of altering trusts. Whereas statutory mechanisms did previously exist for altering mechanical or administrative provisions, the Act facilitates adjustment of beneficial interests. The essential attribute of the Act is that it empowers the court to authorise arrangements on behalf of persons who would otherwise be unable to consent to a variation because of some disability or because they are not ascertainable. It is unclear whether such variation is the result of the court order or whether it is the result of the consent of the beneficiaries. The Act is perplexing because beneficiaries under a trust cannot normally vary it by agreement. They can only bring it to an end (assuming that they are ascertained of full age and sound mind) by calling for their beneficial interests (*Saunders* v. *Vautier* (1841) 4 Beav 115). Yet by the Act a trust may be varied without ending it.

8.1 Beneficiaries on whose Behalf the Court may Approve a Variation

As mentioned above, the broad rationale of the Act is that a variation happens through the mutual agreement of the beneficiaries. In the case of adult beneficiaries of sound mind their consent, with minor exception, must be freely given and the court cannot order a variation where any such person refuses to consent. The court can, however, consent on behalf of the classes of beneficiary specified in s.1 of the Variation of Trust Act 1958. These are:

(a)   infancy and incapacity: s.1(1)(a) covers any person having, directly or indirectly, an interest, whether vested or contingent, under the trusts who by reason of infancy or other incapacity is incapable of assenting, or

(b)   persons with interests subject to two contingencies: s.1(1)(b) covers any person (whether ascertained or not) who may become entitled, directly or indirectly, to an interest in the trust as being at a future date or on the happening of a future event a person of any specified description or a member of any specified class of person, so, however that this paragraph shall not include any person who would be of that description, or a member of that class, as the case may be if the said date had fallen or the said event had happened at the date of the application to court, or

(c)   unborn beneficiaries: s.1(1)(c) covers any person unborn, or

(d)   discretionary interests arising from protective trusts: s.1(1)(d) covers any person in respect of any discretionary interest of his under protective trusts (see Chapter 7) where the interest of the principal beneficiary has not failed or determined.

Non-consenting adults

In the case of adult beneficiaries of sound mind their free consent is needed. If any one adult does not consent then the variation cannot take place. The one exception to this is persons whose only interest is within category (d).

The two main classes of beneficiary who are affected by s.1 are infants and the mentally disabled within (a) and future unborn beneficiaries within (c): for example, any possible future children in a trust for children of a named person. Categories (b) and (d) are not quite so straightforward: (d) relates principally to the spouse of a principal beneficiary under a protective trust as shown in Figure 8.1.

The category which causes most confusion is category (b), upon which there have been several court decisions (*Re Suffert's Settlement* [1961] Ch 1; *Re Moncrieff's ST* [1962] 1 WLR 1344; *Knocker* v. *Youle* [1986] 1 WLR 934). In the first two of these decisions Buckley J has established a two-contingency test that the persons on whose behalf approval may be given are those persons who are capable of fitting within a class description at some future date but excluding those persons who would actually do so at the date of the application to court. In these cases it has been pointed out that a gift to statutory next of kin will establish a class,

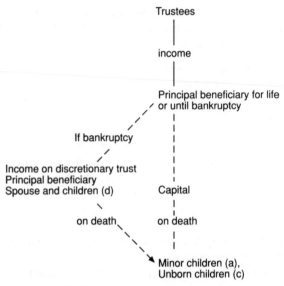

Figure 8.1 Persons within categories (a), (c) and (d) of s.(1) Variation of Trusts Act 1958

the members of which will normally be within (b) as persons who at a future date on the happening of a future event (the death of the person to whom they are next of kin) will be entitled. However, any existing ascertained persons who would be within the class if the event (the death) had occurred at the date of the application to court are not within (b) and the court cannot consent on their behalf (unless they also fall within another category).

Example

If, for example (see Figure 8.2), there is a trust where A has a life interest and there is a remainder in favour of A's next of kin, and at the date of

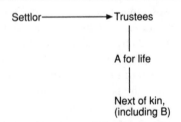

Figure 8.2 Persons within or not within category (b).
(Possible next of kin are within (b) but B is not as he would be entitled if A was dead at the date of the application to court)

the application to court A has one living child, B, who under the rules of intestacy would take absolutely in preference to all other possible next of kin, then other possible next of kin, such as A's brothers and sisters, are within category (b) as persons who may be entitled as members of a class on the happening of a future event, being A's death; but B would be excluded from the category by the proviso, because if at the date of the application to court A had died B would be a member of the class (but A's brothers and sisters would not).

8.2 Benefit

The court's jurisdiction to approve a variation on behalf of beneficiaries within the specified categories is generally limited by the proviso to s.1 which provides that the court shall not approve an arrangement on behalf of any person unless the carrying out thereof would be for the benefit of that person. There is an exception in the case of persons within category (d), presumably because the possible interest of a spouse in the event of his or her partner becoming bankrupt and the trustees then exercising their discretion to pay money to the spouse is so remote that it ought not to stand in the way of a variation.

The term 'benefit' is of course very vague, and not surprisingly it has been the source of much litigation. Understandably the term has been held to embrace financial benefit but, more interestingly, the courts have been willing to give great weight to non-financial considerations.

Financial benefit

In deciding whether a proposed variation is beneficial to the person on whose behalf the court is asked to consent the court's starting point is that the beneficiary should not be materially worse off. Often the proposed arrangement will involve a small risk of loss. This does not necessarily preclude the court from approving the arrangement. The court determines on a balance of probabilities whether the variation is a good bargain, and if the risk is a risk that an adult would take the court will take the same risk on behalf of an infant (see Danckwerts J in *Re Cohen's Will Trusts* [1959] 1 WLR 865; Russel J in *Re Druce's Settlement Trusts* [1962] 1 WLR 363). In *Re Clitheroe* [1959] 1 WLR 1159 an arrangement whereby a beneficiary would receive £100 per annum, instead of remaining a member of a class of discretionary beneficiaries, was held beneficial. The court would not, however, in *Re Cohen* [1965] 1 WLR 1229, approve an arrangement where it was possible (although unlikely) that some beneficiaries would receive nothing under the new arrangement. In a case where there is a small possibility that the beneficiary might be worse off, any objection might be met by taking out insurance against the possibility (*Re Robinson's Trust* [1976] 1 WLR 806).

The extent of the financial benefit and the risks of loss will normally be calculated by an actuary, taking into account return on investments, probable lifespans and any other material factor. The financial benefit sought in many cases is a saving of tax. Provided that there is permitted 'tax avoidance' as opposed to illegal 'tax evasion', the saving of tax is a perfectly acceptable benefit within the meaning of the Act. Goff J in *Re Sainsbury* [1967] 1 WLR 476 said: 'It is quite clear that the motive of the scheme of arrangement to vary the trusts . . . is that it may place certain members of the Sainsbury family in a better position so far as Capital Gains Tax is concerned but it is a perfectly legitimate motive for seeking the court's sanction of the arrangement.'

Not only must there be a financial benefit but there must be such a benefit for all the persons on whose behalf the court is consenting and there should be equity between them so that each receives a fair degree of benefit, although the amount of benefit which each receives does not need to be equal (*Re Van Gruisen's Will Trusts* [1964] 1 WLR 449).

Social and moral benefits

At one time it was thought that 'benefit' was limited to financial benefit, but recent judgments have exhibited a willingness to accommodate the wider meaning of the word so as to include social and moral benefits. Since the concept of morality is a highly contentious one, a reader might expect there to be a plethora of critical comment on the courts' assumption of the moral ground. This has not occurred to the extent expected, perhaps because of the long established practice of the court similarly construing benefit in this wide sense in considering trustees' powers of advancement of capital.

Family benefit

In some cases it may be argued that benefit to a third party may constitute a benefit to the beneficiary himself or herself. Presumably in most cases such an argument should fail, but in the case of family relationships the court may be swayed by the greater good of the family as a whole and the benefit by way of improved relationships which may accrue through a less selfish financial policy. Legal decisions are not consistent on the matter and the law is in need of a decision of the Court of Appeal or House of Lords to clarify the issue. The earliest decision was not sympathetic to a non-financial approach. In *Re Tinker's Settlement* [1960] 1 WLR 1011, the settlor provided that a fund should be held partly on trust for his brother on reaching the age of 30. If the brother died under 30 the gift should pass to the settlor's sister for life and then to

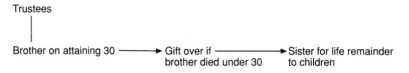

Figure 8.3 *Re Tinker's Settlement*

the sister's children (see Figure 8.3).

By error the trust had not been drafted to provide any benefit to the brother's children if he should die under 30 having fathered children. It was proposed to vary the trust by insertion of a gift over to the brother's children in these circumstances. Russel J refused to give the court's consent on behalf of the sister's children since there would be a clear financial detriment to them in the event that the brother should have children. He threw out an argument that the correction of the error would be beneficial to the family and therefore beneficial to the daughter's children. The decision stands in stark contrast to a later decision of Pennycuick J. In *Re Remnant's Settlement Trusts* [1970] 1 Ch 560 a settlor divided a fund between two daughters for their lives with remainder to their respective children. There was a forfeiture provision that if either daughter became or married a Roman Catholic there was a gift over of income and capital to the other daughter (see Figure 8.4).

Merrill's second husband was a Roman Catholic and she became one herself. She and Dawn proposed a variation to delete the forfeiture provision and to accelerate £10 000 to create trusts for their respective children. The main question was whether there was a sufficient benefit for Dawn's children who were entitled to a larger share of the fund if the forfeiture provision remained. Pennycuick J held that in all the circumstances there was a benefit to the children. On the financial side he accepted that deletion of the forfeiture provisions were detrimental to the children, but on the other hand the acceleration of their interest in £10 000 constituted a financial benefit. More adventurously he took into

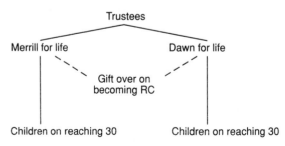

Figure 8.4 *Re Remnant's Settlement Trusts*

account the fact that 'a fortfeiture provision of this kind might well cause very serious dissension between the families of the two sisters'.

A similar leading case is *Re CL* [1969] 1 Ch 587 in which case a settlor left property on trust for his widow for life and then on trust for her adopted daughters. The widow was admitted to a mental home and a proposal was put forward asking for the court's consent on behalf of the widow to a variation surrendering the widow's life interest in favour of the adopted daughters. Cross J held that the widow owed a moral obligation to the adopted daughters and if she was of sound mind she would probably have agreed to the proposal. He therefore approved the arrangement on her behalf.

Delaying a beneficiary's interest

The court's involvement in moral issues has sometimes taken a very 'paternal' turn. In *Re T's Settlement Trust* [1964] Ch 158, and *Re Holt's Settlement* [1969] 1 Ch 100, the courts held that variations which delayed beneficiaries' interests were beneficial even though the delay in receiving property or money is plainly a financial detriment. In *Re T's Settlement Trust* the proposal to change the beneficiary's absolute interest on reaching the age of 21 to a protective trust until the reaching of a later age was approved by Wilberforce J who reasoned that 'it appears to me to be a definite benefit for this infant for a period during which it is to be hoped that independence may bring her to maturity and responsibility to be protected against creditors'. The decision in *Re Holt's Settlement* is more easy to justify without recourse to such 'moral' factors, since in that case the delaying of the beneficiaries' interests was accompanied by an increased share and so some financial advantage could be shown. The paternalistic approach was, however, still evident with Megarry J declaring that 'it is most important that young children should be reasonably advanced in a career and settled in life before they are in receipt of an income sufficient to make them independent of the need to work'.

Exporting trusts

Probably the most controversial extension of the concept of benefit has appeared in relation to proposals to export trusts to other jurisdiction. The most infamous and interesting decision in this field is *Re Weston's Settlement* [1969] 1 Ch 223, where it was proposed to remove a trust from England to Jersey since laws of taxation there were more favourable. The court refused the application partly because some doubt was shed on the evidence that the beneficiaries intended to live there and on the ability of the Jersey courts to administer the trust. More interestingly, on the question of financial benefit Lord Denning MR said that the Court:

should not consider merely the financial benefit to the infants and unborn children, but also their educational and social benefit. There are many things in life more worth while than money. One of these things is to be brought up in this our England, which is still 'the envy of less happier lands'. I do not believe it is for the benefit of children to be uprooted from England and be transported to another country simply to avoid tax.

Lord Denning's view that non-financial factors should prevail over clear financial advantage must remain debatable, as must the question of whether Jersey is a less happy land than England.

In other cases the exporting of trusts has been considered advantageous to beneficiaries. In *Re Seale's Marriage Settlement* [1961] Ch 574 some of the beneficiaries of a settlement had emigrated to Canada, and there was evidence that the other beneficiaries would also settle there. Buckley J approved a variation moving the trust to Canada for the reason that this would facilitate the administration of the trust. Similarly Pennycuick J in *Re Windeatt* [1969] 1 WLR 692 approved the exporting of a trust to Jersey, distinguishing *Re Weston's Settlement* on the ground that the family in *Windeatt* had been in Jersey for nineteen years and the children had been born there.

8.3 **Relevance of Settlor's Intention**

The settlor's intention is not an overriding factor when it comes to variation of a trust under the Act, otherwise almost any proposal could be objected to on this ground since any variation is a deviation from the settlor's original intention. In considering a proposal the court will nevertheless give due weight to any special purpose of the settlor. In particular if the settlor has created a protective trust in order to guard against the claims of creditors of the principal beneficiary, the protection should not be withdrawn lightly (see *Re Steed's Will Trusts* [1960] Ch 407). On the other hand, if the reason for the particular form of trust has effectively ceased the court is more likely to approve the proposal. In *Re Burney's Settlement Trusts* [1961] WLR 545 a marriage settlement of 1927 vested a protected life interest in a husband. By 1960 it was proposed to vary the trust by enlarging the interest into an absolute life interest. Wilberforce J approved the variation since:

the protected life interest was created in 1927 when the husband's circumstances were very different from what they have happily since become. Moreover in 1927 settlors and their advisers were not so alive as they have since become to the desirability of leaving it open to beneficiaries of income to surrender their interests to issue well before their death. In both of these respects the original purpose for which the protected life interest was created has become obsolete.

It should not be thought that the variation will only be approved if the design of the settlor has become obsolete. If necessary the court will overrule the settlor's purpose, as it did in *Re Remnant's Settlement Trust* when it removed the forfeiture provision upon the beneficiary becoming or marrying a Roman Catholic. Pennycuick J commented that the fact that the scheme would defeat the testator's intention was 'a serious but by no means conclusive consideration'.

8.4 Fraudulent Purpose

A variation will not be approved if there is some fraudulent purpose, such as to procure an additional financial advantage for an adult beneficiary. Thus where property is held on trust for A for life and then for such of A's children as he may appoint, a variation will not be approved whereby A appoints part in favour of living children but takes the other part for himself. This has been regarded as a fraud upon the power of appointment (*Re Brook's Settlement* [1968] 1 WLR 1661).

8.5 'Arrangement' or 'Re-settlement'

The Act permits 'any arrangement . . . varying or revoking all or any of the trusts'. This phrase has stimulated much judicial discussion and a distinction has crystallised between a 'variation', which is within the jurisdiction of the Act, and a 're-settlement', which is not. In *Re T's Settlement Trust* [1964] Ch 158 a mother wished to avoid the effect of her immature and irresponsible infant daughter becoming entitled to a large capital sum when she attained the age of 21. She applied to the court for an order transferring the daughter's share to new trustees to be held upon protective trusts for the daughter's life with remainder to her issue. The scheme was turned down by Wilberforce J on the ground that it amounted to a complete resettlement rather than simply a variation.

According to Megarry J in *Re Ball's Settlement* [1968] 1 WLR 899, the question is whether the arrangement 'changes the whole substratum of the trust . . . But if an arrangement, while leaving the substratum, effectuates the purpose . . . by other means, it may still be possible to regard that arrangement as merely varying the original trusts, even though the means employed are wholly different and even though the form is completely changed.' In that case a settlement conferred a life

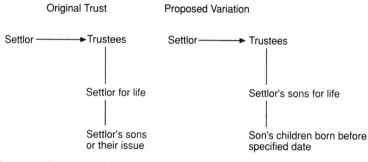

Figure 8.5 *Re Ball's Settlement*

interest upon a settlor and, subject to a power of appointment, the fund was to be divided equally between two sons of the settlor or their issue if either son predeceased the settlor. The proposed arrangement would rescind the original trust and substitute new provisions whereby each half of the fund would be held upon trust for one of the sons for life and then in equal shares amongst such of the sons' children as were alive on, or born before, a certain date (see Figure 8.5).

Megarry J approved the arrangement because it preserved the general drift of the original trust. He explained that although the life interest of the settlor had disappeared, the trusts were 'still in essence trusts in half the fund for each of the two named sons and their children in place of the former provisions for a power of appointment among the sons and their children and grandchildren'.

Although the variation should not replace the substratum of the trust, the material point is one of form and not substance. The machinery or form of the trust may change to a large extent so long as the substantive effect of the trust is similar. By this reasoning a complete revocation of existing trusts is permitted so long as the fresh trust which appears as a replacement is tolerably comparable. Megarry J in *Re Holt's Settlement* [1969] 1 Ch 100 (see also Buckley J in *Re Seale's Marriage Settlement* [1961] Ch 574) analysed the position, noting that an arrangement might be a permitted variation even though effected by the machinery of revocation and resettlement.

8.6 Making Applications

An application should normally be made by a life tenant or other person entitled to the income. It should only be made by the trustees where 'they are satisfied that the proposals are beneficial to the persons interested and have a good prospect of being approved by the court, and further, that if they do not make the application no one else will' (Russel J in *Re Druce's Settlement Trusts* [1962] 1 WLR 363). The settlor may apply and should normally be made a defendant to any action brought by any other person (RSC Order 93 Rule 6(2)).

8.7 Effect of a Court Order

As mentioned above, it is unclear whether the variation takes effect through the consent of the beneficiaries, with the court providing consent on behalf of some, or alternatively whether the court order itself effects the variation. If the variation is by consent of the beneficiaries it is arguable that any dispositions of equitable interests which occur should be in writing to satisfy s.53(1)(c) of the Law of Property Act. Procedurally this would mean that each adult beneficiary should sign a document of variation, and the document of variation would be subject to stamp duty. If there was no signed document the variation would be ineffective. If the variation takes place by the order of the court then no signed document would be necessary. Lord Reid in *Re Holmden's Settlement Trusts* [1968] AC 685 was clearly of the former view when he said:

> the court does not itself amend or vary the trusts . . . Each beneficiary is bound because he has consented to the variation. If he was not of full age when the arrangement was made, he is bound because the court was authorized by the Act of 1958 to approve of it on his behalf and did so by making an order. If he was of full age and did not in fact consent he is not affected by the order of the court and he is not bound. So the arrangement must be regarded as an arrangement made by the beneficiaries themselves. The court merely acted on behalf of or as representing those beneficiaries who were not in a position to give their own consent and approval.

Wynn-Parry J in *Re Viscount Hambleden's Will Trusts* [1960] 1 WLR 82, and Megarry J in *Re Holt's Settlement* [1969] 1 Ch 100, thought that the court order effected the variation and it was not necessary for the beneficiaries to provide writing, but the point remains a moot one.

8.8 Other Means of Variation

Although the Variation of Trusts Act 1958 has become the principal apparatus for varying trusts, a number of other options are available. These other options, set out below, remain of importance because of the procedural limitations which restrict the operation of the 1958 Act: that the consent of *sui juris* beneficiaries must be obtained, and that the court can only approve the arrangement on behalf of other beneficiaries if the variation is for their benefit. Other facilities for variation, though more limited in the substance of the variations possible, are not so restricted by procedural requirements and may be approved by the court even though the consents of *sui juris* beneficiaries are not available.

Inherent jurisdiction of court

A long line of authority recognises that the courts have inherent jurisdiction to vary provisions of trusts where there is good reason to do so. This inherent jurisdiction was reviewed in the leading case of *Chapman* v. *Chapman* [1954] AC 429. The jurisdiction is used mainly to alter the administration of a trust rather than beneficial interests. Four distinct circumstances were recognised by the House of Lords in Chapman.

Conversion

First the courts will intervene in cases in which minors have beneficial interests to authorise the conversion of trust property from personalty to realty or vice versa, where this is for the minor's benefit.

Emergency

Second, where there is an 'emergency' the court may authorise trustees to go outside the terms of the settlement. For instance, the *Re New* [1901] 2 Ch 534, trust assets were affected by a company reconstruction, involving the exchange of ordinary shares for preferences shares, debentures and new denominations of ordinary shares. Under the terms of the trust the trustees were not empowered to invest in any of the new types of security. The Court of Appeal empowered the trustees to do so. However, the jurisdiction cannot be used simply because it is advantageous. In *Re Tollemache* [1903] 1 Ch 955 the Court of Appeal refused to endorse the variation of investment powers merely on the ground that it would be beneficial since there was no real emergency.

Maintenance

Third, there is a limited power to vary beneficial interests by authorising trustees to use income for maintenance of beneficiaries notwithstanding the fact that the settlor has directed that the income should be accumulated. This power was used in *Havelock* v. *Havelock* (1880) 17 Ch D 807 to allow the beneficiaries income for the purposes of their education.

Compromise

Last, in a case where there is a genuine difference between beneficiaries in relation to their respective rights under a trust, the court may approve a compromise arrangement government the rights of all the beneficiaries.

It is not necessary that there should be a contested dispute. In *Mason* v. *Farbrother* [1983] 2 All ER 1078, the trustees sought directions as to the construction of investment powers in a pension fund trust for Co-operative Society employees. One view was that the fund should be invested in the society itself, the other view being that it should be invested in accordance with the Trustee Investments Act 1961. The court held that since there were genuine points of difference, the compromise jurisdiction could be invoked.

S.57 Trustee Act 1925

The Trustee Act confers a jurisdiction on the court to endow trustees with powers which are not available within the trust instrument. The power does not allow any modification of beneficial interests but simply gives trustees the tools necessary for management and administration of the trust. Nevertheless its ambit is wide, and it has been used to sanction expansion of powers of investment (*Mason* v. *Farbrother*, above), and to permit a sale of trust land where a requisite consent could not be obtained (*Re Cockerell's Settlement Trusts* [1956] Ch 372). The court must be satisfied that the variation will benefit the whole trust and not just one particular beneficiary. Any power given under the section should be read into the trust as if it is part of the original settlement (*Re Mair* [1935] Ch 562).

The section can be of particular use where a trust has many beneficiaries, such as a unit trust or pension fund trust, and it would be impracticable to rely upon the 1958 Variation of Trusts Act because under that Act the consent of all *sui juris* beneficiaries must be obtained. Consequently application to extend investment powers of unit trust managers and pension fund trustees tend to be made under s.57.

Settled land

In respect of trusts of land there is a special provision within s.64 of the Settled Land Act 1925 whereby a tenant for life under a strict settlement may apply to the court for approval of any transaction which, in the opinion of the court, is beneficial to the land or to the beneficiaries. This has been held to include a variation of beneficial interests. In *Re Downshire's Settled Estates* [1953] Ch 218 a proposal was made under which the tenant for life would surrender a protected life interest, and provision would be made by insurance for any possible future beneficiaries under the discretionary trust which would have arisen upon forfeiture of the protected life interest. The Court of Appeal held that s.64 should be interpreted widely so as to include such a proposal, especially since it would result in a saving of estate duty.

The rule in *Saunders* v. *Vautier*
In *Saunders* v. *Vautier* (1841) 4 Beav 115 it was held that, where a beneficiary is absolutely entitled to trust property, he can bring the trust to an end by calling for the vesting in him of the property. Similarly where all the beneficiaries are of full age, sound mind and consent they can wind up the trust and take the property, or resettle it on new trusts. They cannot, however, directly vary existing trusts by insisting that the trustees apply the trust property as the beneficiaries direct (*Re Brockbank* [1948] Ch 206).

S.53 Trustee Act
In the case of a minor beneficiary, under s.53 of the Trustee Act 1925 a court may order the vesting of trust property in a particular person for the purpose of applying income or capital for the maintenance, education or benefit of the minor.

Variation in cases of matrimonial dispute
Under the Matrimonial Causes Act 1973 the court has wide powers to order variations of property ownership, including variations of trusts affecting parties to matrimonial proceedings.

Wills
The trusts in a will may be altered in several circumstances. If the will contains a clerical error or if it does not give effect to the wishes of the settlor because solicitors misunderstood his directions then there is a jurisdiction to rectify the will. Also the beneficiaries to a will may agree to a deed varying its terms, and if they do so within two years of the testator's death the variation is not a transfer of value for the purpose of inheritance tax and is not a disposal for the purpose of capital gains tax, and the variation takes effect as if it was made by the deceased. This can be particularly useful if a testator has created a trust with tax disadvantages, such as a discretionary trust.

Reasonable financial provision for dependants
Where a testator does not make reasonable financial provision for family and dependants the Inheritance (Provision for Family and Dependants) Act 1975 empowers a court, upon the application of a person within a specified category of applicants, to make an order that the testator's estate should make reasonable financial provision. In some circumstances this may involve a variation of a previous marriage settlement or an order that a trust created on the testator's death should be varied.

Summary

1 The main procedure for the variation of a trust is the Variation of Trusts Act 1958. However, the court has inherent jurisdiction to vary trusts and there are also a number of other statutory provisions which allow for the variation of trusts, although these all operate in more limited circumstances. In addition, where the rule in *Saunders* v. *Vautier* applies, a trust may be brought to an end by the agreement of the beneficiaries and a new trust established on different terms.

2 Under the Variation of Trusts Act 1958 the court may only consent to a variation on behalf of persons falling within one of the four categories set down in s.1 of the Act. Any beneficiary outside the section must give his/her own consent to the variation.

3 As a general rule the court can only give consent on behalf of persons within s.1 Variation of Trusts Act if the court is satisfied that the variation is for their benefit. However, benefit need not be shown to accrue to beneficiaries falling within s.1(1)(d).

4 The term 'benefit' within the Variations of Trusts Act 1958 has been interpreted by the courts to embrace more than purely financial benefit. In some cases the courts have been willing to give considerable weight to non-financial considerations. The settlor's intention is a relevant, but not overriding, consideration in deciding whether the court will sanction a variation.

5 The Variation of Trusts Act 1958 does not allow the courts to sanction a resettlement. However, even if all the terms of the existing trust are revoked, the court will not regard the arrangement as a resettlement if the sub-stratum of the trust is left intact (i.e., the beneficiaries benefit from the trust in a manner similar to the way that they benefited before the variation).

6 It is unclear whether a variation under the Variation of Trusts Act 1958 takes effect through the consent of the beneficiaries, with the court providing the consent on behalf of those falling within s.1 or, alternatively, whether the court order itself effects the variation. The issue is significant because if the variation is by the consent of the beneficiaries it is arguable that any disposition of equitable interest which occurs under the variation should be in writing in order to satisfy s.53(1)(c) of the Law of Property Act 1925, and will therefore attract stamp duty.

Exercises

1 Explain the circumstances in which a beneficiary will fall within s.1(1)(b) of the Variation of Trusts Act 1958. What is the purpose and effect of the proviso to s.1(1)(b)?

2 In reviewing the reported cases on the Variation of Trusts Act 1958, Cotterrill ((1971) 34 MLR 98) has commented that 'benefit and the measure of it, is what the court says it is'. Explain and discuss this statement.

3 Does the court, in exercising its powers under the Variation of Trusts Act 1958, have to be absolutely certain that the proposed variation is beneficial? What attitude does the court take to the settlor's intention in setting up the trust?

4 Why may it be important to know whether a variation under the Variation of Trusts Act 1958 takes effect through the consent of the beneficiaries or by court order?

5 A trust fund set up in 1970 is held for the settlor's son, Adam (now aged 30), and his daughter, Beryl (now aged 45), in equal shares for protective life interests, with remainder to their respective children equally, and in default of children to their statutory next of kin. There is a forfeiture provision that if any child of Adam or Beryl becomes or marries a Freemason their share should accrue to the other children equally. Beryl is unmarried and has no children. Adam has two children, Charles (aged 16) and Deborah (aged 26). Deborah is engaged to marry a Freemason. Adam, Deborah and Beryl all wish to apply under the Variation of Trusts Act 1958 to vary the terms of the trust in the following ways:

(a) to remove the fortfeiture provision concerning Freemasonry;

(b) Adam wishes to surrender his protective life interest and settle the fund on his children contingent upon their attaining 25 years, this fund to be administered in Guernsey where the family have just settled after ten years' residence in Kenya;

(c) Beryl wishes to have 80 per cent of the capital of her share vested in herself absolutely, the remaining 20 per cent to be held on trust for the persons entitled in remainder under the original trusts.

Explain on whose behalf the court will be required to give consent and whether the application is likely to be successful.

9 Management of Trusts

In many respects a trust fund is similar to any other fund held for the benefit of investors and, although trustees may owe additional particular duties to beneficiaries, the trustees' basic duty is to act as financial managers in maintaining the trust property. The trustees as managers of the trust property must invest it and take reasonable care of it. They must also produce accounts and other information to the beneficiaries.

9.1 Duties and Powers of Investment

The primary duty of a fund manager is to invest the fund with the aim of its maintenance and, if possible, increase; and in the absence of express provision there will be an implied duty upon the trustees to invest any trust monies. In exercising the duty to invest the trustees' scope of investment activity will be limited by the powers in the trust instrument and those implied by law. Any such powers must be exercised impartially with a view to providing a good income for any present beneficiaries and maintaining the capital for those entitled in remainder.

Express powers of investment

Most trust instruments will exclude the statutory powers of investment (see below) and instead will confer extensive express powers. An express power will be construed naturally and liberally rather than restrictively so that, for instance, a power to invest as the trustees think fit' will be construed to confer a general and unrestricted power to invest in any type of investment rather than be limited to those investments authorised by statute (*Re Harari's ST* [1949] 1 All ER 430; *Re Peczenick's ST* [1964] 1 WLR 720).

Although a power to invest will be construed widely to allow any type of investment, the meaning of 'investment' is construed narrowly. It will include the power to invest in land (*Re Wragg* [1919] 2 Ch 58) for the sake of income produced, and possibly capital appreciation (Lawrence J in *Re Wragg* (above). But it has been held not to include the purchase of a house for occupation by beneficiaries (*Re Power* [1947] Ch 572, Jenkins J) although the Law Reform Committee has recommended that this rule be altered. It has also been held that unsecured loans, 'being loans on no security beyond the liability of the borrower to repay ... are not "investments"'', according to Lord Russell of Kilowen in the Privy Council decisions of *Khoo Tek Keong* v. *Ch'ng Joo Tuan Neoh* [1934] AC 529.

Statutory powers
In the absence of express powers of investment there are statutory powers which the trustees may rely upon. These powers may, if desired, be expressly incorporated into the trust. The foremost statute is the Trustee Investments Act 1961, although some other important powers are to be found in the Trustee Act 1925. The statutory powers do not include power to invest in land except that trustees of a strict settlement or trustees for sale may use capital monies to purchase land, at least so long as they retain some land on trust (s.73 Settled Land Act 1925; s.28 Law of Property Act 1925; *Re Wellsted's WT* [1944] Ch 296; *Re Wakeman* [1945] Ch 177). The Law Reform Committee has recognised that the powers given by the 1961 Act are outdated and should be expanded so as to be brought more into line with modern investment practices.

Statutory categories of investment
Schedule 1 of the 1961 Act lists the types of investment authorised and divides them into four categories. The first is 'narrower-range' investments which may be made without taking advice, such as National Savings Certificates and deposits in the Trustee Savings Bank. The second is 'narrower-range' investments which can only be made with advice, including, *inter alia*, fixed interest government securities and mortgages of freehold property. The third is 'wider-range' investments, principally investment in shares in public companies and building societies and investment in unit trusts. The fourth category is 'special range' investment, which means any other investment authorised by the trust (e.g., the trustees may have express power to invest in land).

Division of the fund and purchase and sale of investments
If the trustees have the statutory powers of investment they must comply with the statutory requirements for division of the fund and purchase and sale of investments.

Initial division of fund
If the trustees wish, then subject to their general duties they may invest the entire trust fund in narrower-range investments without following any special procedure. If the trustees wish to invest any monies in wider-range investments they have to comply with the scheme prescribed by s.2 which specifies that a trustee 'shall not have power to make or retain any wider-range investment unless the trust fund has been divided

TRUST FUND

Narrow-range division (50%)	Wider-range division (50%)	Special-range division
This part of the fund may only be invested in narrower-range investments	This part of the fund may be invested in narrower or wider-range Investments, in any proportion, subject to the trustees other duties	E.g. land

Figure 9.1 Division and investment of funds under the Trustee Investments Act 1961

into two parts . . . equal in value at the time of the division', except that any special range property will constitute a third division of the fund (see Figure 9.1).

Use of the monies in each division of the fund

Once the division of the fund has been made s.2 goes on to provide that the narrower-range part of the fund may normally be used for narrower-range investments only. The wider-range part of the fund may be used to purchase narrower-range or wider-range investments, with the initial overall results that anything between 50 per cent and 100 per cent of the fund may be invested in narrower-range investments, but not more than 50 per cent in wider-range investments.

If the trust contains special powers, such as powers of advancement or power to invest in special range property, s.2 allows monies to be withdrawn from either part of the fund in the exercise of such powers. No compensating transfer is required from one part of the fund to another.

Sale of investments

If any investment is sold the proceeds should normally be paid into the part of the fund which was used to effect their purchase, except that if special-range property is sold the proceeds must be divided equally between narrow- and wider-range (Schedule 2(3)).

Although sale proceeds should normally be paid into the part of the fund to which they belong, they may be paid into another part of the fund if this is more convenient from an administrative point of view, although in such case a compensating transfer must be made debiting the part of the fund which has actually received the payment and crediting the part of the fund which should have received the payment.

Restrictions on the exercise of powers of investment

Although express or statutory powers might appear to be quite wide, and in the case of the statutory powers would seem to allow the trustees the unfettered power to use up all of the narrower-range monies in purchasing special-range property or making advancements to beneficiaries, for example, whilst leaving the wider-range part of the fund intact, the trustees' discretion in these matters is restricted by the general requirements that they must exercise reasonable care, take into account the need for diversification and must take proper advice.

Duty of care

The duty to take reasonable care requires the trustees to make their own decisions as prudent men of business would in looking after the interests of others. Although they should take advice they should carefully consider whether the advice should be followed and may be liable for following bad advice. In *Learoyd* v. *Whitely* (1887) 12 App Cas 727 the trustees lent money at 5 per cent on the security of a freehold brickfield, being advised by competent valuers that it was a good security. The valuer's report was based upon the supposition that the business was a going concern. The trustees acted upon the report without making further enquiries. When the security failed, the House of Lords held that the trustees were negligent for simply relying upon the advice given to them and in not making further enquiries to ascertain the strength of the business upon which the money was lent.

The duty to act as prudent men of business precludes the trustees from allowing their own personal values to influence their decisions. In *Cowan* v. *Scargill* [1985] Ch 270, some of the trustees of a pension scheme trust for mineworkers were members of the National Union of Mineworkers and they refused to vote in favour of an investment plan which would include investments overseas and investment in oil because such investment would be against the Union's policy to oppose foreign or competing industries. Sir Robert Megarry v-c held that the trustees must adopt the most financially attractive investment policy, even if they opposed it for extraneous reasons. However, in *Lord Bishop of Oxford* v. *Church Commissioners of England* (*The Times*, 29 October 1991). Sir Donald Nicholls v-c said that charitable trustees, in making investment decisions, could take into account ethical or non-financial considerations provided that such considerations did not significantly jeopardise accepted investment principles. Moreover, where a particular investment conflicted with the aims of the charity, a financially disadvantageous investment decision could be taken.

Diversification

The need for diversification is a factor which a trustee exercising reasonable care would consider but, to remove any doubt, s.6 of the Trustee Investments Act (which applies whether statutory or express powers are being exercised) expressly states that the trustees shall have regard to the need for diversification. In doing so the trustees should take into account the differing needs of the life tenant, who is interested in a good income, and the remaindermen, whose needs are for maintenance of capital.

Advice

Apart from the general duty to take advice as a prudent man of business would the Trustee Investments Act requires the trustee to take advice in relation to specific categories of investment as explained above. S.6 of the Act stipulates that the advice must be advice of a person 'reasonably believed by the trustee to be qualified by his ability in and practical experience of financial matters'. The advice must either be given in writing or, if given orally, it must be confirmed in writing. It is now arguable that advice should be sought of a person authorised to give such advice under the Financial Services Act 1986. Advice must be reviewed periodically at such reasonable intervals as the trustee chooses.

Variation of investment powers

Even though the trustees' powers to invest are prescribed by the terms of the trust or statute they are not set in stone. The courts have jurisdiction to vary the powers under their inherent jurisdiction, under s.57 of the Trustee Act 1925 and under the Variation of Trusts Act 1958, the most appropriate jurisdiction being that under s.57 Trustee Act (*Anker-Petersen* v. *Anker-Petersen* (unreported, 1990). These powers have become of increased importance in the ever-changing climate of investment and finance which has had to be weathered in recent years.

The courts' initially reticent approach (*Re Kolb's WT* [1962] Ch 531) to applications to extend powers of investment has been replaced by a willingness to augment limited powers in times of high inflation and particularly in the case of commercial trust funds such as pension funds (*Mason* v. *Farbrother* [1983] 2 All ER 1078). The courts may, however, impose a condition that the fund should be divided into several parts carrying differing degrees of risk (*Trustees of British Museum* v. *Attorney-General* [1984] 1 WLR 418). Unusually the court did not impose such a requirement in *Steel* v. *Wellcome Trustees Ltd* [1988] 1 WLR 167, but it is submitted that this decision was an exceptional one made during a time when equity investment was highly successful, and might not to be followed in every case. The uncertain state of the share market in recent years may lead to a more cautious judicial approach just as it did in the years following the burst of the South Sea Bubble (see Moffat and Chesterman, pp.375–6).

Liability for wrongful investment

If a trustee makes or retains an unauthorised investment or fails to invest he will be liable for breach of trust. In the case of unauthorised investment the trustee will be liable for any fall in value on sale. If an unauthorised investment is retained the trustee will be liable for the difference between the present value and the price which would have been obtained if it had been sold at the proper time. Trustees failing to invest will be liable to interest. The consequences of such a breach of trust are further considered in Chapter 10.

9.2 Duty of Care

General duty

In exercising their duties and powers as managers of the trust fund the trustees must practise with reasonable care and diligence. Normally the duty is a duty to act as a prudent man of business would act in the management of his own affairs (*Speight* v. *Gaunt* (1883) 9 App Cas 1, HL; *Re Godfrey* (1883) 23 Ch D 483, Bacon v-c) but a higher duty is required when the trustees are investing trust monies, in which case the duty is the stronger duty that would be owed by a prudent businessman acting on behalf of others. This was the view expressed by Lord Watson in *Learoyd* v. *Whitely* (1887) 12 App Cas 727:

> As a general rule the law requires of a trustee no higher degree of diligence in the execution of his office than a man of ordinary prudence would exercise in the management of his own private affairs. Yet he is not allowed the same discretion in investing the monies of the trust as if he were a person sui juris dealing with his own estate. Businessmen of ordinary prudence may, and frequently do, select investments which are more or less of a speculative character; but it is the duty of a trustee to confine himself to the class of investments which are permitted by the trust, and likewise to avoid all investments of that class which are attended by hazard.

The duty should not, however, operate too harshly, at least in the case of unpaid trustees, otherwise it might deter honest men from undertaking the duty of trustee (see Cotton ʟᴊ in *Re Whitely* (1886) 33 Ch D 347), and the trustees are entitled to take the sort of risk that a prudent businessman would take (see Bacon v-c in *Re Godfrey* (1883) 23 Ch D 483). This may include taking the risk of holding on to investments in a falling market (*Re Chapman* [1896] 2 Ch 763).

Paling (1973) 37 Conv. 50, has argued that the ordinary prudent man of business test is inappropriate for unpaid trustees and has proposed a subjective test requiring a trustee to exercise only such skill as he in fact possesses, but the Law Reform Committee in its 23rd Report (1982) Cmnd 8733 has asserted that the objective test should remain.

Professional trustees

'A paid trustee is expected to exercise a higher standard of diligence and knowledge than an unpaid trustee and . . . a bank which advertises itself largely in the public press as taking charge of administration is under a special duty'; so said Harman J in an *obiter dictum* statement (*Re Waterman's Will Trusts* [1952] 2 All ER 1054), where the trustee department of a bank was held liable for failing to secure that it received a sufficient flow of information in respect of a property development project which it had invested in and which subsequently proved inadequate. This view was supported by Brightman J in *Bartlett* v. *Barclays Bank* [1980] 1 Ch 515, where he said:

> I am of opinion that a higher duty of care is plainly due from someone like a trust corporation which carries on a specialized business of trust management. A trust corporation holds itself out in its advertising literature as being above ordinary mortals. With a specialist staff of trained trust officers and managers . . . the trust corporation holds itself out, and rightly, as capable of providing an expertise which it would be unrealistic to expect and unjust to demand from the ordinary prudent man or woman who accepts, probably unpaid and sometimes reluctantly from a sense of family duty, the burdens of a trusteeship . . . so I think that a professional corporate trustee is liable for breach of trust if loss is caused to the trust fund because it neglects to exercise the special care and skill which it professes to have.

Excluding the duty

Many trust instruments are drafted so as to purport to exclude the trustees from liability for negligence except in the case of 'wilful default'. It has been suggested that it is doubtful whether the duties of trustees can be reduced below that required by the Trustee Act (Matthews [1989] Conv. 42), and Goodhart [1980] Conv. 333 has argued that where these clauses are offered as standard terms by professional trustees they may be ineffective and 'unreasonable' under the provisions of the Unfair Contract Terms Act 1977.

9.3 Profits by Trustees

Trustees are not permitted to profit from the trust except to the extent prescribed in the trust instrument. The reason for the rule is that the trustee is in a position of trust (in the 'higher' sense) and in a fiduciary relationship (see Chapter 2). He is not independent of the trust; the trust is dependent upon him to place the interests of the trust first, and his decisions should not be influenced by self-interest. If a trustee were allowed to profit from his position he might take advantage of this fact and put his own interests first, to the prejudice of the trust. For this reason the circumstances in which a trustee may benefit are very limited.

Remuneration of trustees

There is no objection to a trustee being paid for his duties, so long as the trust instrument has made provision for such payment. Some older cases suggested that payment was undesirable as it might be a financial burden upon the trust estate and render it valueless (Talbot LC in *Robinson* v. *Pett* (1734) 3 P Wms 249, p.251), but this view is largely out of date and it is quite common for trustees to be rewarded for their services. Lord Normand in *Dale* v. *IRC* [1954] AC 11, explained that the rule 'is not that reward for services is repugnant to the fiduciary duty, but that he who has the duty shall not take any secret remuneration or any financial benefit not authorized by the law, or by his contract or by the trust deed under which he acts, as the case may be'; so a trustee may be paid for his services where such payment has been authorised by the settlor. Furthermore, in a few circumstances the law will authorise payment even where the settlor did not.

Authority in trust instrument

The trust instrument may of course authorise payment of trustees by the inclusion of a charging clause. Such clauses are, however, construed strictly so as to enable payment only in so far as is clearly stated. The decision in *Re Chapple* (1884) 27 Ch D 582 is a good example. In that case a solicitor was appointed as a trustee and executor. The will authorised him to make the usual professional charges 'as if he, not being a trustee or executor hereof, were employed by the trustee or executor'. The trustee claimed payment for acting as solicitor to the trusts and also for acting as executor. It was held that he was not entitled to payment as executor because the trust only allowed payment as if he was not an executor but was someone employed by the executor.

Authority from beneficiaries

If all beneficiaries are adults and of sound mind and if they unanimously agree, they can authorise payment. The court will treat the agreement with caution, and if there is any hint that the agreement of the beneficiaries was not given freely the court will not enforce the agreement. In *Ayliffe* v. *Murray* (1740) 2 Atk 58 the trustees refused to act in the trust unless the beneficiary would agree to their receiving remuneration. The beneficiary agreed and executed a deed authorising payment. It was subsequently held that the deed should be set aside.

Authority from court

The court has special authority to award remuneration in some cases, such as where it appoints a corporation to act as trustee (s.42 Trustee Act 1925). Although earlier authorities were reluctant to assume an inherent jurisdiction to award or increase remuneration, it now seems to be settled that there is such a jurisdiction, although it should be exercised sparingly. The leading modern authority is *Re Duke of Norfolk's ST* [1982] Ch 61. In 1958 trustees were appointed on the basis that they would receive payment in accordance with their 1958 scale of fees. In 1966 and 1968 further property was added to the trust which involved the trustees in considerable extra work, and the introduction of capital transfer tax in 1975 necessitated further work. The trustees sought an increase in remuneration to compensate them. The Court of Appeal held that the trustees were entitled to extra payment for the additional work already done and further that their general level of remuneration could be increased for the future, although the court's jurisdiction to order the increase should be exercised sparingly, with the court taking into account the level of skill of the trustees, the level of fees levied by other trustees and the nature of the circumstances.

Authority from statute

In exceptional circumstances statute confers power for charges to be made for judicial trustees, the Public Trustee and custodian trustees, who are appointed by the court (see section 9.6 below).

Indemnity for expenses

If the trustee has incurred expense in connection with the trust and has paid from his own pocket he is entitled to be indemnified (s.30(2) Trustee Act 1925), and such costs are a first charge on both the capital and income of the trust estate (*Stott* v. *Milne* [1884] 25 Ch D 710).

Incidental profits

As mentioned above, the extent to which a trustee may benefit from a trust is quite restricted and, although it is increasingly common for trustees to receive remuneration, they are not generally allowed any other profit because of the risk that they might put self-interest before their duty to the trust. The rule is a strict one and may be applied even though the trustee claims to have acted honestly and even though the trust may have benefited. Lord Herschell in *Bray* v. *Ford* [1896] AC 44 at p.141 and p.28, 46 gave the classic statement of the rule:

It is an inflexible rule of a Court of Equity that a person in a fiduciary position ... is not, unless expressly provided, entitled to make a profit; he is not allowed to put himself in a position where his interest and duty conflict. It does not appear to me that this rule is, as has been said, founded upon principles of morality. I regard it rather as based on the consideration that, human nature being what it is, there is a danger in such circumstances of the person holding a fiduciary position being swayed by interest rather than by duty, and thus prejudicing those whom he was bound to protect. It has therefore been deemed expedient to lay down this positive rule. But I am satisfied that it might be departed from in many cases without any breach of morality, without any wrong being inflicted, and without any consciousness of wrong-doing. Indeed, it is obvious that it might sometimes be to the advantage of the beneficiaries that their trustee should act for them professionally rather than a stranger, even though the trustee were paid for his services.

Although it is now quite common for trustees to be paid for their services the basic rule still applies, and trustees and other persons in similar fiduciary roles should not be able to take advantage of their positions and profit from the trust. To hold otherwise would put the trustee in a position where self-interest could conflict with the interests of the trust. The rule is a strict one so that it is irrelevant that the trustee might have acted fairly. The fact is that there is a risk that some unfair advantage could be taken, and to deter trustees from succumbing to the temptation of taking such advantage the courts prohibit trustees from profiting in almost all cases. The rule has many branches, as the examples discussed below demonstrate.

Use of trust property

One conspicuous illustration of breach of fiduciary duty is where the trustee uses trust property for his own benefit. If, for instance, the trustee occupies trust land without the authority of the trust instrument, there is a clear breach. In *Webb* v. *Earl of Shaftesbury* (1802) 7 Ves 480, a trustee was allowed to appoint gamekeepers to the trust estate as he thought proper, and to be reimbursed for the wages of any such gamekeeper. The trustee's claim for reimbursement was initially disallowed. The court confirmed that a gamekeeper could only be appointed if necessary to the management of the estate, and in so far as the appointment may have been made purely for pleasure reimbursement would not be permitted.

Accretions to trust property

As a logical extension of the rule that a trustee must not use trust property for his own benefit, it has been decided that a trustee must not have the benefit of any accretions to the trust property, and that any accretion arising becomes trust property even though the accretion might not have occurred but for the acts of the trustee. The classic case of the rule is *Keech* v. *Sandford* (1726) Sel Cas t King 61, where the trust property included a lease of the profits of a market, and the beneficiary was an infant. Prior to the expiry of the lease the trustee applied to the lessor for a renewal of the lease but the lessor refused on the ground that the beneficiary, being an infant, would not be liable for the rent. The trustee then took a lease for himself, but litigation ensued and the Court of Chancery held that the trustee should not have the benefit of the lease but should assign it to the infant.

The principle has been extended to the purchase of the freehold by the trustee of a lease, so that the trustee of the lease who acquires the freehold must hold it upon the trusts. Hanbury and Maudsley (pp.562–3) state that the position is unclear, but the trend of the modern cases has been to hold the trustee liable. For example, in *Protheroe* v. *Protheroe* [1968] 1 WLR 519 (see also *Thompson Trustees* v. *Heaton* [1974] 1 WLR 605) a husband held a lease of the matrimonial home on trust for himself and his wife. The husband then purchased the freehold in his own name. When he sold the freehold the Court of Appeal decided that he must account to his wife for one-half of the proceeds of sale. Lord Denning MR said that 'There is a long established rule of equity from *Keech* v. *Sandford* . . . downwards that if a trustee, who owns the leasehold gets in the freehold, that freehold belongs to the trust and he cannot take the property for himself.'

Self-dealing

If a trustee employs himself (*Bray* v. *Ford* [1896] AC 44) or enters into business transactions with the trust in respect of which he is interested (*Williams* v. *Barton* [1927] 2 Ch 9) the trustee will be obliged to disgorge any profits made or any commission or remuneration received. The position of a solicitor trustee is slightly more complicated. A solicitor trustee is not entitled to receive payment for non-litigious work done in connection with the trust (*Re Barber* (1886) 34 Ch D 77). However, if litigious work is needed then the solicitor's profit costs may be charged (*Cradock* v. *Piper* (1850) 1 Mac & G 664). In addition, a trustee is entitled to profit costs for work done directly as a solicitor for the beneficiaries, even though their costs might be recovered from the trust estate (*Re Barber*, above).

Of course, if the trust instrument authorises the trustee to employ himself or his business then the benefit may be retained by the trustees provided that no undue advantage has been taken. In *Re Sykes* [1909] 2

Ch 241, the trust property included a business of licensed victualer. The trust instrument declared that the trustees could carry on the business as if they were absolute owners and that they could exercise all powers and discretions notwithstanding that they might have a personal interest in the exercise of the powers. The trustees were also wine merchants and they took advantage of their position as trustees by supplying the trust's public houses with wines and spirits at a profit, but at less than marked prices. The Court of Appeal held that the terms of the trust clearly allowed the trustees to keep their usual profits.

Purchase of trust property

The rule against self-dealing also operates in cases where the trustee purchases trust property. In the case of such a purchase there is an apparent risk of conflict of duty and interest since the trustee as vendor has the duty to obtain the highest price, whereas the trustee as purchaser is interested in paying the lowest price. The rule is not that the purchase cannot take place, or that the transfer of property is void, but that 'Any trustee purchasing the trust property is liable to have the purchase set aside, if in any reasonable time the cestui que trust chooses to say he is not satisfied with it' (see Arden MR in *Campbell* v. *Walker* (1800) 5 Ves 678). So the beneficiary has an option to avoid the sale to the trustee within a reasonable time. The rule is a strict one so that the beneficiary has the option even though the sale appears to have been a fair one by auction (*Ex Parte Lacey* (1802) 6 Ves 625), because there is a risk of the trustee having an advantage over other persons bidding; and even if there is an independent valuation (*Wright* v. *Morgan* [1926] AC 788) because the trustees can still fix the time of valuation and sale.

Purchase by nominee company

The rule applies to a sale by a trustee to a company which is acting as his nominee, because the company is wholly owned by the trustee or because the trustee otherwise has control of the company, perhaps through a majority shareholding and directorship (*Re Thompson's Settlement* [1986] Ch 99). But a sale to a company of which the trustee is merely a member is probably not voidable, at least if the trustee can prove that the price was fair and no advantage was taken (*Re Thompson's Settlement*). Similarly, if the trustee sells or leases to a member of her family or another person in whom she is interested the rule is not applied strictly but the burden will fall upon the trustee to prove that the deal is fair (*Ferraby* v. *Hobson* (1847) 2 Ph 255).

Options to purchase

The strict rule also applies to options to purchase which are exercised by trustees, except that if a trustee was granted an option to purchase before assuming the trusteeship, the option may be validly exercised by the trustee (*Vyse* v. *Foster* [1874] LR 7 HL 318), but in the exercise of the option no advantage should be taken, particularly in the fixing of the price.

Subsequent purchasers

The transaction can be set aside not only against the trustee but also against any subsequent purchaser with notice of the fact that the trustee purchased from the trust (*Cookson* v. *Lee* (1853) 23 LJ Ch 473). But once the trust property has passed through the hands of a bona fide purchaser the sale cannot be set aside, but the beneficiary has a restitutionary remedy against the proceeds of sale in the hands of the trustee (*Hill* v. *Langley*, *The Times*, 28 January 1988).

There is no prohibition upon a trustee purchasing ex-trust property provided that there is a completed intermediate sale to a bona fide purchaser, but so long as the contract for sale from the trust to a purchaser has not been completed the trustee cannot enter into a contract for the sub-sale of the property to him, as he still has duties as trustee to perform in the sale of the property (*Parker* v. *McKenna* (1874) 10 Ch App 96).

Ex-trustees

Similarly there is no prohibition upon an ex-trustee purchasing trust property provided that a reasonable time has elapsed since retiring from the trust. But if the trustee arranges the sale during her trusteeship, resigns soon after and then completes the purchase five years later the the sale can be set aside (*Wright* v. *Morgan* [1926] AC 788).

Strict rule

Generally the rule has been applied strictly irrespective of whether the trustee acted fairly or paid a proper price, but in exceptional cases the courts have shown some willingness to allow trustees to keep the trust property where it is quite obvious that the trustee has taken no advantage. In *Holder* v. *Holder* [1968] Ch 353, a testator left his estate on trust to be divided amongst his children. The trust property included two farms which one of the children had farmed during the testator's lifetime, and that child wanted to buy them. He had been made one of the executors and he purported to renounce his executorship and bought them at auction. Later one of the other beneficiaries sought to have the sale set aside. The Court of Appeal held that the sale should stand for two reasons. First, the beneficiary had acquiesced in the sale by accepting his share of the proceeds and not challenging the sale earlier. Second, there was no breach of duty by the executor because he had taken only minimal steps in the administration of the estate and any special knowledge which he had about the property was not acquired in his capacity of executor but in his earlier capacity as tenant of the property. Some critics thought that the decision in *Holder* was to herald a relaxation of the strict rule against receiving benefit from fiduciary positions, but the strict rule was recently confirmed in *Re Thompson* (above).

Purchase of beneficiary's interest: fair dealing

If a trustee wishes to purchase from a beneficiary his beneficial interest the question is a quite different one. There is no danger of the trustee acting as both vendor and purchaser since the beneficial interest is a piece of property quite distinct from the trust property itself and the beneficiary is free to sell his interest to any purchaser. The trustee is, however, in a position where some advantage might be taken because the value of the beneficial interest is affected by the value of the trust property and the trustee may have knowledge of matters which affect the value of the trust property. For this reason a sale of a beneficial interest from a beneficiary to a trustee will be carefully scrutinised, and if the trustee has been guilty of any unfair dealing the sale may be set aside. In order to assess whether the deal was a fair one the courts will explore the adequacy of the consideration (*Coles* v. *Trecothick* (1804) 9 Ves 234) and whether the trustee has relevant information which he does not disclose to the beneficiary, such as a valuation of the trust estate (*Dougan* v. *Macpherson* [1902] AC 197) and whether the sale was at the initiative of the beneficiary (*Morse* v. *Royal* (1806) 12 Ves 355).

Director's fees

It is now becoming increasingly common for trust property to include a substantial shareholding in a company. Sometimes a trustee may become a director of a company in which the trust has a shareholding. In such a case the trustee may receive remuneration in his capacity of company director and the question arises as to whether the trustee can retain the director's fees or whether he must account to the trust for them. The basic principle is that if the trustee acquired the directorship as a result of his position as trustee then she must account for the fees received (*Re Macadam* [1946] Ch 73). On the other hand the trustee can retain the fees if she was a director before he became a trustee (*Re Dover Coalfield's Extension* [1908] 1 Ch 65, although it is doubtful on the facts of that case that the trustee should have been allowed to retain the fees), or if he is voted in as a director independent of the trust shareholding (*Re Gee* [1948] Ch 284); and if the trust instrument makes it clear that the

trustees may be appointed directors the trust instrument may be construed so as to authorise the retention of the fees (*Re Llewellins WT*
[1949] Ch 225). Furthermore, if the directorship results in the trustee
doing substantially more work than was originally contemplated when
the trust was created, the court may authorise the trustee to retain some
or all of the fees (*Re Keeler's ST* [1981] Ch 156), although it is submitted
that the proper analysis of this jurisdiction is that the trustee must
account to the trust for all the fees received but is entitled to receive
remuneration for the extra work done for the trust under the principle in
Re Duke of Norfolk's ST [1982] Ch 61 (see above, section 9.3).

Competition with the trust

A further obvious instance where a conflict of duty and interest will arise
is where the trust includes the carrying on of a business and the trustee is
interested in a competing business. If the trustee was carrying on the
business before his appointment then there should normally be no
objection; but if, whilst trustee, he proposes to set himself up in a similar
business then a court order may be obtained to prohibit him from doing
so (*Re Thompson* [1930] 1 Ch 203) since there is a clear possibility that
the trustee's self-interest in his own business will conflict with his duty to
the trust business.

Taking other opportunities

Other illustrations of taking opportunity may not fit into the categories
described above, but the same principles apply, and if an opportunity
comes the way of the trustee as a result of the fact that he is a trustee then
he will be liable to account for all benefit which he has received. It is
immaterial that the trustee or other fiduciary has acted bona fide, or that
the trust has benefited from the actions of the trustee. The leading
modern authority is the case of *Boardman* v. *Phipps* [1967] 2 AC 46 in
which case a solicitor to a trust which had a large shareholding in a
company realised that profit could be made by re-organising the company, and since the majority of the trustees were not interested in taking
the opportunity the solicitor took the opportunity himself. He was held
to be in breach of his fiduciary duty to the trust even though he had acted
in good faith. The case is discussed fully with other authorities in section
2.4.

No duty to compromise own interest

The trustee's duty not to permit a conflict of interest and duty does not
extend to preventing the trustee from taking advantage of some interest
of his own, and there is no duty to compromise his own interest in the
interest of the trust. In *Sargeant* v. *National Westminster Bank Plc, The*

Times, 10 May 1990, trustees of sale of land were also agricultural tenants of the land under tenancies granted to them by the testator (their father). Under the terms of the trust they owned two-thirds of the beneficial interest and also had power to purchase trust property. They proposed to purchase the freehold of the largest farm and sell the other two for development. The third child had died but his personal representatives opposed sale subject to the tenancies on the ground that the best price would not be obtained. It was held that they could sell subject to their tenancies. As tenants they were under no duty to co-operate in a sale with vacant possession (*Boardman* v. *Phipps*, above, was distinguished).

Beneficiary's remedies for breach of fiduciary duty

The remedies available to a beneficiary vary according to the nature of the breach. If, for example, the breach is a purchase by the trustee of trust property then the primary remedy available to the beneficiary is to elect to avoid the sale of the property within a reasonable time. In other cases the trustee may be held liable to account for profits received or may possibly have to hold some property upon trust for the beneficiaries. It is important to distinguish between the remedy of account and the constructive trust. These last two remedies are considered in Chapter 11 (see section 11.4).

Defences

Although the rule against taking advantage is normally a strict one, defences may be available in some cases. The clearest defences are that the trust instrument authorised the transaction or that it was entered into with the full consent of the beneficiaries. In *Holder* v. *Holder* (above) the plaintiff could not have a sale of trust property to the trustee set aside where with full knowledge of the facts he had affirmed the sale. Similarly, if there is long acquiescence under a sale to a trustee, that 'ought to be taken as evidence that as between the trustee and the cestui que trust the relation had been abandoned in the transaction; and, that in all other respects it was fair' (see Eldon LC in *Parkes* v. *White* (1805) 11 Ves 209).

9.4 Delegation of Duties

The trustees' duties as managers of the trust fund may encompass a wide variety of tasks. The trustees may wish to delegate some of these, either because they are mundane matters which do not justify the use of the trustee's time or because they require skills which are outside their expertise. The traditional view was that, since the trustees were themselves delegates of the settlor, they should not delegate their duties. Lord Langdale MR in *Turner* v. *Corney* (1841) 5 Beav 515, said: 'trustees who take on themselves the management of property for the benefit of others have no right to shift their duty on other persons'. This strict approach has been modified and some degree of delegation is currently allowed to trustees.

Appointment of agents

Trustees have always been able to appoint agents to undertake work which, in the ordinary course of business, called for the skill of another. For example, a trustee can employ a solicitor to do legal work and can employ a stockbroker to deal with investments (*Speight* v. *Gaunt* (1883) 22 Ch D 727); but the old rule was that a trustee should not employ agents to do work where it was not necessary to use the agency of another. It is thought that the position has been relaxed by s.23 of the Trustee Act 1925 which provides that 'Trustees ... may, instead of acting personally, employ and pay an agent, whether a solicitor, banker, stock-broker, or other person, to transact any business or do any act required to be transacted or done in the execution of the trust. The effect of this, according to Maugham J in the leading case of *Re Vickery* [1931] 1 Ch 572 is that a trustee 'is no longer required to do any actual work himself, but he may employ a solicitor or other agent to do it, whether there is any real necessity for the employment or not'.

Delegation of responsibilities

Although trustees can delegate tasks to agents, this does not absolve the trustees from their primary duty of taking decisions in respect of the trust. Thus although trustees may employ a stockbroker to advise on investments and for the mechanics of investments, the trustees must make the investment decisions themselves.

In limited circumstances only can trustees delegate their primary duties. These are set out below.

Inherent jurisdiction of the court

The court may authorise the trustees to delegate in a particular case. In *Steel* v. *Wellcome Trustees Ltd* [1988] 1 WLR 167 the court approved a power to delegate investment decisions to advisers: but only up to a maximum of two percentage points of the value of the trust fund, and even in this case the advisers had to report to the trustees quarterly and the trustees would be liable if they failed to exercise adequate supervision.

Foreign property

In the case of property situated outside the United Kingdom, s.23(2) of the Trustee Act 1925 allows the trustees power to delegate the management, administration and sale of the property.

Power of attorney

A 'trustee may by power of attorney, delegate for a period not exceeding twelve months the execution or exercise of all or any of the trusts, powers and discretions vested in him as trustee, either alone or jointly with any other person or persons' (s.25(1) Trustee Act 1925). Under this statutory authority a trustee can delegate discretions and decision-making. The drawback from the trustee's point of view is that the trustee remains liable for any acts done by the attorney. The formalities for creating such a power are contained in the Powers of Attorney Act 1971 and the Enduring Power of Attorney Act 1985.

The limitations on the trustees' ability to delegate have been criticised by Hayton [1990] 106 LQR 87 as being inadequate to cope with the complex financial transactions which are associated with modern trusts, and he suggests that the advantages of employing an investment manager under the Financial Services Act 1986 make it desirable that s.23 of the Trustee Act should be extended to cover appointment and payment of an investment manager.

It should be noted at this point that delegation leads to difficulties when the agent commits some breach of trust. In section 10.3 it will be considered whether the trustee may be held responsible for the acts of the agent.

9.5 Accountability of Trustees

The trustees manage the trust fund for the benefit of the beneficiaries and it is only proper that there should be some degree of accountability to the beneficiaries and to the courts. The extent of accountability is, however, quite limited; otherwise trustees might be unduly hampered in the carrying out of their obligations and the exercise of their powers.

Accounts and audit

Any fund manager is subject to a duty to keep accounts and the trustee is no exception. The trustee must disclose the completed accounts to the beneficiaries if the beneficiary so requires and pays for a copy (*Pearse* v. *Green* (1819) 1 Jac & W 135). The accounts may be audited, subject to the discretion of the trustees, but not more than once in three years unless the nature of the trust makes a more frequent audit appropriate (s.22(4) Trustee Act 1925).

Trust documents and information
A further degree of accountability of the trustee is induced by the fact
that the beneficiary is entitled to a reasonable amount of information
about the trust. The beneficiary should be told that he has an interest in
the trust (*Hawkesley* v. *May* [1956] 1 QB 304). The beneficiary can also
demand to inspect most documents relating to the trust 'because they are
trust documents, and because he is a beneficiary. They are, in this sense,
his own' (see Lord Wrenbury in *O'Rourke* v. *Darbishire* [1920] AC 581
626 HL). The beneficiary is, for example, entitled to inspect deeds of title
deeds of trust property (*Re Cowin* (1886) 33 Ch D 179) and minutes of
meetings of the trustees (*Re Londonderry's Settlement* [1965] Ch 918;
CA), but not letters passing between a trustee and beneficiary (*Re
Londonderry's Settlement*).

The litigation in *Talbot* v. *Marshfield* (1865) 2 Dr & Sm 549 neatly
highlights the distinction between those documents with the quality of
trust documents and those which do not have that quality. In that case
trustees took counsel's opinion on whether they should exercise a power
of advancement. Other beneficiaries took proceedings to prevent the
advancement and the trustees obtained another opinion advising them
whether they had a good defence to the beneficiaries' action. The court
found that the first opinion was a trust document (and could be seen by
the beneficiaries) because it was obtained for the benefit of the trust. The
second opinion was not a trust document (and could not be inspected by
the beneficiaries) because it was purely for the trustees' benefit.

The obligation to disclose trust documents is not an absolute one as it
has to be balanced against the privilege accorded to trustees in relation to
their reasons for making decisions. The general rule is that the trustees'
duty to provide information is qualified by the fact that trustees do not
have to give reasons for their decisions. In *Re Londonderry's Settlement*
(above) a beneficiary sought minutes of meetings relating to the trustees'
decision in relation to the exercise of a power of appointment. Although
it was recognised that minutes of meetings were trust documents, the
duty to disclose them was overriden by the privilege protecting the
trustees from disclosing their decisions. Samuels (1965) 28 MLR 220, has
criticised the privilege protecting the trustees' reasoning and says that
trustees should be fully accountable for their decisions and the reasons
for making them.

Control of trustees

By beneficiaries
The accountability of trustee to beneficiary does not extend to the trustee
being subject to the control of the beneficiary. The trustee has powers

vested in him which were vested in him by the settlor and which are his to exercise. In *Re Brockbank* [1948] Ch 206, beneficiaries wanted a trustee, in exercising a power of appointing a new trustee, to appoint Lloyds Bank. The trustee refused to exercise his power in this way and the court refused to interfere with the trustee's discretion at the instigation of the beneficiaries.

The law is not, however, clear on this point due to the Court of Appeal decision in *Butt* v. *Kelson* [1952] 1 Ch 197, in which case the beneficiaries wanted the trustees to use the voting power of shares owned by the trust in a particular way. The court took the view that the beneficiaries were the owners of the shares and were entitled to have them voted as they wished. The decision was doubted in *Re Wichelow* [1954] 1 WLR 5 by Upjohn J who took the opportunity to distinguish the decision. On the facts before him he refused to allow the beneficiaries to direct the trustees how to use the voting power carried by the trust shareholding, on the ground that it was not possible to consult with possible unborn beneficiaries.

By court

The courts do, of course, exercise supervision over the trustees, but this will be kept to a minimum. Lord Truro LC in *Re Beloved Wilkes' Charity* (1851) 3 Mac & G 440 expressed the principle thus:

> It is to the discretion of the trustees that the execution of the trust is confided, that discretion being exercised with an entire absence of indirect motive, with honesty of intention, and with a fair consideration of the subject. The duty of supervision on the part of this Court will thus be confined to the question of the honesty integrity and fairness with which the deliberation has been conducted, and will not be extended to the accuracy of the conclusion arrived at.

The court will consider interfering with a trustee's discretion if it has been exercised dishonestly or capriciously (*Re Manisty* [1974] Ch 17; *Re Lofthouse* (1885) 11 Ch D 272, CA). In *Klug* v. *Klug* [1918] 2 Ch 67 one of the trustees was the beneficiary's mother and refused to approve an advancement of money to the beneficiary because the beneficiary had married without her approval. Neville J did not hesitate in interfering since the trustee was allowing her personal animosity to guide her discretion. Similarly the court will interfere if the trustee has not really exercised the discretion at all. In *Turner* v. *Turner* [1984] Ch 100, trustees exercising powers of appointment did not exercise their own judgment but simply did as the settlor instructed them. Mervyn Davies J held the trustees to be in breach of trust for failing properly to exercise their discretion. However, a court will not interfere in the exercise of a discretion just because it is convenient to do so or because the trustees wish to surrender their discretion to the court (*Re Allen-Meyrick's WT* [1966] 1 WLR 499).

9.6 Appointment and Removal of Trustees

Who can be a trustee?
In general any legal personality, whether individual or corporate, may be a trustee. The only statutory limitation is that a minor cannot own land (s.1 Law of Property Act 1925) and by s.20 Trustee Act 1925 a minor cannot be appointed trustee of land or personalty. In other cases eligible persons who have initially been appointed may be removed by the court if they are undesirable because of financial irresponsibility (*Re Barker* (1875) 1 Ch D 43) or if they have been guilty of a crime of dishonesty (*Coombe* v. *Brooks* (1871) LR 12 Eq 61).

Although a beneficiary may be appointed as a trustee this is generally not desirable because of the possibility of conflict and interest, at least if there are other beneficiaries.

Whereas a minor cannot be expressly appointed as trustee there are some circumstances in which a minor may become a trustee by operation of law, principally in the area of resulting trusts. In *Re Vinogradoff* (1935) WN 68 a woman transferred stock into the joint names of herself and her granddaughter, aged four. After the death of the woman it was resolved that the granddaughter held the stock on a resulting trust for the woman's estate.

On occasions, special types of trustee may be appointed apart from ordinary individuals and corporations. First, as distinct from an ordinary corporation, is a special type of corporation known as a trust corporation. This is a corporate body, often within the same company group as a bank, which undertakes the business of acting as trustee and has a large issued capital of an amount specified by statute or, if it does not satisfy this financial requirement, has been appointed by a court to act as a trustee. A trust corporation can do any act which is required by statute to be performed by two individual trustees.

Other special types of trustee include the Public Trustee, custodian trustees and judicial trustees. The Public Trustee is a corporation sole created by the Public Trustee Act 1906, whose special function is the administration of small estates where there are no trustees to act or an additional trustee is desirable. A custodian trustee is a corporation which has the role of holding the trust property whilst leaving the administration of the trust under the control of managing trustees. The purpose of so doing is usually so that once trust property is vested in his name it will not be necessary for any other appointment of new trustees. Finally, judicial trustees are appointed by the court where it is desirable that the administration of the trust should be subject to the close scrutiny of the court (e.g., where there has been impropriety or the administration of the trust has broken down).

How many trustees should there be?

Any number of trustees may be appointed as a general rule but there are special cases where minima and maxima must be observed. Furthermore it is normally wise to appoint more than one trustee in order to reduce the possibility of misconduct or neglect which might be more likely to occur in the case of a sole trustee. The special cases are as follows:

(a) in the case of land held upon trust for sale or under a strict settlement the maximum number of trustees permitted is normally four (s.34 Trustee Act 1925);

(b) although there needs only to be one trustee of land normally there must be two or more to give a valid receipt for capital money on the sale of the land (s.14 Trustee Act 1925);

(c) where under a will or intestacy property is to be held upon trust for a minor and no trustees have been appointed, the personal representatives may appoint not more than four trustees (s.42 Administration of Estates Act 1925);

(d) where a trustee wishes to retire, but it is not proposed to appoint a new trustee in his place, there must be at least two remaining trustees (s.39 Trustee Act 1925).

First appointment

When a settlor creates a trust he normally names trustees to act. Occasionally there will be no trustee (e.g., where the trust is created by will and the trustees named have predeceased the testator), or the named trustees may refuse to act. In these cases trustees may be appointed by some power in the trust instrument or failing such the court will appoint trustees for 'the court will not allow a trust to fail for want of a trustee'. If, however, 'it is of the essence of a trust that the trustees selected and no-one else shall act as the trustees of it and those trustees cannot or will not undertake the office, the trust must fail' (see Buckley J in *Re Lysaght* [1966] 1 Ch 191).

Change of trustee

A number of events may call for the subsequent appointment of a new trustee or trustees: the death of a trustee, retirement, refusal to act, disclaimer, unfitness to act, incapacity or mental disorder, for instance.

Upon some such events the trust instrument may provide machinery for the appointment of new trustees. Alternatively appointment of new trustees may be authorised by statute or may be within the power of the court.

Out of court

New trustees may be appointed out of court by an express trust power or by virtue of statutory authority. The basic position is set out in s.36 of the Trustee Act 1925 which provides that where a trustee:

(a)   is dead, or
(b)   remains out of the United Kingdom for more than twelve months, or
(c)   desires to be discharged from all or any of the trusts or powers reposed in or conferred on him, or
(d)   refuses or is unfit to act therein, or
(e)   is incapable of acting therein, or
(f)   is an infant,

then new trustees may be appointed by:

(a)   the persons nominated in the trust instrument;
(b)   the existing trustees;
(c)   the personal representatives of the last surviving trustees;
(d)   the beneficiaires in certain cases
(e)   the court (see below).

If a trustee wishes to retire he can do so under s.39 of the Trustee Act, which provides that where a trustee by deed declares that he wishes to retire, and after his discharge there will remain a trust corporation or at least two individuals to act as trustees, then if the co-trustees and any other person empowered to appoint new trustees consent by deed to the retirement, the retiring trustee will be discharged. Otherwise a trustee may be discharged by the consent of all of the beneficiaries or by the authority of a court order.

By court

The court may appoint a new trustee whenever it is 'inexpedient difficult or impracticable to do so without the assistance of the court' under s.41 Trustee Act 1925. The jurisdiction will be useful where a sole surviving trustee dies intestate, where there is disagreement between the trustees, where a trustee is incapable of acting or resides abroad and there is no other trustee capable of making an appointment.

Summary

1 Trustees are under a duty to invest trust property. There are a number of statutory powers of investment, the most important of which is the Trustee Investment Act 1961. As the Trustee Investment Act 1961 is complex to administer and the investments permitted largely outdated for modern economic circumstances, there are usually extensive express powers of investment contained in the trust instrument. Even if an investment is authorised by statute or by the trust instrument, this does not necessarily mean that it will not involve a breach of trust. Trustees must act like the prudent man of business investing someone else's money and therefore avoid investments attended with hazard. In their selection of the type of investment, trustees must balance the interests of any competing beneficiaries, and they should have regard to the need for diversification in so far as it is appropriate to the circumstances of the trust. Furthermore, trustees must always select investments in the best interests of the trust even though this may conflict with their own personal values.

2 The general standard of care owed by trustees in the administration of the trust is that of the ordinary prudent man of business conducting his own affairs. A higher standard of care is owed by professional trustees and is that which is appropriate to the degree of skill and expertise they hold themselves out as having in trust administration.

3 As the trustee/beneficiary relationship is a fiduciary relationship a trustee must not make a profit from his position or put himself in a position of conflict between his duty to the trust and his personal interest. This principle has resulted in the general rule that a trustee is not entitled to remuneration for the administration of the trust. However, many exceptions have developed to the general rule, and today most trustees receive remuneration under an express clause in the trust instrument. There are also important statutory powers to remunerate certain types of trustees and the court has extensive powers under its inherent jurisdiction to remunerate trustees where this is in the best interests of the trust. Trustees are entitled to legitimate and reasonable expenses incurred in the administration of the trust.

4 Purchase of the trust property by a trustee is subject to the self-dealing rule which means, subject to exceptions, the sale to the trustee will be voidable at the option of the beneficiaries. Sales of trust property to a relative (not acting as nominee for the trustee) and to a company in which the trustee has less than a controlling interest are subject to the fair-dealing rule which requires that the purchaser establish that the trustee took reasonable care to find a purchaser and that the best price attainable was paid.

5 Where a trustee acquires a directorship as a result of shares held on trust, unless expressly or impliedly authorised by the trust instrument he or she is not, as a general rule, entitled to keep any fees paid. However, the court has inherent jurisdiction to allow a trustee to keep fees paid in whole or in part if it is satisfied that the trustee has put in effort over and above that which would be expected of a director appointed to represent a majority share holding and that the trustee can prove he/she is the best person to do the job.

6 S.23 Trustee Act 1925 now allows trustees to delegate all acts done in the administration of the trust. A discretion vested in a trustee, can however, only be delegated by the grant of a power of attorney, and suffers the penalty that the trustees are automatically liable for any wrongful acts of the attorney.

7 Trustees are under a duty to keep accounts and to have them audited, and to provide information to the beneficiaries about the management of the trust on request. As a general rule, beneficiaries are entitled to inspect trust documents, but if a trust document contains information about how the trustees have exercised a discretion, they need not reveal this part to the beneficiaries as trustees are not bound to give reasons for how they have exercised discretions. (However, if the trustees do give reasons, the court will consider the adequacy of the reasons.)

8 Subject to exceptions, as a general principle so long as the trust continues the beneficiaries cannot interfere with the running of the trust affairs. A beneficiary may only make representations to the trustees. However, if all the beneficiaries are of full age and full mental capacity and absolutely entitled between them, under the rule in *Saunders* v. *Vautier* they could agree to terminate the trust and, if they wish, bring into being a new trust.

9 Apart from a minor, any legal person (whether an individual or corporation) may be expressly appointed a trustee. Minors may become trustees by operation of the law (e.g., under a resulting trust). Usually the first trustee(s) are appointed by the settlor/testator. Where there is not such person available or willing to act, and the trust instrument contains no express power to appoint trustees, the court will appoint trustees. Subsequent to the setting-up of the trust new trustees may be appointed out of court, by virtue of some express power in the trust instrument or under s.36 Trustee Act, or alternatively by the court under s.41 Trustee Act.

Exercises

1 In what circumstances (if any) can a trustee be liable for a breach of trust despite the fact that the trust property has been invested in an asset expressly authorised by the trust instrument?

2 Why is it undesirable to place reliance on the Trustee Investment Act 1961 as a source for the trustees' powers of investment?

3 By Henry's will Thelma and Tom were expressly appointed as trustees for sale of Greenacre, freehold land, which was to be held on trust for Ronnie for life, with remainder to Ronnie's children in equal shares. The will contained no express power of investment. A few years ago the trustees sold Greenacre and invested the £70 000 proceeds of sale in authorised unit trusts. They later sold all the units for £60 000 and bought a freehold dwelling house in which Ronnie and his children now live rent free. Consider the liability of Thelma and Tom to the beneficiaries with regard to the transactions which have taken place.

4 For some years Good and Reliable have been unpaid trustees of the Nussbourn family trust, being relatives of the settlor. As the fortunes of the trust have increased the business has become more complex and time consuming and Good and Reliable now wish to retire as trustees and to appoint Adder and Subtract of Deadly, Dull, Boring and Company

(Accountants) in their place. The trust instrument contains no express power to appoint trustees and has no provision for remuneration of trustees. Advise Adder and Subtract.

5 What standard of care is owed by (a) an unpaid trustee and (b) a paid trustee in the general administration of the trust? Do you think the standard expected of an unpaid trustee is too high, especially when compared to the position of a paid trustee? (See Paling (1973) 37 Conv. 50.)

6 Quick and Sharp are trustees of the Equinox trust, the funds of which were originally invested in a 30 per cent share holding in Alpha Limited. However, six years ago the trustees sold all the trust shares in Alpha Limited to Beta Plc of which Quick was a director. The proceeds of sale were invested in a 40 per cent share holding in Gamma Limited, a company in which Sharp already had a personal share holding of 20 per cent. Sharp subsequently became a director of Gamma Limited and has been paid a substantial fee ever since. The value of shares in Alpha Limited have risen considerably whereas Gamma Limited shares have fallen in value.

The beneficiaries of the Equinox trust are questioning the sale of the Alpha shares, and furthermore wish to know whether they have a valid claim to the director's fee Sharp has received from Gamma Limited.

Advise the beneficiaries.

7 To what extent may trustees delegate their functions as trustees?

8 By his will Sir Samuel Stirling left his residuary estate to George and Mary to hold on discretionary trust for his children living at the date of his death. You are approached by Victor, William and Xavier, the only living children of Sir Samuel, who are all adults. They are dissatisfied with George and Mary's management of the trust fund and wish the trustees to be removed and Enterprise Management Co. to be appointed in their place. They claim that Mary (their stepmother) is hostile to their interests and George is aged 89 and losing his memory.

Advise Victor, William and Xavier.

10 Breach of Trust

Trustees may be found to be in breach of their duties for many different reasons. They may have acted outside the scope of their powers by making an unauthorised investment; they may have been negligent in the manner in which they have invested; they may have exercised a discretion capriciously; or they may have been in breach of fiduciary duty by making a personal profit from the position of trusteeship. In these cases and others the trustees may be held accountable for their breaches as appears below.

10.1 Joint Liability of Trustees to Beneficiaries

Since trustees are jointly responsible for the management of the trust they are also jointly liable for any wrongdoing or neglect in the execution of the trust in which they are involved, whether actively or passively. A trustee may be liable to a beneficiary even though a breach has actually been committed by a co-trustee if the commission of the breach was facilitated by his inaction. As Hayton and Marshall (8th edn, p.725) have explained, a trustee may find that he is sued by beneficiaries in respect of acts of co-trustees in the following circumstances:

1. If he leaves a matter in the hands of his co-trustee without enquiry.
2. If he stands by while a breach of trust, of the facts of which he is cognizant, is being committed by his co-trustee. In the words of Lord Cottenham in Styles v Guy, (1849) 1 Mac. & G. 422, at 433, it is the duty of executors and trustees to watch over, and, if necessary, to correct, the conduct of each other.
3. If he allows trust funds to remain in the sole control of his co-trustee, 'The duty of trustees' said Kay J. in Re Flower (1884) 27 Ch D 592 'is to prevent one of themselves having the exclusive control over the money, and certainly not, by any act of theirs, to enable one of themselves to have the exclusive control of it.'
4. Apparently also if, becoming aware of a breach of trust committed or contemplated by his co-trustee, he takes no steps to obtain redress.

In cases where a trustee has not himself been involved in wrongdoing and has taken every care in the administration of the trust, but in circumstances beyond the innocent trustee's control and responsibility a co-trustee perpetrates a breach (such as a misappropriation of trust property), the innocent trustee is not liable for the acts of the co-trustee. S.30 of the Trustee Act 1925 provides that: 'A trustee shall be chargeable only for . . . his own acts, receipts, neglects of defaults, and not for those of any other trustee . . . unless the same happens through his own wilful default.' It has been suggested that s.30 should have the effect that a trustee is only liable for his own acts and never for those of a co-trustee. In *Re Brier* (1884) 26 Ch D 235, however, Lord Selbourne said that the section did not substantially alter the previous law, that all trustees were equally liable, and it should be emphasised that if a trustee neglects to do as much as he or she should, and thus enables a co-trustee to act in breach, he or she is liable for the neglect, and the section expressly refers to such neglect.

The trustees are jointly and severally liable, so that beneficiaries can opt to sue any one or more of the trustees who are found to be liable through active breach or passive neglect. As between the trustees, however, the liability may be different. If one trustee is sued he or she will usually have a right to claim a contribution from the other trustee or trustees, and in some circumstances a trustee is entitled to a complete indemnity from the other trustee or trustees (see below).

10.2 Liability of Trustees *inter se*

Rights of contribution

Since liability of trustees is joint and several there is a right, if one trustee is sued separately, to a contribution from the other trustees, so that all of the trustees bear a share of the liability. This right exists even though one trustee is more culpable than another. The reason for the joint liability between trustees was succinctly stated by Cotton LJ in *Bahin* v. *Hughes* (1886) 31 Ch D 390, when he said: 'It would be laying down a wrong rule to hold that where one trustee acts honestly though erroneously the other trustee is to be held [not liable] who by doing nothing neglects his duty more.' In *Bahin* v. *Hughes* itself there were three trustees. Two of them effected an unauthorised investment on the security of leasehold property. The third was informed by letter, but she did not take any action. When the security proved insufficient it was held that all three trustees were liable; the third had to contribute and was not entitled to an indemnity from the others.

The measure of contribution is normally equal, although it has been suggested that s.2 of the Civil Liability (Contribution) Act 1978, which gives the court a discretion to order such contribution as is just and equitable (including a complete indemnity), might result in trustees receiving different proportions of contributions according to culpability. It is submitted, however, that it is unlikely that the Act makes any difference since the rationale is that all trustees should take equal responsibility, and one should not be liable to make a smaller contribution because of a failure to take such equal responsibility.

Rights of indemnity

Although liability of trustees is normally joint and the liability to contribute is equal, there are some exceptional circumstances in which a trustee who has been sued by a beneficiary is entitled to a complete indemnity from the co-trustee in departure from the general rule in *Bahin* v. *Hughes* (above). The general gist of the cases is that if one trustee was either solely responsible for or took the sole benefit of the breach, he or she should bear sole responsibility, so that if he or she is sued there will be no right of contribution; and if the other trustees are sued they are entitled to a complete indemnity from the trustee at fault.

Solicitor/trustee

The first exception is that if a breach of trust is committed as a result of a complete reliance by one trustee upon another trustee who is a solicitor, then the solicitor trustee must indemnify the co-trustee. In *Re Partington* (1887) 57 LT 654, the two trustees were a solicitor and the testator's widow. The solicitor undertook most of the trust administration and was paid costs for his professional work. He negligently made an unauthorised investment of mortgage in respect of which the widow relied entirely upon his advice. In these circumstances it was held that the widow was entitled to a complete indemnity from the solicitor trustee.

The mere fact that one trustee is a solicitor is not enough to entitle the co-trustee to indemnity if the other trustee has been active and did not rely upon the solicitor trustee. In *Head* v. *Gould* [1898] 2 Ch 250, one solicitor was a trustee and the other was the daughter of the life tenant. They both agreed to sell a house, and instead of reinvesting the proceeds to pay them to the life tenant, in breach of trust. It was decided that there was no right of indemnity from the solicitor trustee since the non-solicitor had actively colluded in the breach.

The exception is based upon the reliance by one trustee upon his co-trustee for some good reason. Stirling J in *Re Partington* (above) said: 'if there is a relationship existing between the co-trustees which will justify the court in treating one of them as solely responsible for the breach of trust then the other trustee is entitled to indemnity from him'. Because of the width of this reasoning the exception may not be limited to the case of a solicitor trustee and might, for example, apply where an accountant trustee provided financial advice or in any other analogous case where one trustee has a particular skill which the other relies upon.

Trustee/beneficiary

The second occasion when one trustee is entitled to a complete indemnity from the other is where the other trustee is also a beneficiary and has actively participated in a breach of trust with the intent of obtaining a benefit for himself in his capacity as beneficiary. In *Chillingworth* v. *Chambers* [1896] 1 Ch 685 there were two trustees, one of whom was also a beneficiary. Together they made an unauthorised investment by lending money on security of a mortgage of leasehold property. The security proved insufficient and the loss was made good out of the interest of the trustee who was a beneficiary. It was held that he was not entitled to a contribution from the other trustee who, if sued, would have been able to claim a complete indemnity. Kay LJ expressed the general principle that where a trustee who is also a beneficiary 'has received, as between himself and his co-trustee, an exclusive benefit by the breach of trust, [he] must indemnify his co-trustee to the extent of his interest in the trust fund, and not merely to the extent of the benefit which he has received'.

Indemnity from beneficiary

Just as a trustee is entitled to indemnity from a co-trustee who is a beneficiary and has participated in a breach of trust, a trustee may obtain a complete indemnity from a beneficiary who is not a trustee but who has instigated or requested the breach of trust. The courts' inherent jurisdiction is applicable if either the beneficiary instigated or requested the breach of trust so as to obtain a personal benefit (even if no benefit was in fact received), or if the beneficiary passively concurred in the breach and actually received a personal benefit. Statute has extended the jurisdiction so that the beneficiary's equitable interest may be impounded irrespective of the question of benefit. S.62 of the Trustee Act 1925 states:

> Where a trustee commits a breach of trust at the instigation or request or with the consent in writing of a beneficiary, the court may, if it thinks fit ... make such order as to the court seems just, for impounding all or any part of the interest of the beneficiary in the trust estate by way of indemnity to the trustee.

Although the drafting of s.62 appears to be quite wide, it is subject to the serious limitation which applied to the earlier case law: namely, that it has to be proved not only that the beneficiary instigated or consented to the acts of the trustees but that he knew of all the facts making the act of the trustees a breach of trust. In *Re Somerset* [1894] 1 Ch 231 a beneficiary requested that the trustees should invest money upon the security of a mortgage of property, an investment which in itself would not be unauthorised. The trustees made the investment and did so negligently in that the value of the property made it inadequate security. When the beneficiary sued the trustees for negligence, the trustees claimed indemnity. It was held that, although the beneficiary had consented to the investment, the beneficiary was not aware that the property was inadequate security and that for this reason the trustees should not have an indemnity from the beneficiaries. Lindley LJ explained that:

> if a cestui que trust instigates, requests or consents in writing to an investment not in terms authorized by the power of investment, he clearly falls within the section; and in such a case his ignorance or forgetfulness of the terms of the power would not I think protect him . . . But if all that a cestui que trust does is to instigate, request, or consent in writing to an investment which is authorized by the terms of the power, the case is I think very different. He has a right to expect that the trustees will act with proper care in making the investment, and if they do not they cannot throw the consequences on him.

Fraud

A trustee may be entitled to a complete indemnity from another in respect of a breach of trust if the other trustee has acted fraudulently and the first trustee has not. In *Re Smith* [1896] 1 Ch 171 one trustee dishonestly accepted a bribe to induce him to make an unauthorised investment. It was held that the other trustee who had acted innocently was entitled to a complete indemnity.

10.3 Liability for Acts of Agents

In addition to liability for his own acts and those of his co-trustee, a trustee may find that he is liable for the acts of an agent who has been appointed to assist in the administration of the trust. S.23 of the Trustee Act 1925 allows the trustees to delegate some of their functions with a reasonable degree of freedom (see above, section 9.4), but the trustees should bear in mind that they may take the ultimate responsibility for any misapplication on the part of the agent. The position of the trustee is at present unclear, due to the equivocal drafting of ss 23 and 30 of the Trustee Act, and judicial decisions upon these provisions.

The sections provide that the trustee should not be liable for the acts of an agent so long as the agent was 'employed in good faith' (s.23) and so long as any loss did not happen through the trustee's 'wilful default' (s.30). One might have thought that the effect of the provisions would be that the trustee will not normally be liable for an agent's acts, but it is not clear what is meant by 'wilful default', and whether a trustee who simply leaves an agent to get on with his delegated job is in default in doing so.

The leading case, although a first instance decision only, is *Re Vickery* [1931] 1 Ch 572, where the executor of a will employed a solicitor to wind up the estate. At the time of appointment he knew nothing about the solicitor to suggest that he should not be appointed, but three months later one of the beneficiaries told the executor that the solicitor had previously been suspended from practise although he was now allowed to practise again. The executor refused to take the matter away from the solicitor who ultimately absconded, after having taken financial advantage of the trust. The beneficiary sued the executor. Maugham J resolved that the solicitor had been appointed in good faith and the executor was not guilty of wilful default. He purported to apply the decision of Romer J in *Re City and Equitable Fire Ins* [1925] Ch 407 (in which case Romer J said that wilful default was where a person 'knows that he is committing and intends to commit a breach of his duty, or is recklessly careless in the sense of not caring whether his act is or is not a breach of duty'), and said 'wilful default' is 'a consciousness of negligence or breach of duty, or recklessness'. This reasoning has been severely criticised. Jones (1959) 22 MLR 381 (1931) 47 LQR 330, p.463, has argued that the reasoning is wrong on four counts:

(a)   the Trustee Act is consolidating and s.30 re-enacts s.31 Law of Property Act 1859 under which *Re Brier* (see section 10.2 above) was decided;
(b)   *Re City and Equitable Fire Ins* [1925] Ch 407 was not a trust case;
(c)   it is difficult to reconcile this interpretation with s.23(3)(a);
(d)   it does not reconcile s.23 and s.30.

In addition Stannard [1979] Conv. 345, has pointed out that common law cases in contract on the meaning of wilful default use a very different meaning to the cases in equity which traditionally adopt a test of 'failure to do what is reasonable'.

If Jones and Stannard are correct the trustees still have substantial responsibility where they delegate duties, and they would be liable whenever they failed to do that which was reasonable. In a decision subsequent to *Re Vickery* a trustee was held to be liable for exercising insufficient supervision over an agent. In *Re Lucking* [1968] 1 WLR 866 the trust property consisted of a controlling shareholding in a company and the sole trustee procured the appointment of an old friend as managing director of the company. The trustee signed blank cheques and allowed the friend to complete the cheques and countersign them. The friend applied considerable sums for his own purposes. It was held that the trustee was liable for the misapplications as he had not acted as a prudent man of business and was in breach of duty himself by not exercising sufficient control over the agent. The Law Reform Committee Report recommended that the law should be clarified to the effect that a trustee should not be liable if it was reasonable to employ an agent and if reasonable steps were taken to ensure that the agent was competent and the work done competently. This would make it clear that the trustee still has substantial responsibility even where an agent is appointed.

10.4 Defences and Relief from Liability

Assuming that there is a clear breach of trust the trustees will normally be fully liable for such breach (subject to the possibilities of contribution and indemnity mentioned above). In some cases, however, a trustee or trustees may be absolved wholly or partly from liability as appears below.

Participation in, or consent of beneficiary to a breach

It is clear that a beneficiary who is *sui juris* and who knowingly concurs in a breach of trust cannot afterwards complain of it unless the trustees know or ought to have known that the beneficiary's concurrence was the result of duress or undue influence. The principle is fully explained by Wilberforce J in *Re Pauling's ST* [1964] Ch 303:

> The court has to consider all the circumstances in which the concurrence of the cestui que trust was given with a view to seeing whether it is fair and equitable that, having given his concurrence, he should afterwards turn round and sue the trustees; that subject to this, it is not necessary that he should know that what he is concurring in is a breach of trust, provided that he fully understands what he is concurring in, and that it is not necessary that he should himself have directly benefitted by the breach of trust.

Of course, it is the consenting trustee only who is prevented from suing the trustees, and other beneficiaries who have not consented may pursue an action for breach. In these circumstances it might be noted from a practical point of view that the beneficiary who consented to the breach is liable to have his or her interest impounded (see section 10.2 above), and if the interest is sufficient to make good the breach the trustee will ultimately incur no liability.

Acquiescence

Even if a beneficiary did not initially consent to a breach of trust he may be found to have subsequently acquiesced in the breach if with knowledge of the facts which constitute the breach he elects not to take any steps in respect of the breach. It is not necessary that the beneficiary should know of his legal right to challenge the act of the trustee, just that he is aware of the facts. In *Holder* v. *Holder* [1968] Ch 353, where it was alleged that a trustee had purchased trust property in breach of his fiduciary duty, a beneficiary was held to have acquiesced in the breach by receiving his share of the proceeds of sale of the trust property. It was irrelevant that he did not know that he might have had a legal right to challenge the sale. Delay in making a claim will not in itself amount to acquiescence, but a long delay is certainly an important factor which will be taken into account.

Statutory relief

S.61 of the Trustee Act 1925 empowers the court to relieve trustees from the repercussions of a breach of trust. It provides:

> If it appears to the court that a trustee . . . is or may be personally liable for any breach of trust, whether the transaction alleged to be a breach of trust . . . but has acted honestly and reasonably, and ought fairly to be excused for the breach of trust and for omitting to obtain the directions of the court in the matter in which he committed such breach, then the court may relieve him either wholly or partly from personal liability for the same.

The provision of such a power has been criticised (Maugham (1898) 14 LQR 159) on the basis that trustees can always go to the court for directions on matters which they are not sure of and that they should not be excused if they have committed a breach; but the jurisdiction, being statutory, is of course well established.

Although there are quite a few decided cases on the section the effect of the section is not entirely clear. The section provides that the trustees must have complied with three tests. They must have acted honestly, reasonably and ought fairly to be excused. There seems to be an overlap in respect of these last two tests since in *Perrins* v. *Bellamy* [1898] 2 Ch 521 Kekewich J said that:

> in general and in the absence of special circumstances, a trustee who has acted 'reasonably' ought to be relieved, and that it is not incumbent on the court to consider whether he ought fairly to be excused, unless there is evidence of a special character showing that the provisions of the section ought not to be applied in his favour.

Although the basic test may be somewhat vague, there are at least a few solid principles which may be extracted from the cases. First, a trustee will not be relieved under the section if his only excuse is that he relied upon the advice of his co-trustee. Second, he will not be excused simply as a result of relying upon the advice of the settlor or the settlor's solicitor. Third, the mere fact that the trustee took independent legal advice will not relieve him, particularly if he then fails to sue the lawyer who advised him wrongly (*National Trust Co of Australasia* v. *General Finance Company of Australasia* [1905] AC 373). It should also be noted that the courts will be less willing to exercise their discretion in the case of professional or paid trustees than in the case of non-professional or unpaid trustees (*Re Waterman's Will Trust* [1952] 2 All ER 1054).

10.5 Limitation and Laches

It is a general rule of law that a person who has a legal claim should make it within a reasonable period of time. This general rule has crystallised in the Limitation Act 1980, s.21 which, in the case of actions for breach of trust, provides that a beneficiary should pursue her cause of action within six years of the breach. There is a proviso that in the case of future interests, such as the reversionary interest of a child where a parent is entitled to a prior life interest, time does not run until the reversionary interest falls into possession. So, in *Re Pauling's ST* [1964] Ch 303, where trustees made improper advancements of capital it was held that the interests of the children were future interests and time did not run from the date of the advancement but from the date that the children's interests vested in possession. The six-year rule does not apply if the trustees have been guilty of fraud or if the action is in respect of trust property which is, or the proceeds of which are, in the possession of the trustee. In these cases there is no time limit and the trustees may be sued at any time (subject to the doctrine of laches).

The Limitation Act does not deal with all claims which may be made in respect of breach of trust. It does not deal with actions for equitable relief by way of injunction, specific performance, rescission or rectification, or for the setting aside of a purchase of trust property by a trustee. In these and any other circumstances not within the Act the defendant trustee may be able to rely upon the equitable doctrine of laches. This doctrine, briefly stated, is that delay by a plaintiff in pursuing an equitable remedy may afford the defendant with an equitable defence. There is no strict rule as to what period of delay is necessary to give rise to the defence, but a period of 20 years has been suggested (*Weld* v. *Petre* [1929] 1 Ch 33) as a guide, although if one draws an analogy with the periods under the statute a rather shorter period might be appropriate.

10.6 **Measure of Liability**

The general rule is that the remedy for the trustee's breach of trust is to compensate the trust fund for the loss sustained. The beneficiaries may be able to take advantage of both personal and proprietary remedies as explained in Chapter 11.

Summary

1 A breach of trust is committed where a trustee fails to carry out a duty or improperly exercises a power. The breach may be positive or negative (i.e., failure to do something), and it may be innocent, negligent or fraudulent.
2 As trustees are under a duty to act jointly in the management of the trust, they are jointly and severally liable to the beneficiaries. A trustee is also liable for any other act of a co-trustee which causes loss to the trust if the loss occurs through the trustee's failure to exercise reasonable supervision over the co-trustee.
3 If one trustee is alone sued by the beneficiaries he is generally entitled to a contribution from his co-trustee(s). However, there are some situations in which the trustee will be entitled to an indemnity from one or more of his co-trustees. Where the indemnity is from a trustee/beneficiary who has participated in a breach of trust intended for his own benefit, it should be remembered that the duty to indemnify will only extend to the full amount of the beneficial interest.
4 S.23 Trustee Act 1925 allows trustees to delegate all acts done in the administration of the trust. If an honest but foolish appointment is made under s.23, the trustees will only be liable for subsequent acts of the agent if they occur through the trustee's own 'wilful default' (s.30). *Re Vickery* defines this narrowly to involve recklessness on the part of the trustees, but the better view is that a trustee will be liable on the basis of 'wilful default' if he or she fails to exercise reasonable supervision over the agent. If the agent is appointed in bad faith the trustees are liable for all acts done by the agent.
5 A trustee may have one or more of three defences to an action for breach of trust: first, with regard to the Limitation Act 1980, it should be remembered that there is no limitation period where there has been a fraudulent breach of trust or a trustee has converted trust property to his own use, although the equitable doctrine of laches may limit the time in which an action may be brought. Where a limitation period is specified, the general rule is that an action must be brought within six years of the date of the breach of trust. Second, to obtain relief under s.61 Trustee Act 1925, a trustee must establish that he has acted each of (a) honestly, and (b) reasonably, and (c) he ought fairly to be excused. Because of the latter requirement a paid trustee is unlikely to succeed in the defence. Third, the defence of consent of the beneficiary acts at common law and under s.62 Trustee Act 1925. In either case the consent is only valid if it is given by a beneficiary of full age and sound mind who had full knowledge of all the material facts. The defence only operates against a beneficiary who has

consented; those who have not consented may still bring an action for breach of trust.

6 The general purpose of an action for breach of trust is to effect restitution of the trust fund (i.e., compensate for loss sustained). However, where a fraudulent breach of trust has been committed the amount of interest payable by the trustee may be increased as a penalty.

Exercises

1 Quick (a solicitor) and Slow (a retired civil servant) are trustees of a trust, the assets of which are invested in land. Slow leaves the management of the trust wholly to Quick. Quick employs Sharp (an estate agent) to collect rents from the tenants of the trust land. Sharp has disappeared with all the rents collected in the last two months.

Advise Quick and Slow as to their liability.

2 Globetrotter has recently returned from abroad to find Grabber, his co-trustee, has misappropriated £2000 of trust money. In his absence Laidback has acted for Globetrotter under a power of attorney. He had no knowledge of the misappropriation by Grabber as he failed to take any interest in the administration of the trust.

Advise Globetrotter as to his liability (if any) to the beneficiaries. (In addition to Chapter 10 see also section 9.4.)

3 Smart (a solicitor) and Gullible (a poet) are both trustees of a trust fund. The beneficiaries are currently suing Smart alone for a breach of trust on the grounds that some years ago he wrongly invested trust funds in a property in which Gullible's son, Hopeless (a beneficiary of the trust), now resides, paying a market rent. The investment was made at the instigation of Gullible and Hopeless and only after taking counsel's opinion on the precise ambit of the investment clause of the trust instrument, but the advice has turned out to be incorrect.

Advise Smart:

(a) whether he has any defences to breach of trust; and

(b) whether, if he is liable to the beneficiaries, he can recover all or anything from his co-trustee Gullible.

4 Examine the decision in *Re Vickery* [1931] Ch 572. What does Maugham J say about the liability of trustees for the acts of an agent? Do you agree with his view or do you consider that trustees ought to have greater responsibility for the acts of their agents? (See Law Reform Committee 23rd Report (1982) Cmnd 87 33 para. 4 6–8; Stannard [1979] Conv. 345; Jones (1959) 22 MLR 381.

11 Personal and Proprietary Remedies against Trustees and Others

11.1 Nature of Beneficiaries' Remedies

If there is a breach of some duty by trustees the beneficiaries have rights to sue the trustees for breach of trust, as explained in Chapter 10. The beneficiaries may also have rights against other persons who have interfered, whether wittingly or unwittingly, with the trust affairs or property. The basic remedies available to the beneficiaries are designed to be restitutionary in the sense of requiring the restoration of any loss to the trust, although in some cases penal liability may be imposed upon a wrongdoer.

Unjust enrichment

There is a growing trend to associate the restitutionary remedies with the concept of 'unjust enrichment'. The leading proponents of this approach (Goff and Jones, *The Law of Restitution*, 3rd edn; and Birks, *Introduction to the Law of Restitution*) hold that there should be a coherent body of rules whereby restitution is available to prevent or reverse any unjust enrichment. For example, a trustee or stranger to the trust may have been unjustly enriched by receiving trust property; or by taking part in some fraud or dealing with trust property the trustee or stranger may have unjustly enriched himself or assisted another person in the receipt of an unjust enrichment. It should be emphasised, however, that the principle of unjust enrichment is relatively new to English law and it is possible that in some circumstances there may be no remedy even though a person may have been unjustly enriched. The notion of unjust enrichment as a cause of action has now received the recognition of the House of Lords, in *Lipkin Gorman* v. *Karpnale* [1991] 3 WLR 10. In that case a partner in a firm of solicitors wrongfully used money withdrawn from the firm's client account to finance his gambling at a casino. The casino acted innocently throughout and was not aware that it had received money stolen by the partner from the firm's account. The firm claimed restitution of the monies to the extent that they had not been repaid by the partner. Alliott J, at first instance, and the Court of Appeal had approached the question of liability from the point of view of 'knowing receipt' or 'knowing assistance' (see sections 11.3 and 11.5 below), but the House of Lords decided that once it was shown that the casino had received monies to which the firm was entitled at law the casino was liable to reimburse the firm for the reason that the casino was unjustly enriched at the expense of the firm. Lord Templeman said, 'the law imposes an obligation on the recipient of stolen money to pay an equivalent sum to the victim if the recipient has been "unjustly enriched" at the expense of the true owner'.

Enrichment by subtraction and by wrong

There are two essential categories of enriching event which may give rise to restitutionary claims and which are of assistance for the purposes of this chapter. First, a plaintiff beneficiary may claim where another person has been enriched at the expense of the beneficiary because some value has been subtracted from the beneficiary. For instance, if trust property has been mixed with a trustee's own property or if it has passed into the hands of a third party, beneficiaries may have restitutionary rights to the return of the trust property or its value. Such rights may exist even though there has been no conscious wrong done (perhaps because the property was transferred to a third party due to a mistake).

Second, a person may have been enriched as a result of a wrong done to the plaintiff beneficiary, even if there has been no subtraction of value from the beneficiary; for example, in *Boardman* v. *Phipps* [1967] 2 AC 46 (see above, section 2.4), a solicitor who had profited from a breach of fiduciary duty without causing any loss to the beneficiaries under the trust was held liable to account for his enrichment.

Claims to value received and value surviving: tracing

Where a restitutionary claim is in respect of property it may be a claim to value received or to value surviving (see Birks, *Introduction to the Law of Restitution*, p.358). In the context of a trust this means that the beneficiary might claim against a trustee or third party either the value of the property at the date that it was misapplied (the *value received* by the trustee or third party), or alternatively the value of the property at the date that the beneficiary makes a claim (the *value surviving*). The latter claim, to value surviving, is likely to be made if the property has increased in value so that it is presently worth more than when it was received by the trustee or third party. Even if the value of the property has diminished the demand for value surviving is likely to be made if the trustee or third party has become insolvent and the beneficiary wishes to make a proprietary claim, for the reasons explained under the heading

'Personal and proprietary remedies' below.

The exercise of identifying the value surviving is customarily called 'tracing'. As property passes from the trust through the hands of other persons its passage may be followed or traced. If the property is exchanged by the wrongdoer for some other property the exchange product may, at least in most cases, be treated as a substitute for the trust property. Once the destination of the property or its exchange product has been identified by tracing, the beneficiaries can seek personal or proprietary remedies as explained in section 11.4 below.

Personal and proprietary remedies

A restitutionary claim may be satisfied by a personal remedy, suing the trustee or third party for compensation, or by a proprietary remedy, procuring specific recovery of the trust property itself or, where the trust property has been exchanged for, intermingled with, or invested in other property, some other proprietary interest in that other property. Where the recipient of the property is liable, and able to pay the full value of the property whether on the basis of the value received or the value surviving, the personal remedy will be just as good as the proprietary remedy. In some circumstances, however, it will be useful to have a proprietary remedy. If, for example, the recipient of the property has become bankrupt the personal remedy against the recipient will only allow the beneficiary to prove in the recipient's bankruptcy as an unsecured creditor. If there is only enough money in the bankruptcy to pay half of the recipient's unsecured debts the beneficiary may only receive half of the amount of his or her claim. If the beneficiary is able to assert a proprietary right, to the effect that certain property is not that of the bankrupt but is that of the beneficiaries, the beneficiaries will have a right to the property itself in priority to all other creditors; and if the trustee in bankruptcy uses the property for the benefit of creditors generally, the trustee in bankruptcy may be personally liable.

It should be noted that there has been a great deal of academic debate about the precise analysis of beneficiaries' rights to trace, and in particular whether the rights are rights *in rem* (giving *rights* of recovery) or alternately personal possessory rights (where recovery *may* be ordered but there is *no right* to recovery). It is not proposed to deal with this debate in this introduction to the subject and readers who wish to investigate the theory in more depth should read Scott (1966) 7 WALR 463, 481; Pearce (1976) 40 Conv. 277; and Goode (1976) 92 LQR 360.

Proprietary claims in equity and the need for a fiduciary relationship or proprietary interest

As will be seen below, rules of law and equity differ when a proprietary claim is being made to a mixed fund including property of the claimant and property of the recipient, with the rules of equity being more flexible than the rules of law. There is authority which indicates that the rules of equity can only be relied upon when there is an equitable fiduciary relationship (*Re Hallett's Estate* (1880) 13 Ch D 696). In the context of a claim by a beneficiary against a trustee the point should give rise to no difficulty since the relationship between the parties clearly fulfils the description of an equitable fiduciary relationship. What, however, if the beneficiary is trying to trace the property into the hands of a third party? Apparently the beneficiary is able to claim so long as the third party has acquired the property from the trustee. There does not need to be a direct fiduciary relationship between beneficiary and the recipient, but only an initial fiduciary relationship between the beneficiary and the trustee. In *Re Diplock's Estate* [1947] Ch 716, in the administration of an estate there was an initial fiduciary relationship between personal representatives and next of kin. The personal representatives made wrongful distributions of property. It was held that the initial relationship between next of kin and personal representatives was sufficient to enable the next of kin to make claims against third-party recipients of property.

The requirements of a fiduciary relationship has been stretched to the limits in some cases where it is very doubtful that any fiduciary relationship existed. In *Sinclair* v. *Brougham* [1914] AC 398 depositors in a building society were held entitled to make proprietary claims in the winding-up of the society notwithstanding the fact that the relationship between them and the society would normally be regarded as simply contractual and not fiduciary. Probably the better view is simply that the claimant must prove an equitable proprietary interest. In *Chase Manhattan Bank NA* v. *Israel British Bank (London) Ltd* [1981] Ch 105 monies of the plaintiff had been paid by mistake to a New York bank and forwarded to the defendant. Although there was no fiduciary relationship in the ordinary sense between plaintiff and defendant, Goulding J held that 'A person who pays money to another under a factual mistake retains an equitable proprietary interest in it and the conscience of that other is subjected to a fiduciary duty to respect his or her proprietary right.' On this basis there should be a right to trace in equity whenever the plaintiff can prove an equitable proprietary interest; it should not be necessary otherwise to examine the relationship between plaintiff and defendant.

11.2 Claims for Breach of Trust

In Chapter 10 the beneficiaries' claims against trustees for breach of trust were considered. The trustee may be in breach by having misappropriated trust property, or by breach of some duty or wrongful exercise of a power. In a case involving misappropriation, the legal title to the property will have passed (since that would have been vested in the trustees by the terms of the trust), but the equitable proprietary interest remains with the beneficiaries who, accordingly, can pursue a personal remedy for restitution in the measure of value received or surviving, or may seek restitution by way of a proprietary remedy against the trustee or third party.

Personal claims

The general rule is that the remedy for the trustee's breach of trust is to compensate the trust fund for the loss sustained. This may be achieved by requiring restitution in either measure of value received or surviving. In other cases the remedy is in damages for the loss caused to the trust by the breach.

Breaches relating to investment

Many breaches by trustees involve improper dealings with investments. The basic rule is that if the trustees have failed to invest the beneficiaries are entitled to a remedy in damages equal to interest which could have been earned if the trustees had acted properly; the normal measure will be that the trustee will be liable to pay interest upon the trust fund which has been left dormant (*Shepherd* v. *Mouls* (1845) 4 Hare 500).

If trust monies have been used for unauthorised investments, the beneficiaries are entitled to damages in the measure of reinstatement of the fund together with interest. The recent approach of the courts is to bring the rate of interest into line with commercial rates, so that a rate at a percentage above bank base rate is paid. The trustee is not normally made subject to penal damages, but if a trustee has been fraudulent the court may express its displeasure by increasing the amount of interest payable by the trustee.

In some cases the beneficiaries may elect to take something other than interest. If, for example, the trustees have made an unauthorised investment which has increased in value, the beneficiaries may opt to adopt the unauthorised investment (*Re Patten* (1883) 52 LJ Ch 787); in other words, to have restitution in the measure of value surviving. If the trustees sell an investment which they were not authorised to sell the beneficiaries may choose to sue for an amount which would represent the present value of the investments which have been sold (*Re Bell's Indenture* [1980] 1 WLR 1217).

Other breaches

In the case of other breaches, such as misapplication of trust money, the trustee must replace the money with interest. If the trustee has used the money in his or her own business he or she may be liable to pay compound interest. Similarly in cases of fraud the trustee may be liable to compound interest or an increase in the rate of interest, as the court decides.

Proprietary claims: unmixed property

Normally trustees will keep trust property separate from their own and in such a way that it is quite clear that the property is trust property. Trust monies, for instance, will be kept in a separate trust account. Other property, such as land, will have title documentation which shows that the property is the subject-matter of a trust. In such cases there is no difficulty for the beneficiaries in making a proprietary claim. This is so even if the trustee or other wrongdoer has converted the property into some other form (e.g., by using trust money to acquire land, company shares or other property). The common law and equity have long held that an owner of an interest in property may trace it into the hands of a third party and into a product for which the property was exchanged. The most cited authority is that of *Taylor* v. *Plumer* (1815) 3 M&S 562, in which case Sir Thomas Plumer entrusted a stockbroker, Walsh, to purchase bonds on his behalf. Walsh instead bought American investments and bullion with the intention of boarding a boat for America. Walsh was, however, apprehended and the investments and bullion were seized and returned to Sir Thomas Plumer. On Walsh's bankruptcy his trustees sought to recover the bullion and investments from Plumer. It was held that the investments and bullion were the ascertainable product of Plumer's money and were owned by him. Lord Ellenborough emphasised:

> It makes no difference in reason or law into what other form, different from the original, the change may have been made, whether it be into that of promissory notes for the security of the money which was produced by the sale of the goods of the principal . . . or into other merchandise, . . . for the product of or substitute for the original thing still follows the nature of the thing itself, as long as it can be ascertained to be such, and the right only ceases when the means of ascertainment fail, which is the case when the subject is turned into money, and mixed and confounded in a general mass of the same description.

The right of a beneficiary to trace into the 'exchange product' extends not only to an exchange of physical assets such as coins, grain or oil, but also to exchanges involving choses in action, such as bank-notes and bills of exchange. It has recently been suggested that if the common law has to be relied upon (which should not be the case where there is a trust) monies cannot be traced when they are transferred by telegraphic transfer (see Millett J in *Agip (Africa) Ltd* v. *Jackson* [1990] Ch 265 affirmed by the Court of Appeal at [1991] 3 WLR 116), on the ground that the common law 'can only follow a physical asset such as a cheque or its proceeds, from one person to another. It can follow money but not a chose in action.' It is submitted that the reasoning of his Lordship is muddied and that there is no fundamental reason why a transfer of monies by telegraphic means cannot be traced (although there may be problems of mixing: see below). His Lordship is wrong in so far as he may be regarding the rights in a cheque to be physical. A cheque is merely written evidence of a debt; and evidence of a debt created by electronic means should be just as good as that created when molecules of ink attach to paper. Further, it is quite clear that a chose in action can be traced at common law, and into any exchange product (see Lord Goff in *Lipkin Gorman* v. *Karpnale* [1991] 3 WLR 10, 29).

Proprietary claims: mixed funds

The closing words of Lord Ellenborough's statement above refer to the difficulty which arises when the trustee mixes the trust property with his own. In such circumstances it is no longer possible clearly to identify which is the trust property; for instance, if the trustee has deposited trust money to the credit of his personal bank account in which he already has money of his own. Due to the impossibility of ascertainment on such occasions the common law, according to most commentators (but see Goode (1976) 92 LQR 360, Pearce [1976] Conv. 277, Khurshid and Matthews (1979) 95 LQR 78), would not permit tracing into the mixture. The rule was recently recognised by the House of Lords in *Lipkin Gorman* v. *Karpnale* [1991] 3 WLR 10, although the restriction on tracing at common law was considered only to bar a proprietary claim and not a personal claim for money had and received. In other words, so long as it can be shown that a person has recieved money, it can be 'traced' in the sense that it is identified as having been received by the recipient, and a personal claim may be made against the recipient to prevent his or her unjust enrichment, but if the money is mixed with other money the claimant cannot establish a proprietary right to it.

Although the rules of common law might restrict tracing in some cases of admixture, as far as a trust is concerned the rules of equity are not so restricted and will allow beneficiaries to identify the value surviving and continuing proprietary right of the beneficiaries even though the trust property has been mixed with that of a third party. As Atkin LJ explained in *Banque Belge pour L'Etrange* v. *Hambrouck* [1921] 1 KB 321, 'The question always was, had the means of ascertainment failed? But if in 1815 [the date of *Taylor* v. *Plumer*] the common law halted outside the banker's door, by 1879 equity had the courage to lift the latch, walk in and examine the books: Re Hallet's Estate.' Once the trust property has been 'traced' into the mixed fund there may be several alternative proprietary remedies (explained below) available to the beneficiary.

First charge over the mixed fund

Although in equity, trust property which is mixed with that of a trustee or third party is no more capable of identification than it is in common law, equity will allow the beneficiaries' claim over a mixed fund to prevail over that of a trustee who has wrongfully mixed trust property with his own. In many cases it is possible to distinguish the separate contributions of the trustee and beneficiary to the admixture, and in terms of the monetary value of the respective contributions. In such cases the primary remedy of the beneficiary is to have a first charge on the mixed fund or any property purchased with it. If the mixed fund is of money it is treated as security for the repayment of the trust money. If the fund decreases in value the charge is unaffected and the claim of the beneficiaries must prevail over that of the trustee's irrespective of the fact that the trustee also contributed to the mixed fund. The facts of *Re Oatway* [1903] 2 Ch 356 provide a good example of the remedy. Many students misunderstand the effect of the charge. A clear understanding of *Re Oatway* will avoid such misunderstanding. Trust money of £3000 was mixed in an account with the trustee's own money. At a time when the balance exceeded £5137 the trustee purchased shares to the value of £2137. Later the money in the account was dissipated and the beneficiaries and the trustee's personal representatives contested the ownership of the shares. Although it could be argued that at the time of the purchase there were £3000 of trust money in the account and £2137 of the trustee's own money, it was decided that the shares were not owned by the respective parties in such proportions. The trust had a charge over the mixed fund and the shares for repayment of the £3000 trust money, and until this was repaid to the trust the trustee could not assert any claim to a proportion of the mixed fund or the shares which were purchased with the mixed fund. Thus the trust had a charge for repayment of £3000 over the shares purchased for £2137, and the trust could enforce the charge by obtaining an order for the sale of the shares, and the proceeds (up to a maximum of £3000) could be claimed by the trust.

Example: A trustee has £5000 of his own money in his personal bank account. He wrongly pays into the account £5000 trust money, to make a balance of £10 000. He then spends £5000 on shares and later spends the remaining £5000 on a holiday.

Bank Account	Trust	Trustee	Balance
Initial balance	£0	£5 000	£5 000
Payment in of £5000 trust money	£5 000	£5 000	£10 000
Purchase of shares and holiday	£0	£0	£0

Despite the fact that the shares were bought at a time when there was enough of the trustee's own money to buy them, the beneficiaries will be entitled to a first charge over the shares so that they can be sold and the proceeds of sale used to repay the beneficiaries, in full if they are of sufficient value, or in part if they have decreased in value.

First charge over all of the trustee's assets?

It has been said that the beneficiaries' rights extend not only to a charge over the mixed fund itself, but also over the whole of the trustee's assets on the basis that the trustee has mixed trust property with his own and that his assets should therefore be subject to a general floating charge until repayment of the monies (Lord Templeman in *Space Investments Ltd* v. *Canadian Imperial Bank of Commerce Trust Co. (Bahamas) Ltd* [1986] 1 WLR 1072). Hanbury and Maudsley (13th edn, p.630) suggest that such a view would be unfair to the general creditors of the trustee.

Claim to the entire admixture

The onus is upon the trustee to prove which part of the admixture belongs to him, and in so far as he is unable to do so equity will allow the beneficiaries to claim the property for themselves. In *Lupton* v. *White* (1805) 15 Ves 432, the defendant had mixed an unascertainable amount of the plaintiff's lead ore with his own. Lord Eldon held that:

> if a man, having undertaken to keep the property of another distinct, mixed it with his own, the whole must both at law and in equity be taken to be the property of the other until the former puts the subject under such circumstances, that it may be distinguished as satisfactorily, as it might have been before that unauthorized mixture upon his part.

It will be rare that the beneficiary will actually be able to claim the entire property since, if the extent of the contribution is clear, it would be unjust to allow the beneficiary to claim the whole and he may instead have a first charge over the admixture or may be regarded as tenant in common of the mixture (*Indian Oil Corporation Ltd* v. *Greenstone Shipping Co. SA (Panama)* [1987] 3 WLR 869).

Proportionate shares: increases in value of the mixed fund

Sometimes the beneficiaries' primary remedy of a charge over the mixed fund may be considered less than adequate. If the fund has increased in value and it is apparent that a profit will be made by it, it would be against principle to limit the beneficiaries' claim to a charge for the amount of trust money originally utilised whilst permitting the defaulting wrongdoer to retain the profits for himself. Although the point remains a moot one, the commentators strongly argue that 'the appropriate remedy in such a situation is to allow the beneficiary to claim, if he wishes, a share of the fund in the proportion which the original trust funds bore to the mixed fund at the time of the mixing' (Hanbury and Maudsley, p.638; and see *Re Tilley's WT* [1967] Ch 1179 and *Indian Oil Corporation Ltd* v. *Greenstone Shipping Co. SA (Panama)* [1987] 3 WLR 869). It is submitted that there is merit in this view but that there is a further argument that if the wrongdoer has acted in a clear breach of duty he should be held accountable for all profits received by him and should not be allowed a proportionate share of the profit made in breach of trust and partly by use of the trust monies. This is the normal rule where there is a breach of the wrongdoer's fiduciary duty (see *Boardman* v. *Phipps* [1967] 2 AC 46).

Special rules for current bank accounts

Special rules apply when the mixing occurs in a current bank account, and the claim is to the balance of monies remaining in the account, probably once the trustee has become bankrupt. The basic rule is, of course, that the beneficiary has a first charge over the bank account for the repayment of the trust monies. Where, however, there have been withdrawals and payments in there are two special rules. First, any withdrawal by the trustee for his own purposes is deemed to be a withdrawal of his own money. Although this has been justified for the reason that it should be presumed that the trustee has not acted in breach of trust (*Re Hallett's Estate* (1880) 13 Ch D 696), the main effect (and probably reason) for the presumption is that the beneficiaries' claim is not reduced by such withdrawals. The second rule peculiar to current bank accounts is that any payment in of the trustee's own money is to be credited to the trustee and not appropriated to the trust to make good any deficiency in trust money (*Roscoe* v. *Winder* [1915] 1 Ch 62). The combined effect of these rules is often described in terms that the beneficiaries' claim is to the lowest intermediate balance in the account.

Example: Suppose a trustee has £500 of his own money in a personal current bank account and he then pays into the account £500 of trust money. Later he withdraws £600 to purchase company shares. £500 of the withdrawal is assumed to be his own money under the rule in *Re Hallett*; the other £100 will of course be trust money and the £400 remaining in the account is deemed to be trust money. If the trustee then pays in £100 of his own money it is not deemed to replace the £100 deficiency in trust money and accordingly the intermediate balance of £400 is the limit of the beneficiaries' claim.

Bank Account	Trust	Trustee	Balance
Initial balance	£0	£500	£500
Payment in of £500 trust money	£500	£500	£1000
Withdraws £600 for shares	£400	£0	£400
Pays in £100 own money	£400	£100	£500

Property purchased with the mixed fund

It should be noted that the rules are only adopted for the purpose of analysing the claim to the remaining balance and they do not prevent the normal rules from operating in respect of property purchased with the mixed fund. Returning to the example above, the beneficiaries would have a charge over the shares purchased with the mixed fund to secure the repayment of the £500 trust money, notwithstanding the fact that employment of the special rules might indicate that only £100 of trust money could have been used in the purchase of the shares (see *Re Oatway* above).

Mixing of two trust funds

If the trustee pays money from two trust funds into his own account the two categories of claimant do not share rateably but the rule in *Clayton's Case* (1816) 1 Mer 572, is applied so that the first payment into the account is deemed to be the first payment out.

Example: Suppose a trustee, T, has £1 in her own bank account and then pays in £399 belonging to trust A, and then £400 belonging to trust B. T then withdraws £400 which is spent on living expenses, thus leaving £400 in the account. It is assumed that the £400 withdrawn represents the first moneys paid in (i.e., the £1 of her money (on the basis of *Re Hallet*) and the £399 of trust A's money (on the basis of Clayton's Case). The £400 remaining in the account belongs to trust B, with the result that trust A bears the loss £399.

Goff and Jones (*The Law of Restitution*) criticise this application of Clayton's Case:

> If an active banking account contains a mixed fund composed of the moneys of beneficiaries under two different trusts, any loss as between the two trusts is borne in accordance with the arbitrary rule in

Clayton's Case, namely, first in first out, which was conceived to apply as between a banker and his customer. Judge Learned Hand condemned this particular manifestation of the rule in the following words: 'There is no reason in law or justice why [the fiduciary's] depredations upon the funds should not be borne equally between them. To throw all the loss upon one through the mere chance of his being earlier in time, is irrational and arbitrary and is equally a fiction as the rule in Clayton's Case. When the law attempts a fiction, it is, or at least it should be, for some purpose of justice. To adopt it here is to apportion a common misfortune through a test which has no relation whatever to the justice of the case.' This denunciation is, in our view, most convincing. The loss should be borne *pari passu*. Both groups of beneficiaries can show an equitable title to the mixed fund; accordingly they should share it rateably according to their contributions.

11.3   Persons in Knowing Receipt of Trust Property/ Trustee *de son tort*

A distinction needs to be drawn between a trustee de son tort and other persons in knowing receipt of trust property.

Trustee *de son tort*

The term 'trustee *de son tort*' has been used in different ways. It is here used in the meaning adopted by A.L. Smith LJ in *Mara* v. *Brown* [1896] 1 Ch 199 as someone who, although not appointed as a trustee and who also has no authority from a trustee, nevertheless takes it upon himself to intermeddle with trust affairs or to do other acts which are characteristic of the office of a trustee. In so doing, such a person makes himself a trustee of 'his own wrong' and as such a constructive trustee. A trustee *de son tort* is therefore in effect someone who positively assumes the role of a trustee. In *Selangor United Rubber Estates* v. *Craddock (No 3)* [1968] 2 ALL ER 1073 Ungoed-Thomas J said that the distinguishing features of a trustee *de son tort* included (a) that he did not claim to act in his own right but for the beneficiaries' and (b) that his assumption to act is not of itself a ground of liability but merely creates the liability to account in respect of the property over which he has assumed the duties of trustee. Thus a trustee *de son tort*'s status as constructive trustee precedes the event which becomes the subject of the claim against him. Once it is established that a person is a trustee *de son tort* it is irrelevant to the question of liability that he may be well intentioned and act honestly (*Lyell* v. *Kennedy* (1889) 14 App Cas 437). All that is required is to establish that the trust property is vested in him or is under his control to such an extent that he could require it to be vested in him (*Re Barney* [1892] 2 Ch 265).

Knowing receipt or dealing

Knowing receipt or dealing arises where a person:

(a) knowingly receives trust property in breach of trust: or

(b) receives trust property other than as a bona fide purchaser for value but subsequently becomes aware that it is trust property and then deals with it in a manner inconsistent with the trust; or

(c) receives trust property without a breach of trust, but knowing that it is trust property and subsequently deals with it in a manner which is inconsistent with the trust.

In *Agip (Africa) Limited* v. *Jackson* [1990] Ch 265, at first instance Millett J expressed the view that a vital characteristic of a person falling within the 'knowing receipt or dealing' category is that the person has received the property for his own use or benefit. He subsequently elaborated upon this in an article ('Tracing the proceeds of fraud' (1991) 107 LQR 71), saying that the party must receive the property 'in the sense of setting up his own title to it'; someone who has merely handled property (e.g., as an agent, nominee or trustee) can only be liable to account on the ground of 'knowing assistance' (see section 11.5 below). It is very important to distinguish clearly between cases of 'knowing receipt or dealing' and 'knowing assistance' as the bases and circumstances of liability are very different.

It should be noted that it is not necessary in cases of either 'knowing receipt or dealing' or 'knowing assistance' to establish a formal trust. Directors of limited companies, for example, by reason of their fiduciary duties are treated as though they are trustees of the company funds which come into their hands or under their control. Consequently, if a director misapplies company funds he commits a breach of trust. If the fund then falls into the hands of someone who receives them with knowledge of the breach, that person becomes a constructive trustee of the misapplied funds. An example of knowing receipt or dealing is seen in *Belmont Finance Corporation* v. *Williams Furniture Limited (No 2)* [1980] 1 All ER 393. This involved an arrangement to finance and acquire a company (Belmont Finance Corporation) which not only involved a breach of fiduciary duty by Belmont's directors but was also unlawful under what was then s.54 Companies Act 1948. Williams Furniture Limited, the defendant company, owned all the shares in CIF Limited, which in turn owned all the shares in Belmont. Grosscurth and two others, who between them owned all the shares in another company (MF Ltd), wished to acquire Belmont Finance Corporation but needed finance.

Grosscurth, therefore, proposed to finance the purchase by selling MF Ltd to Belmont. It was agreed that Belmont would buy all the shares in MF Ltd for a sum grossly in excess of their value and that Grosscurth, the Chairman of MF Ltd, would buy all the shares held by CIF Limited in Belmont (see Figure 11.1).

Belmont was subsequently declared insolvent, and the receiver sought to recover from CIF Limited and its directors £489 000 which CIF had received from the sale of the Belmont shares, on the ground that they were in breach of fiduciary duty. The Court of Appeal held that CIF Limited was a constructive trustee of the proceeds of sale because the payment to Grosscurth for the MF Ltd shares was a misapplication of company funds. CIF Limited and its directors were liable because they had received the money knowing all the circumstances of the transaction, including the breach of trust by the directors of Belmont Finance Corporation in purchasing MF Ltd at a greatly inflated price, against Belmont's best interests.

In the case of 'knowing receipt or dealing' liability is as a constructive trustee. Liability does not depend upon proof of an intention to do wrong (no dishonesty was established in the Belmont case) or on proof of acquisition of some personal advantage or unjust enrichment. Liability in categories (a) and (c) cited above arises out of the very receipt of the trust property, and in category (b) it arises from the date of notice that the property is trust property. It seems that it is not necessary to pove that the stranger has knowledge of the precise facts which establish the breach of trust. In *Nelson* v. *Larholt* [1948] 1 KB 339, an executor of a will issued eight successive cheques to the defendant, who cashed them in good faith. The defendant was, nevertheless, held liable as a constructive trustee as the reasonable man would have been put on enquiry as to whether a breach of trust was involved in these circumstances. It was therefore irrelevant that the defendant had no actual knowledge of the breach of trust.

The main difficulty in 'knowing receipt or dealing' cases has been as to

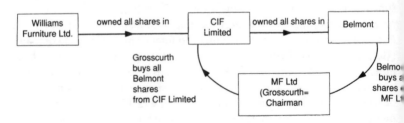

Figure 11.1

the nature or type of the knowledge sufficient in order for a constructive trust to arise.

In *Baden, Delvaux et Lecuit* v. *Société Générale pour Favoriser le Développement du Commerce et L'Industrie en France* SA [1983] BCLC 325 (on the facts, a case of 'knowing assistance' rather than 'knowing receipt': see section 11.5), Peter Gibson J identified five mental states which he considered would be sufficient knowledge to give rise to liability:

(a) actual knowledge;
(b) wilfully shutting one's eyes to the obvious;
(c) wilfully and recklessly failing to make such enquiries as an honest and reasonable man would make;
(d) knowledge of circumstances which would indicate the facts to an honest and reasonable man; and
(e) knowledge of circumstances which would put an honest and reasonable man on enquiry.

According to Peter Gibson J, a person within category (b) or (c) will be taken to have actual knowledge, whilst a person in category (d) or (e), will be regarded as having constructive knowledge. In *Re Montagu's ST* [1987] Ch 264, Megarry V-C took the view that only knowledge within categories (a)–(c), as outlined in the Baden Delvaux case, would be sufficient to found a case of 'knowing receipt or dealing'. (For criticism of this view see Harpum (1987) 50 MLR 217.) This view was also taken by the Court of Appeal in *Lipkin Gorman* v. *Karpnale Ltd* [1989] 1 WLR 1340 (NB: on appeal to the House of Lords the case was not approached from the point of view of either 'knowing receipt' or 'knowing assistance'). However, in *Agip (Africa) Ltd* v. *Jackson* (see above), without expressing a final view on the matter, Millet J suggested that constructive knowledge (categories (d) and (e)) would also be sufficient in cases of 'knowing receipt or dealing'. The reason he gave for this is that liability arising out of 'knowing receipt or dealing' is not 'fault-based' but is 'receipt-based'. He went on to express the view that: 'Tracing claims and cases of "knowing receipt" are both concerned with rights of priority in relation to property taken by a legal owner for his own benefit.'

However, in the more recent decision of *Eagle Trust plc* v. *SBC Securities Ltd*, *The Times*, 14 February 1991, Vinelott J reverted to the view taken in *Re Montagu's ST* and *Lipkin Gorman*, holding that only actual knowledge (i.e., categories (a)–(c) of the Baden Delvaux classification) was sufficient to give rise to a constructive trust on the grounds of 'knowing receipt or dealing'. The statement is, nevertheless, made *obiter dicta*, as on the facts it is a case of 'knowing assistance'. It is submitted that Millet's view is to be preferred (see further Millet (1991)

LQR 71). It is also in line with the view of the Court of Appeal in *Belmont Finance Corporation* v. *Williams Furniture Ltd (No 2)*.

A further issue relating to the nature of the knowledge required for 'knowing receipt or dealing' to arise out of *Re Montagu's ST* was whether knowledge could be imputed to a principal where the agent had the requisite degree of knowledge. Megarry v-c doubted whether this was so. In 1923 the future 10th Duke of Manchester had assigned certain chattels to which he was entitled in remainder on the death of the 9th Duke to trustees on trust on the death of the 9th Duke to select such chattels as they thought fit for inclusion in the family settlement and to hold the remainder, if any, for the 10th Duke absolutely. The 9th Duke died in 1947 but no selection of chattels was ever made by the trustees. The chattels were therefore released to the 10th Duke, and the Duke's solicitor (who had at one time known of the clause relating to the chattels) informed him that he was free to sell the chattels. The 10th Duke died in 1977 and the 11th Duke claimed, among other things, that the 10th Duke was a constructive trustee of the chattels, as he had knowingly received trust property in breach of trust. Megarry v-c made two significant points. First, a person is not to be taken to have knowledge of facts which he once knew, but has genuinely forgotten about at the time in question; and second, a donee or beneficiary of property will not be fixed with all the knowledge his solicitor had provided that he has not employed the solicitor to investigate his claim to property and has done nothing else which can be treated as accepting the solicitor's knowledge as his own.

The judicial precedents discussed above must now be considered in the light of the recent decision of the House of Lords in *Lipkin Gorman* v. *Karpnale* [1991] 3 WLR 10 (see section 11.1 above), concerning the receipt by a casino of monies misappropriated by a solicitor from his firm's client account. In the House of Lords the action proved successful on the basis that the casino had received money to which the solicitors had title at common law and the casino should not be unjustly enriched at the expense of the claimants. This approach, if expanded upon, may lead to the previous case law becoming largely redundant.

Remedies available

It would appear that the extent of liability is similar for both the express trustee and the third-party intermeddler becoming constructive trustee. Just as an express trustee may be liable in damages for breach of trust, the intermeddler may be liable in tort (*Belmont Finance Corporation* v. *Williams Furniture (No 2)* [1980] 1 All ER 393), presumably in fraud or conversion, and may be made to pay damages with simple or compound interest. Alternatively the intermeddler may be liable to make good the loss to the trust in the restitutionary measures, and the personal or proprietary remedy may be chosen as is convenient (see section 11.2 above).

11.4 Claims for Breach of Fiduciary Duty

In Chapters 2 and 9 it was explained that a trustee or other person in a fiduciary position is not normally permitted to take advantage of that position by making some personal profit. If a trustee does profit from his or her position there is strict liability and the beneficiaries have a cause of action irrespective of whether the trustee acted honestly or not. Although there is a clear cause of action it is not obvious what remedies are available to the beneficiaries.

Personal remedies

Any profits arising in the course of administration of the trust belong more properly to the trust rather than the trustee, who is not permitted any profit beyond that which the terms of the trust allow. If, therefore, a trustee seeks to retain an unauthorised profit, this amounts to unjust enrichment of the trustee at the expense of the beneficiaries, and in order to undo or prevent such unjust enrichment equity allows the beneficiaries the right to require restitution of the amount to them, and they clearly have a personal remedy for such restitution, requiring the trustee to account to them on a personal basis for the value of the property received.

As an alternative to the restitutionary claim the beneficiaries may find that in some circumstances an action for damages for fraud or breach of trust will enable them to claim a higher amount. In *Maheson* v. *Malaysia Housing Society* [1978] 2 WLR 444, Maheson was an agent employed to buy land. The land found by him was worth $456 000 but he colluded with the vendor to inflate the price to $944 000, $122 000 of which Maheson would receive by way of bribe. It was held that the plaintiff government department could either claim the $122 000 bribe as money had and received, or damages of $443 000 for loss suffered. Damages for loss suffered may in an appropriate case include either simple or compound interest (*Wallersteiner* v. *Moir (No 2)* [1975] QB 373).

Proprietary claims

Whether the beneficiaries have a proprietary interest in the profit made is a much more difficult question. The answer may to some extent depend upon the source of the profit.

Profit from the trust itself

A recent authority indicates that if the profit came directly from the trust itself, the claim is proprietary, presumably because the property was originally trust property and it has been improperly acquired by the trustee or other person owing fiduciary duties to the trust. This sort of situation is analogous to that where a person is in knowing receipt of trust property. In *Guinness Plc* v. *Saunders* [1990] 2 AC 663, a company director received a payment from the company (to whom he owed a fiduciary duty) in connection with a contract in which he had a personal interest. It was held that the failure of the director to make disclosure to a meeting of the full board of directors of his interest rendered him liable to repay the remuneration paid to him by the company under the contract. In the company's action for restitution it was held that the director could not maintain a cross-claim for reasonable payment for work done (a 'quantum meruit') for work done by him because he 'held the money as a constructive trustee for [the company]. The existence of some cross-claim for a quantum meruit or allowance did not impeach or determine that trust.'

It is likely that in other cases where the breach of duty includes the receipt of property from the trust or the beneficiary there will be a proprietary claim: for example, if a trustee purchases trust property or the beneficial interest of a beneficiary. *Hill* v. *Langley*, *The Times* 28 January 1988, is a case of the latter description in which a trustee had purchased a beneficiary's interest. Although the trustee had subsequently sold the interest on to a bona fide purchaser it was held that the beneficiary could trace into the proceeds of sale in the trustee's hands.

Profit from use of trust property

Recently commentators have argued that there should only be a proprietary right if the profit derives from the use of trust property (see Hanbury and Maudsley, p.578), whereas if trust property has not been used and the profit derives from an outside source only there should be personal accountability.

Although the distinction between profits arising directly from trust property and profits arising from an outside source can no doubt be made, it is suggested that there is little to recommend the distinction, which may be criticised on at least two grounds. First, if a proprietary right is to be available wherever trust property has been used to make a profit, it might be argued that information acquired by the fiduciary from his position is trust property. If so, there will be few, if any, cases where a proprietary right in the profit does not exist. The idea that information may be trust property was accepted in *Boardman* v. *Phipps* [1967] 2 AC 46. A second criticism which might be levied at the distinction made between profits arising from trust property and other profits is that in either case there may be no loss to the beneficiaries, so that the technical distinction might make no practical difference (see further Gearty (1986) 45 CLJ 367 and Martin [1987] Conv. 209).

Profits from outside sources

Some authority suggests that if the profit comes from an outside source the liability will be a personal liability to account only. In *Lister & Co.* v. *Stubbs* (1890) 45 Ch D 1, an agent had secretly received commissions from parties with whom he was dealing for his principal. He had converted some of the commissions into investments and land. In the course of proceedings against him by his principal it was sought to obtain injunctions to prevent him from dealing with the property. It was held that his liability was a personal liability to account only and that no order could be made against the property itself, since the commissions were never property of the principal.

Whether the analysis in *Lister* v. *Stubbs* is correct is debatable. It does not necessarily follow that property deriving from an outside source cannot be the subject of a trust. In the case of an express trust, a situation might arise where profits are made on trust investments, or on the carrying on of some business or transaction by the trustees for the trust. It is quite clear that such profits are, on receipt by the trustees, held upon trust for the beneficiaries, even though previously they were never trust property. It can, it is submitted, be strongly argued that a trustee should have no better right to retain an unauthorised profit than he would have to retain a profit made in the normal course of the trust's dealings, and that the fact that the profit derives from an outside source is not in itself a bar to a proprietary claim (the student should see also Goff and Jones, *The Law of Restitution*, 3rd edn, p.657).

Effect of dishonesty

It was explained earlier (Chapter 2 and Chapter 9) that there might be breach of fiduciary duty irrespective of whether the trustee or other fiduciary acts honestly or dishonestly. Although it is well established that liability exists irrespective of honesty it has been argued that the extent of liability should vary according to whether the breach is an honest one or a dishonest one, so that an honest fiduciary should be liable to account personally whilst a dishonest fiduciary should be subject to a proprietary claim by way of constructive trust (Jones (1968) LQR 472). It is suggested that the idea that a dishonest breach should be 'penalised' by a constructive trust is emotional and illogical. If the person in breach has enough money to satisfy the claim it matters little whether liability is personal or proprietary, at least so long as any personal claim can be made in both measures of value received and value surviving (before any subsequent dissipation of the property). If the trustee in breach of duty is bankrupt the competition will be between the beneficiaries and the other creditors of the trustee. In these circumstances it is submitted that if there has been no subtraction of value from the trust there is no reason why the beneficiaries should not rank equally with the other creditors.

Effect of honesty and admixture of effort

As explained in Chapters 2 and 9, a person in breach of fiduciary duty is liable even though there was no dishonesty. Even if the 'wrongdoer' invested his or her own money and effort he or she is liable to account for the profits received. In these circumstances, however, the courts are willing to show some flexibility and the fiduciary may be able to claim an indemnity for expenses and remuneration for the effort involved. In section 2.4 the case of *Boardman* v. *Phipps* [1967] 2 AC 46 was explained; it will be recalled that a solicitor had, in breach of his fiduciary duty to the trust, taken advantage of an opportunity to re-organise a company in which the trust had a large shareholding. He had invested his own money and time to improve the financial position of the company. Although he was held liable to account for the profit which he had made, the court resolved that he should receive generous remuneration for work done.

Comment

Some of the situations studied above might lead to an alternative hypothesis for determining whether a claim is to be personal or propriet-ary. There would be some justice in recognising a proprietary right where the profit derives from the trust and represents a subtraction in value from the trust, as in *Guinness Plc* v. *Saunders* (above), whilst allowing a personal remedy in account only if the profit derives from some other source and there is no subtraction of value from the trust, as in *Lister* v. *Stubbs* and *Boardman* v. *Phipps* [1967] 2 AC 46.

11.5 **Persons Knowingly Assisting in a Fraudulent Design**

'Knowing assistance' occurs where a person knowingly assists in a fraudulent design on the part of the trustees or other fiduciaries, even though no part of the trust property may ever have come into his or her hands and without such person purporting to act as a trustee. Here the liability is 'fault-based' and not 'receipt-based' as with 'knowing receipt or dealing' (see section 11.3 above). In *Baden, Delvaux et Lecuit* v. *Société Générale Pour Favoriser Le Développement du Commerce et L'industrie en France SA* [1983] BCLC 325, Peter Gibson J expressed the view that this categorisation of 'intermeddler' is equally applicable to a stranger who does receive trust property, and in *Agip (Africa) Ltd* v. *Jackson* [1990] Ch 265, Millett J thought that a case of 'knowing assistance would arise, as opposed to 'knowing receipt or dealing' where a person received trust property in breach of trust, but not for their own benefit.

Where in a case of 'knowing assistance' the stranger does not receive any trust property, it would seem incorrect to describe him or her as a constructive trustee, as in order for a constructive trust to arise there needs to be trust property.

In the Baden Delvaux case Peter Gibson J set down four elements which must be present in order to succeed on the ground of 'knowing assistance'. He went on to say that although it was useful to isolate the various elements, at the end of the day the court must be satisfied that the stranger was a party or privy to dishonesty on the part of the trustee. In *Lipkin Gorman* v. *Karpnale Ltd* [1979] 1 WLR 1340, Alliott J put it another way when he said that 'want of probity is a key aspect in the approach the court should take'. The four elements cited by Peter Gibson J as being necessary to establish 'knowing assistance' are:

(a) the existence of a trust. As with cases of 'knowing receipt or dealing' this is not confined to a formal trust. It is enough that there is a fiduciary relationship between the 'trustee' and the property of the other person; and

(b) the existence of a fraudulent and dishonest design on the part of the trustees of the trust. In *Selangor United Rubber Estates Limited* v. *Craddock (No 3)* [1968] 2 All ER 1073, Ungoed-Thomas J expressed the view that there is no difference in the meaning of 'fraudulent' or 'dishonest' in the context. The Court of Appeal in *Belmont Finance Corporation Limited* v. *Williams Furniture Limited* said that the requirement should not be extended to fall short of actual dishonesty on the part of the trustees; and

(c) the assistance of the stranger in the design (the assistance of the stranger in the design is purely a question of fact); and

(d) knowledge on the part of the stranger.

The question of knowledge needs to be examined more closely. There are two issues: (a) what must the stranger know (i.e., the extent of the knowledge); and (b) what is the nature of the knowledge necessary? With regard to the extent of the knowledge there is very little authority. It seems the stranger must know of the trust, and of the fraudulent and dishonest design, although he or she need not know every detail of the precise nature of the fraud (*Agip (Africa) Limited* v. *Jackson*). Furthermore, the relevant knowledge must relate to facts and not merely allegations (see *Carl-Zeiss-Stiftung v. Herbert Smith (No 2)* [1979] 2 Ch 276).

As to the nature of the knowledge required, it is necessary to refer to the five mental states identified by Peter Gibson J in the Baden Delvaux case (see section 11.3 above). The greater weight of authority establishes that actual knowledge (i.e., categories (a)–(c)) will only suffice for 'knowing assistance' cases. In many decisions the view has been taken that the nature of the 'knowledge required' is, and should be, the same for cases of 'knowing receipt or dealing' and 'knowing assistance'. However, in *Agip (Africa) Limited v. Jackson*, Millet J considered that this view is mistaken, as the basis of liability in 'knowing receipt or dealing' cases differs from that of cases of 'knowing assistance'. 'Knowing receipt or dealing' cases are concerned with rights of priority in relation to property taken by a legal owner for his own benefit, whereas 'knowing assistance' cases are concerned with fraud. In the words of Millet J (p.1389): 'Although dishonest furtherance of a dishonest scheme is a sound basis of liability, negligent but honest failure to appreciate that someone else's scheme is fraudulent, is not.' Nevertheless he did not appear to rule out categories (d) and (e) of the Baden Delvaux classification as being insufficient to found an action on the basis of 'knowing assistance' as he says: 'I gratefully adopt the [Baden] classification but would warn against over refinement or a too ready assumption that categories [d] or [e] are necessarily cases of constructive notice only. The true distinction is between honesty and dishonesty.' Similarly, Fox LJ on appeal [1991] 3 WLR 116 seemed to accept that, whilst dishonesty was a requirement in 'knowing assistance' cases, any of the five mental states identified in the Baden Delvaux case would be sufficient.

Remedies available

It is clear that the person who knowingly assists in a fraudulent design is liable in a personal action to make restitution personally. Although such a person is described as a constructive trustee there is no trust property of which he or she is in possession. Whereas cases of 'knowing receipt' are concerned with rights of priority in relation to property (see above) 'cases of "knowing assistance" are concerned with the furtherance of fraud' according to Millet J at first instance in *Agip (Africa) Ltd v. Jackson* [1990] Ch 265. Such a person is not, strictly speaking, a trustee since there is no property to be the subject-matter of a trust, but since a person is liable to account in respect of the fraud as though he or she were a trustee.

However, the cause of action is in tort rather than breach of trust, and the relevant torts where several persons have assisted knowingly in a fraudulent design are probably fraud and conspiracy (*Belmont Finance*

Corporation v. *Williams Furniture (No 2)* [1980] 1 All ER 393). The primary remedy in damages will include simple interest, and in an appropriate case the wrongdoer may be made liable to compound interest (*Wallersteiner* v. *Moir (No 2)* [1975] QB 373).

Of course the restitutionary remedy of account is also available, but whether proprietary remedies are available is unclear. Such persons have not received trust property, but they may have made profits from their fraud, in which case it is suggested that their liability is similar to that of persons in breach of fiduciary duty (see section 11.4 above), and in the Belmont Finance case the court considered that the personal remedies available were the same in both cases.

11.6 Innocent Recipients of Trust Property

Bona fide purchasers

If the trust property has passed into the hands of a bona fide purchaser of the legal interest for value and without notice that the property was trust property, the right to trace is extinguished since the beneficiaries and the purchaser are both innocent parties and the purchaser's legal ownership takes precedence over the equitable interest of the beneficiaries.

Innocent volunteers

Proprietary claims for restitution

If the recipient of trust property is an innocent volunteer (possibly a beneficiary of another trust) – that is, a person receiving the property without having given value, and without knowledge that the property was trust property – the recipient is considered in equity to be in a similar position to the beneficiaries under the trust. If the problem is simply that the volunteer has received trust property which remains identifiable as separate property the interest of the beneficiary, being first in time, will prevail and the volunteer will be bound to return the trust property to the trust.

Mixed fund

If the trust property has become mixed with that of the volunteer's in such a way as no longer to be clearly identifiable, the beneficiaries and the volunteer will share *pari passu* (proportionately according to their respective contributions) in the mixed fund, and in any property acquired by means of the mixed fund (*Sinclair* v. *Brougham* [1914] AC 398 and *Re Diplock* [1948] Ch 465).

Personal actions for restitution

Apart from the proprietary claim against an innocent volunteer there is also a personal claim for money had and received in order to prevent the unjust enrichment of the recipient. The claim was recently successful in the House of Lords decision of *Lipkin Gorman* v. *Karpnale* (see above, section 11.1), which concerned a claim against an innocent recipient of stolen money. Previously the claim had been established where beneficiaries of a deceased person's estate sought restitution from volunteers who received trust property by mistake from personal representatives. The action was, however, subject to the important limitation that the beneficiaries must first exhaust their claim against the personal representatives who distributed the property by mistake. In *Re Diplock* [1951] AC 251 a testator made a gift by will which included non-charitable purposes and accordingly the gift was void. The testator's personal representatives in ignorance of the invalidity of the gift made distributions of property to volunteers. The testator's next of kin claimed to recover the property from the recipients of it. It was held that the next of kin could pursue both the proprietary claim and that they also had a personal claim against the recipients.

It should be noted that there is an additional limitation on the personal claim against an innocent volunteer. In *Agip (Africa) Ltd* v. *Jackson*, Millet J said that it only subsists so long as the volunteer still retains the property (or presumably the exchange product), since it would be unjust to make the innocent party liable to account to any greater extent.

11.7 Loss of the Restitutionary Claim

Chapter 10 reviewed the defences of trustees to a claim for breach of trust. In addition the restitutionary claims of the beneficiaries of the trust may be lost in a variety of ways. In general the proprietary claim is more likely to be lost than the personal claim, which will persist irrespective of what happens to the property, except in the case of an innocent volunteer who will not be subject to a personal action once the property is no longer traceable in his or her hands.

Property ceases to be identifiable

First, the proprietary claim of the beneficiaries will be lost if the property becomes altogether unidentifiable, if a trustee or volunteer has simply spent trust money received without exchanging it for some other type of durable property (for instance, on food which has been consumed, or on a holiday which has been taken before the claim is made).

If trust money has been used to pay off debts of the recipient (whether trustee or volunteer) the money is irrecoverable. It is no longer in the hands of the first recipient and the creditor who has received the money is a purchaser for value from the debtor trustee or volunteer. It has been argued that in such circumstances the beneficiaries whose money has been used to pay the debts of a volunteer should take over the position of the creditor so that the volunteer owes a corresponding debt to the beneficiaries (a process called 'subrogation') but, in *Re Diplock* [1948] Ch 465, it was held that the debt was altogether extinguished and the beneficiaries could not claim to be in the position of the creditor who had been paid.

Change of position
If the recipient has changed his position in reliance upon his entitlement to the money or property received, it might be argued that it is inequitable to allow a restitutionary claim, whether proprietary or personal, to be made against him. It has been held that the defence is available in respect of the proprietary claim, but it is not clear whether it is available in respect of the personal claim. In *Re Diplock* (above), some of the money paid by mistake by the personal representatives had been used by the recipients in the improvement of land owned by the recipient. It was held that there should be no proprietary claim for a charge over the land since it would be inequitable that the innocent recipient's land should be subject to possible sale to enable the beneficiaries to recover the money.

Although there was a defence to the proprietary claim in *Re Diplock* there was not a similar defence to the personal restitutionary claim, although in earlier cases the defence has succeeded (*Deutsche Bank (London Agency) v. Beriro* [1895] 1 Com Cas 123). It now seems likely that the defence will be available where a personal claim is made. In *Lipkin Gorman* v. *Karpnale* (see section 11.1 above) solicitors claimed restitution of client monies which had been misappropriated by a partner and spent at a casino. The claim was a personal claim for money had and received by the casino to the use of the solicitors. Although their Lordships rejected the defence of change of position on the particular facts, they recognised that in principle the defence could have been available notwithstanding that the claim was a personal one.

It should be appreciated that a mere change of position is not enough to found the defence. The change of position must have occurred in reliance upon the receipt of the property. So if money has been paid by mistake to an innocent recipient and the innocent recipient uses the money for usual expenses there will be no defence since the recipient would have incurred the expenditure even if the mistake payment had not been made (*Baylis* v. *Bishop of London* [1913] 1 Ch 127).

Further, even if there is a change in position in reliance upon receipt of the money, the defence is not available unless it would be unjust to require the recipient to make restitution. In *Lipkin Gorman* v. *Karpnale* where a thief spent stolen money at a casino, the fact that the casino changed its position by allowing the thief to gamble and taking the risk of having to pay winnings to the thief was not sufficient to found the defence, since taking into account the laws of chance and both winning and losing bets it would not be unjust that the casino should make restitution.

Estoppel

Sometimes trust money may be transferred to a recipient in such circumstances as to amount to a representation which induces the recipient to do some detrimental act in reliance upon the payment. In such a case the payer may be estopped from recovering the money paid. In *Deutsche Bank (London Agency)* v. *Beriro* [1895] 1 Com Cas 123, a bill of exchange was drawn by B in favour of the defendants. The defendants then endorsed the bill to the plaintiffs on the basis that, when the bill was paid by B, the plaintiffs would make a payment to the defendants, and the defendants would then make a payment to B. The plaintiffs then mistakenly thought that the bill had been paid and therefore made a payment to the defendants, who accordingly paid B. When the plaintiffs discovered that B had not paid the bill and that they had paid money by mistake they sought restitution from the defendants. It was held that the defendants had two defences: first, change of position (see above); and second, that the mistaken payment by the plaintiffs amounted to a representation which induced the defendants to act to their detriment with the result that the plaintiffs were estopped from seeking restitution.

If a trustee mistakenly made a payment in similar circumstances, amounting to a representation, it might be argued that any estoppel was binding upon the trustee but not upon any beneficiaries, particularly since the mistaken payment could not be considered to be within the powers of the trustee. It is suggested, however, that the estoppel should equally prevent the beneficiaries from recovering from the innocent party who has changed his or her position in reliance upon the representation. Since change of position without a representation may found a defence to the proprietary claim (*Re Diplock*) or a personal claim (*Lipkin Gorman* v. *Karpnale*, above), estoppel must *a fortiori* provide a defence in both cases.

Summary

1 A claim in respect of trust property or for breach of duty may be made by means of a personal action for compensation against the trustee(s) or a third party, or it may be made by means of the proprietary technique of tracing.

2 Tracing arises where a legal or equitable owner of property is able to assert 'title' to a particular asset (which may have undergone a change of form) by following it into the hands of another. Where the property ceases to be identifiable or has been dissipated no tracing action will lie. The remedy of tracing exists at common law as well as in equity, but it is not possible to trace at common law once the property claimed has been mixed with other property or where the claimant has a merely equitable interest (e.g., that of a beneficiary under a trust).

3 In order to trace in equity it is necessary to establish the existence of a fiduciary relationship, or possibly simply an equitable proprietary interest, although such a relationship need not exist between the parties to any tracing action. It is not possible to trace in equity into the hands of a bona fide purchaser in good faith.

4 Where a tracing action is brought the following principles apply:
(a) where the property has not been mixed with other property but has undergone a change in form, the beneficiary may either elect to take the exchange product or to have a charge on the first property to the extent of the trust money;
(b) where property other than money is mixed by a trustee or by someone who has knowledge of a breach of trust, to the extent that such a person is unable to establish which property is his own, the property is treated as belonging to the trust;
(c) where trust money is mixed with the trustee's own money, the beneficiaries merely have a first charge on any property purchased from the mixed fund (the weight of case law authority suggests that a beneficiary cannot trace to any increase in value of property purchased from a mixed fund);
(d) where trust money is mixed in a current bank account, as regards withdrawals from the account, the trustee is deemed to use his own money first. However, once the trustee has drawn on the trust money, the beneficiary cannot generally trace to subsequent sums of the trustee's own money paid into the account. Where a trustee mixes in a current bank account money from two or more trust funds with his own money as between the two trust funds the rule in Clayton's Case applies (i.e., first in, first out).

5 A personal action or proprietary action may lie against an innocent volunteer in receipt of trust property. A personal action will lie where an innocent volunteer receives trust property by mistake. In a tracing claim, the claimant may recover the trust property from the innocent volunteer where it remains unmixed. Once the property is mixed the claimant and the innocent volunteer rank *pari passu*. It will not be possible to trace to funds spent on improvements or alterations to an existing asset of an innocent volunteer.

6 A personal action will lie against a stranger who intermeddles with trust property where: (a) he is a trustee *de son tort*, or, (b) he knowingly receives trust property in breach of trust or receives trust property either without knowing it is trust property or knowing it is trust property but not that it is transferred in breach of trust and then deals with the property in a manner inconsistent with the trust, or; (c) where he knowingly assists in a fraudulent or dishonest design on the part of the trustees, whether or not such any trust property passes into his hands. It is not necessary to prove fraud or dishonesty on the part of the stranger to make him liable as a trustee *de son tort* or for knowing receipt or dealing. It is unclear as to the type of knowledge that needs to be established for 'knowing receipt or dealing' and 'knowing assistance'; the weight of authority suggests that constructive knowledge as outlined in *Baden Delvaux* will not be sufficient for 'knowing assistance', although there is disagreement as to whether it may be enough in a case of 'knowing receipt of dealing'.

Exercises

1 In what circumstances may it be advantageous to pursue a tracing remedy against a trustee rather than bringing a personal action for breach of trust?

2 Should the law require a fiduciary relationship before a claimant can trace in equity? (See (1983) 103 LQR 433 R.M. Goode.)

3 How do the principles of tracing against an innocent volunteer differ from those of tracing against a trustee? Do you think the limitations on tracing against an innocent volunteer put such a party in too favourable a position? (See Hanbury and Maudsley, 13th edn pp.639–44.)

4 Pickwick is a trustee of trust fund A and trust fund B. On 4 December he sold assets of trust fund A and paid the £10 000 proceeds of sale into his personal bank account which at that date had a balance of £5000. On 6 December he withdrew £11 000 of which he gave £5000 to his daughter for a deposit on a house (which has increased in value). He invested a further £5000 in shares (which have decreased in value) and he spent the remaining £1000 on a holiday. On 8 December he paid £2000 of his own money into the same account and on 9 December he paid in £3000 belonging to trust fund B. On 11 December he withdrew £5000 with which he bought shares which were subsequently registered in his name, and finally on 12 December he withdrew £2000 for a trip to see Father Christmas in Lapland. On 13 December Pickwick was declared bankrupt.

   Advise the beneficiaries of trust funds A and B on the possibilities of their successfully making a tracing claim.

5 (a) Why is it important to distinguish between cases of 'knowing receipt or dealing' and cases of 'knowing assistance'?
   (b) Distinguish between actual and constructive knowledge in the context of intermeddling cases. Should constructive knowledge be sufficient to found an action (i) for knowing receipt or dealing and (ii) knowing assistance?

6 Twister, a director of Tinpot Ltd, received a £10 000 cash deposit from a client of Tinpot Ltd before the company went into liquidation. He misappropriated this sum for his own use. He subsequently gave £5000 of it to his wife who used the money to purchase a car for her own and Twister's use. The car was not insured and has since been written off in

an accident. The remaining £5000 Twister paid to Loyal, a business friend in satisfaction of a personal debt Twister owed him. Loyal was surprised to be paid by Twister as he had recently heard from a mutual friend that Twister was under threat of bankruptcy, but he accepted the £5000 without question.

Twister has now been declared bankrupt and the liquidator has discovered his fraud concerning the £10 000. He wishes to know whether a personal action lies against either or both of Twister's wife and Loyal.

Advise the liquidator.

Part IV

Purposes, Unincorporated Associations, Charities and Trusts

12 Private Purpose Trusts

12.1 Introduction

A purpose trust is one where the objects of the trust are a cause or purpose as opposed to the trust being for the benefit of a person (which term includes a corporation) or persons. The general rule is that such trusts are void for one or both of two reasons: first, the so-called 'beneficiary principle', and second, perpetuity.

The beneficiary principle

The 'beneficiary principle' was explained by Grant MR in *Morice v. Bishop of Durham* (1804) 9 Ves Jr (p.404) where he stated that 'there must be somebody in whose favour the court can decree performance'. In other words, as a trust creates an obligation there must be someone who can compel the trustees to carry out their duties. Charitable trusts form a major exception to the rule that purpose trusts are void as such trusts are enforceable by the Attorney-General. Examples of the types of gift which would fall foul of the 'beneficiary principle' can be seen in such cases as *Re Astor's Settlement Trusts* [1952] Ch 534 which involved a trust for the maintenance of good understanding between nations and the preservation of the independence of newspapers, and *Re Wood* [1949] Ch 498 where the trust was for the objects of the appeals made on BBC Radio 4's programme 'The Week's Good Cause' (since the appeals were not necessarily charitable, in which case any purpose trust would have been enforceable by the Attorney-General).

It is worth noting that many of the reported cases on the validity or otherwise of a purpose trust have also involved the trust failing to satisfy the requirement of certainty necessary for the creation of a trust (see Chapter 3) as the objects of the trust are uncertain. In *Re Endacott* [1960] Ch 232, where a testator left his residuary estate 'for the purpose of providing some useful memorial to myself', the trust failed for uncertainty as it was not clear what was meant by 'useful' as well as for the fact that it was a trust for a purpose which fell foul of the 'beneficiary principle'. Very broadly defined purposes are likely to be held to be void. *Re Astor's Settlement*, where the objects could be described as being somewhat broad, failed not only on account of the beneficiary principle, but also because the words used to describe the purposes were uncertain in meaning.

Perpetuity

With regard to perpetuity, there are two aspects to the principle. First, the rule relating to vesting provides that, in the case of future interests, it must be possible within a certain period of time (known as the perpetuity period) to say with certainty who is entitled to the gift. Second, the property once vested in the trustees must not be rendered inalienable. This aspect of the rule is concerned with the duration of the trust once it has come into existence and it is this aspect which is relevant to the question of the validity or otherwise of a private purpose trust. A gift is inalienable if some provision or the terms of the gift itself prevents it from being disposed of within a certain period of time. A gift will be void if it is not certain that it will in principle be possible for the interest of the trust to be alienated before the end of any life or lives in being and 21 years (i.e., the perpetuity period). The reason for the principle is that it is against the public interest for the property to be out of general circulation indefinitely if it is not for a purpose which is of general benefit to the community. Charitable purpose trusts once again escape from the difficulties experienced by private purpose trusts; they are not subject to the rule relating to inalienability as a charitable trust is required to be of public benefit. The need for the principle is seen when one considers that potentially large sums of money could be tied up for totally idiosyncratic purposes. For instance, in *Brown* v. *Burdett* (1882) 21 Ch D 667, a fund of money was set aside to keep a house maintained, in this case only for 20 years, with all but four of its rooms blocked up, and in a Scottish case *McCaig's Trustees* v. *Kirk-Session of United Free Church of Lismore* [1915] 1SLT 152, income from a fund was to be applied for the purpose of building life-size bronze statues of the testator and his family.

Although the 'beneficiary' and perpetuity principles were developed for very laudable reasons they have led to an undesirable situation whereby, in some cases, gifts which most people would consider ought to be valid potentially fall foul of either one or both of the principles. This has occurred partly due to the fact that the concept of what is charitable has been fairly narrowly defined (arguably influenced by the extensive tax concessions afforded to such gifts (see section 14.2 below) and partly as the principles have been applied in some circumstances to gifts made to unincorporated associations (see Chapter 13). The judiciary have sought to find ways of giving effect to private purpose trusts in meritorious cases. This chapter investigates the extent to which, despite the 'beneficiary' and 'perpetuity' principles, private purpose trusts may nevertheless be given effect. The next chapter will consider the problems which the principles have created for unincorporated associations.

12.2 **Trusts of Imperfect Obligation**

Trusts of imperfect obligation are exceptions to the rule that private purpose trusts are void. They are so called because, on the one hand, no one can compel the trustees to carry out the trust yet, on the other, no one can prevent the trustees from doing so if they wish; hence the *imperfect* obligation. In effect one is saying that what is an invalid trust may nevertheless take effect as a valid power.

Trusts of imperfect obligation were described by Roxburgh J in *Re Astor's Settlement Trusts* [1952] Ch 534 as being 'concessions to human weakness or sentiment' and by Harman LJ in *Re Endacott* [1960] Ch 232 as 'merely occasions when Homer has nodded'. There are three basic categories:

(a) trusts for the maintenance of particular monuments and graves;
(b) trusts for the saying of masses for the dead;
(c) trusts for the maintenance of one or more specific animals.

It should be noted that trusts for these kinds of purpose may in some circumstances be valid and enforceable as charitable gifts. A trust for the maintenance of monuments and graves generally, as opposed to one set up for the maintenance of a particular monument or grave, will fall within the ambit of a charity (being for the advancement of religion), as will most of the trusts set up for the saying of masses for the dead following the decisions in *Re Hetherington* (see section 14.5, below). Likewise, although a trust for a particular animal(s) will not be charitable, a trust which benefits humanity and is either for a species of animals or animals generally will normally be charitable (see section 14.7, below).

It is not totally clear whether trusts of imperfect obligation have to be confined to the perpetuity period in order to be valid, so that the only 'concession' offered is exemption from the 'beneficiary principle'. The issue of perpetuity has sometimes been glossed over or applied with flexibility, particularly in the 'animal cases'. In *Pettingall* v. *Pettingall* (1842) 11 LJ Ch 176 a legacy of £50 a year for the maintenance of a black mare was held to be valid, the case making no reference to the perpetuity period. In *Re Dean* (1889) 41 Ch D 552 the court upheld a bequest for the maintenance of the testator's horses and hounds for a period of 50 years if they lived that long. The bequest should have been limited to 21 years, but the decision as to the validity of the gift seemed to be based on the (erroneous) view that animal lives can be 'lives in being' for the purpose of ascertaining the perpetuity period. The better view is that all trusts of imperfect obligation should be limited in duration so as to ensure the trust does not exceed any human life or lives in being and 21 years. It seems that the alternative fixed period not exceeding 80 years (now allowed under s.1 Perpetuities and Accumulations Act 1964), does not apply to the duration of purpose trusts.

It looks unlikely that the categories of trusts of imperfect obligation will be extended beyond the three categories set out above. In *Re Thompson* [1934] Ch 342 an extension of the 'animal cases' was upheld, allowing a legacy of £1000 to be applied by the legatee for the promotion of fox hunting but, in the light of later cases showing a far stricter approach, it is doubtful whether the decision will be followed.

12.3   Trusts Directly or Indirectly for Ascertainable Individuals

Provided that a trust is limited to a duration within the perpetuity period it seems that where a trust, although expressed as being for a purpose, is (directly or indirectly) for the benefit of ascertainable individuals it will fall outside the mischief of the 'beneficiary principle'. In *Re Denley's Trust Deed* [1969] 1 Ch 373 land was conveyed to trustees for a non-charitable purpose: namely, to hold on trust to maintain a sports-ground for a limited time, within the perpetuity period. The trust deed, however, went on to provide that the sportsground was intended primarily for the employees of a particular company and secondarily for the benefit of such other person or persons, if and as the trustees may allow to use the same. Goff J held that the trust was valid and enforceable. He drew a distinction between purpose or object trusts which are abstract and impersonal, such as those found in *Re Astor's Settlement Trusts* (above) and *Re Wood* (above), which are void on account of the beneficiary principle, and those which are indirectly or directly for the benefit of ascertainable individuals (on the facts of the case, the employees of the company), which are valid. The court could prevent misuse of the trust by ordering the trustees to admit the employees entitled to use the land. It is vital to note that it is not only necessary to establish that the trust is directly or indirectly for the benefit of individuals, but also that those individuals are 'ascertainable'. Thus in *R* v. *District Auditor, ex p. West Yorkshire Metropolitan County Council* (1986) 45 CLJ 391 (C. Harpum) where the trust involved was for the benefit of 'any or all or some of the inhabitants of the County of West Yorkshire', the gift could not be saved by the *Re Denley* line of reasoning as there were no ascertained or ascertainable beneficiaries. Even if the term 'inhabitant' was sufficiently certain, the class of 2 500 000 potential beneficiaries was so large that the trust was in any case unworkable (see section 3.4).

The *Re Denley* approach to purpose trusts seems commendable in that it may operate to prevent a perfectly acceptable but nevertheless non-charitable purpose from failing. However, whether it is consistent with existing authorities is more debatable. First, Goff J failed adequately to discuss the Privy Counsel decision in *Leahy* v. *Attorney-General* [1959] AC 457 (see section 13.2, below) which appears to take an inconsistent view. Second, the distinction drawn by Goff J in distinguishing earlier authorities, between purposes which are 'abstract and impersonal' on the one hand, and those 'directly or indirectly for the benefit of ascertainable individuals' on the other, seems nebulous. Arguably, a better approach to ensuring that 'acceptable' non-charitable purpose trusts are given effect to would be to adopt the principle that an invalid trust is a valid power, and by this means allow gifts to be given effect to provided they are limited to the perpetuity period. Alternatively, the law should be reformed to separate the 'trust law benefits' from the tax concessions granted to charitable trusts to encourage the latter category of trusts to be widened. In the meantime, a simple practical solution to ensuring a private purpose is carried into effect is to incorporate a society to advance the particular purpose(s). The law of trusts would not then be relevant. Furthermore, as a corporation is a legal person no problems occur on account of the 'beneficiary principle' and there need be no problems.

12.4 Trusts to Carry out a Commercial Purpose

So far we have only considered private purpose trusts in the non-commercial sphere, but it was noted in section 3.1 that it is common for parties to commercial agreements to make use of the trust since it can be particularly useful for giving effect to some commercial purpose or in providing priority to beneficiaries in the event of insolvency. In this section it is intended to examine what will be necessary to establish that a trust to carry out a commercial purpose has been created.

Such trusts, being indirectly for ascertainable individuals will, it is submitted, fall within the *Re Denley* principle discussed above (see section 12.3), and will therefore not fall foul of the beneficiary principle. Care should be taken to ensure that the trust is established on such terms that it will not fall foul of the rules relating to perpetuity and inalienability (see section 12.1).

The leading decision is *Barclay's Bank Ltd* v. *Quistclose Investments Ltd* [1970] AC 567. A company, Rolls Razor, was in financial difficulty.

It had exceeded its agreed overdraft at Barclays Bank which was threatening to petition for its winding-up. In order to appease the Bank, Rolls Razor obtained a loan from Quistclose Investments Ltd, but the loan was made on the condition that the money was used only to pay an ordinary share dividend which had been declared by Rolls Razor. The money was put in a special account at Barclay's Bank on the condition (agreed with the bank) that the account would only be used to pay the dividend. Rolls Razor subsequently went into voluntary liquidation without having paid the dividend. Barclay's Bank wanted the money in the special account to reduce Rolls Razor's overdraft. The House of Lords, however, decided that Barclay's Bank held the money on the secondary trust (see section 3.1, above) for Quistclose Investments Ltd, which was able to recover the entire sum. It had never been the intention of either Rolls Razor or Quistclose Investments that the money should become part of the assets of Rolls Razor. The money had been advanced on trust for a particular purpose only (i.e., payment of the dividend). As the dividend could not be paid, the primary purpose trust (see section 3.1) had failed and the money should be returned to Quistclose Investments Ltd in execution of the secondary trust.

In order to establish a trust for a commercial purpose, as opposed to a simple loan, and thus to be able to recover all monies advanced in the event of insolvency and if the purpose fails, at least two elements must be established: first, the money or other property is to be used for a specific purpose *and no other*; and, second, the purpose is known to the recipient. In *Barclay's Bank* v. *Quistclose Investments Ltd*, the money was paid into a special account. This factor influenced the court in finding a mutual intention to create a trust of the money, rather than an intention that the money should become part of the general funds of Rolls Razor. It is, however, apparent from *Re EVTR* [1987] BCLC 646 that the setting up of a special account is not necessary to the finding of a trust; other factors may be sufficient. Here, the appellant agreed to assist a company for whom he had worked to purchase new equipment. He deposited a sum of money with the company's solicitors, authorising them to release it 'for the sole purpose of buying new equipment'. The money was not paid into any special fund, but was paid out by the company for the purpose of acquiring the equipment. The Court of Appeal held that the appellant could recover his money (after agreed deductions) on the basis of the reasoning applied in the Quistclose case: that is, a trust of the money for the purpose of purchasing new equipment had been created. As on the facts of the case part of the equipment ordered was never delivered, and the money had been refunded to the company by the seller, the purpose had failed and the appellant could therefore recover this part.

Peter Gibson J summed up the key principles in the establishment and operation of a trust for commercial purpose in *Carreras Rothmans Ltd* v. *Freeman Matthews Treasure Ltd* [1985] Ch 207, p.222 as follows:

> equity fastens on the conscience of the person who receives from another property transferred for a specific purpose only and not, therefore, for the recipient's own purposes, so that such a person will not be permitted to treat the property as his own or to use it for other than the stated purpose . . . if the common intention is that property is transferred for a specific purpose and not so as to become the property of the transferee, the transferee cannot keep the property if for any reason that purpose cannot be fulfilled.

The decision in Carreras Rothmans Ltd is of particular significance in that it appears that, in order to establish a trust of a commercial purpose, it matters not that the party advancing the money on trust is (at the time of the creation of the trust) contractually bound to repay the money to another as opposed to having made a voluntary loan or disposition, as in *Barclay's Bank* v. *Quistclose* and *Re EVTR*. In Carreras Rothmans Ltd (CR Ltd) cigarette manufacturers had employed FMT Ltd as its advertising agency to carry out the creation and placement of advertisements in the media. CR Ltd originally paid FMT Ltd a monthly fee, not only for its services but also a sum to cover all expenditure incurred by FMT Ltd on the placement work. It subsequently became apparent that FMT Ltd was in financial difficulties and, in order to protect third parties, CR Ltd agreed with FMT Ltd to pay a monthly sum into a special account at FMT Ltd's own bank, the money to be used only for the purposes of meeting the accounts of the media and production fees of third parties directly attributable to CR Ltd's involvement with the agency. When FMT Ltd went into liquidation, CR Ltd successfully claimed that the monies in the special account was held by FMT Ltd for CR Ltd upon trust for the sole purpose of applying it towards the debts owed to the third parties, and thus in default of that purpose being carried out there was a resulting trust to CR Ltd. The case is of further significance as on the facts Peter Gibson J made an order requiring the liquidator of FMT Ltd to carry out the primary trust (i.e., make the payments from the account to the third parties). This is to be contrasted with both *Barclays Bank Ltd* v. *Quistclose Investments* and *Re EVTR*, where the primary trust could not be carried out, and the party advancing the money took on resulting trust.

The decision in *Re Kayford* [1975] 1 WLR 279 is another example of the use of trust in furthering a commercial purpose (for the facts, see sections 1.4 and 3.1, above). The decision takes the Quistclose principle further by holding that, in opening up a separate bank account (called a 'Customer Trust Deposit Account') into which the mail-order company paid the customer's purchase money, the debtor/creditor relationship was excluded and the obligations of the mail-order company were turned into those of a trustee. Consequently, on the winding-up of the mail-order company, the customers were not mere creditors of the company but beneficial owners of the money in the account until such time as their goods had been delivered. Thus it can be seen that the trust can be used to protect customers on liquidation who would otherwise have been merely unsecured creditors.

Summary

1 Purpose trusts are generally void on account of either or both of the 'beneficiary principle' and the perpetuity rule, but there are important exceptions to this rule.
2 Basic questions to determine whether a purpose trust is valid or void:

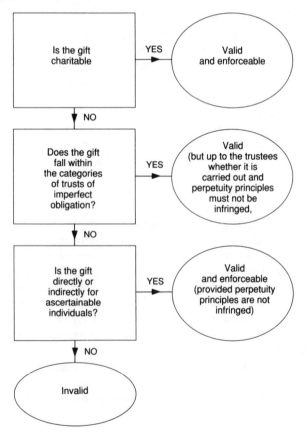

3 A purpose trust may be created in order to give effect to some commercial purpose and it has proved especially effective in providing protection on insolvency. In order to establish a trust as opposed to a simple loan agreement, when money or other property is transferred to another, it is necessary (a) to show that the money or other property is to be used for a specific purpose and no other, and (b) that the purpose is known to the recipient.

Exercises

1 For what reason(s) is (are) private purpose trusts generally held to be void?

2 When will a purpose trust be valid?

3 The will of a testator who died recently provides, *inter alia*:
(a) 'I give £4000 to my trustees to maintain my collection of snakes';
(b) 'I give £15 000 to my trustees to maintain my croquet lawn primarily for the benefit of the employees of the Kimberton Estate, but secondarily for such other persons as my trustees may in their absolute discretion think fit.'
Are these gifts valid and enforceable?

4 Moneypots Investment Company advanced £60 000 to Pennyless Launderers Ltd 'to be used for the sole purpose of purchasing new plant and machinery'. Pennyless Launderers Ltd has now gone into liquidation having only used £10 000 of the £60 000 for the purchase of plant and machinery. Advise Moneypots Investment Company whether it is entitled to recover the £60 000 or any part thereof in preference to other creditors of Pennyless Launderers Ltd.

13 Unincorporated Associations

13.1 Introduction

In *Conservative and Unionist Central Office* v. *Burrell* [1982] 2 All ER 1 Lawton LJ described an unincorporated association as being: 'two or more persons bound together for one or more common purposes . . . by mutual undertakings, each having mutual duties and obligations, in an organisation which has rules which identify in whom control of it and its funds rests and upon what terms and which can be joined or left at will'. He went on to point out that the bond of union between the members of an unincorporated association has to be contractual. The purpose or purposes for which the members come together may be many and varied; it may be to pursue a common interest (such as gardening, poetry or reading), to fight a common cause (perhaps abolition of the Arms Trade), or simply as a social club. The purpose may be charitable or non-charitable. If it is non-charitable problems may arise as to the validity of gifts made to the unincorporated association since such associations are not legal persons and in consequence, with the exception of trade unions, cannot own property or be the subject of legal rights and duties. This may lead to difficulties with either or both the beneficiary principle and the perpetuity rule outlined in Chapter 12. In this Chapter it is proposed to consider first the validity of gifts to unincorporated associations, and second the entitlement to an association's property on its dissolution.

13.2 The Validity of Gifts to Unincorporated Associations

If the assets of an unincorporated association are held by its officers or trustees upon charitable trusts, no problem will arise as to the validity of gifts made to the association. A charitable gift may exist for a purpose and may continue for ever (see section 14.2, below). Thus, for example, a gift to a society which exists to promote and preserve the organ works of J.S. Bach, would be valid as an educational charity even if the gifts were not limited in duration to the perpetuity period. It is only gifts to non-charitable unincorporated associations which may be rendered invalid on account of either or both the beneficiary and perpetuity principles. Whether this is the case depends upon the particular construction of the gift. It appears from the decision in *Re Recher's Will Trusts* [1972] Ch 526, that there are four possible interpretations of a gift to an unincorporated association.

A gift to individual members of the association at the date of the gift as joint tenants or tenants in common

Where a gift is made to the individual members of the association at the date of the gift as joint tenants or tenants in common this involves an absolute gift and not one made by way of trust (see Figure 13.1). In effect one is saying that the association name is simply used as a convenient label to define the members of the class. If this construction is placed on the gift it will be valid. As it is a gift to the members, the gift will not fall foul of the beneficiary principle.

The question arises, therefore, as to the types of circumstances in which this construction of a gift would be feasible. In the first place a distinction needs to be drawn between 'inward looking' and 'outward looking' associations. An 'inward looking' association is one which exists for the benefit of the members, such as a social club. An 'outward looking' association would include one established to carry out a benevolent or philanthropic purpose, or further a particular cause (such as campaigning against nuclear dumping). The construction of a gift to the individual members of the association at the date of the gift would normally only be appropriate for a gift made to an 'inward looking' association. It was held in *Re Ogden* [1933] Ch 678 that this construction may be appropriate for a gift to an 'inward looking' association even where the gift is made for the general purposes of the association; provided that the constitution of the society does not prohibit the gift from being divided between the individual members, it does not matter that the donor did not clearly envisage this result. However, it is likely that many gifts which were previously held to fall within this category, and especially one which was construed as being for the general purposes of the association, would today be explained on the basis of the contract-holding theory (see below, p.238). As Vinelott J observed in *Re Grant's Will Trusts* [1980] 1 WLR 360, cases in this category are 'relatively uncommon'.

A gift to be held on trust for present and future members either forever or for an indefinite period

A trust for present and future members would only be appropriate for an

donor ——————————➤ members of the association

Figure 13.1

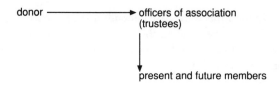

Figure 13.2

'inward looking' association (see Figure 13.2). It would not encounter problems with regard to the beneficiary principle as it is a trust for individuals and not a purpose. In *Neville Estates* v. *Madden* [1962] Ch 832 Cross J thought there would be a problem with regard to remoteness of vesting in future members if the gift was not limited to the perpetuity period, but the Perpetuity and Accumulations Act 1964 (applying to dispositions made after 15 July 1964) would seem to resolve the problem. Under the Act a gift is treated as valid until it is apparent that the gift must vest outside the perpetuity period. S.4(4) allows, in the case of a class gift, for members of the class not ascertained within the perpetuity period to be excluded from the class. The gift would therefore take effect in favour of members who are ascertained within the perpetuity period. It is important to note, however, that a gift could be invalid on account of its duration if the capital is to be retained as an endowment and the members are only to receive the income. The trust will then be void as a perpetual trust. In *Carne* v. *Long* (1860) 2 De GF & G 95, where a testator left certain land to the trustees of Penzance Public Library (the library was not charitable as the books were only available for the use of subscribers of the library) to hold for ever for the maintenance and support of the library, the gift was held to be void as it was a gift for present and future members of the library and the land was required to be held indefinitely.

A gift to the trustees or proper officers of the association on trust to carry into effect the purposes of the association
Where the gift is construed as being one to the officers of the association on trust to carry out the purposes of the association, the gift may be void on account of both the beneficiary and perpetuity principles (see Figure 13.3). In *Leahy* v. *Attorney-General for New South Wales* [1959] AC 457 a testator made a gift of a sheep station to be held on trust for 'such order of nuns of the Catholic Church or the Christian Brothers as my executors and trustees shall select'. The gift was held to be void. The gift was not charitable as some of the orders were purely contemplative orders (see section 14.5, below) which deprived the gift of the necessary element of public benefit to be charitable. Furthermore, the Privy Council decided

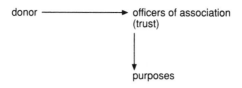

Figure 13.3

that there was no intention to create a trust for individual members of selected orders, causing the gift to fall foul of the beneficiary principle. Moreover, as the testator was found to have intended to establish an endowment, the trust was perpetual and, as it was not limited to the perpetuity period, the gift was also void on account of perpetuity principles.

It may, however it seems, be possible to construe a gift as being to the officers of the association on trust to carry out the purposes of the association without the gift offending the beneficiary principle. Such was held in *Re Lipinski's Will Trusts* [1976] Ch 235 which relied upon the reasoning in the earlier decision of *Re Denley's Trust Deed* [1969] 1 Ch 373 (see section 12.3, above). It will be remembered that *Re Denley's Trust Deed* was not concerned with a gift to an unincorporated association but with a gift of land conveyed to trustees on trust to maintain a sportsground (a non-charitable purpose), primarily for the benefit of employees of a certain company and secondarily for the benefit of such other person or persons as the trustees allow to use the same. Goff J held that, although expressed as being for a purpose, the gift was directly or indirectly for the benefit of ascertainable individuals and therefore outside the mischief of the beneficiary principle. Despite the fact that *Re Denley* is arguably inconsistent with the earlier Privy Council decision of *Leahy* v. *Attorney-General for New South Wales* (above), it was followed and applied to a gift to an unincorporated association by Oliver J in *Re Lipinski* (above). Here the testator had left part of his estate to the Hull Judean (Maccabi) Association, specifying that it was to be used solely in the work of constructing a new building for the association and/or improving existing buildings. One of the lines of reasoning (see next section for the other) adopted by Oliver J in holding the gift to be valid was that, although the gift was expressed as being for a purpose, it was clearly for the benefit of ascertained individuals, these being the members of the association for the time being. It should, however, be noted that in *Re Grant's Will Trusts* [1980] 1 WLR 360 Vinelott J said that *Re Denley* had no application to gifts to unincorporated associations but was confined to discretionary trusts. In *Re Lipinski* itself Goff J limited the scope for applying this construction and thereby circumventing the beneficiary principle by indicating that the purpose must benefit the members. It would therefore be an inappropriate construction for a gift to an outward looking association.

A gift to the existing members of the association beneficially, but on the basis that the subject-matter of the gift is given as an accretion to the funds of the association and is governed by association rules, to which all the members are contractually bound

This is sometimes known as the contract-holding theory and the courts today tend to lean towards such a construction of a gift to an unincorporated association. It is essentially different from the first construction in that an individual member, although beneficially entitled, cannot claim his or her share except with the agreement of the majority or with unanimity. Moreover, an individual member's share accrues to other members on his or her death or resignation (see Figure 13.4). This aspect of the theory is difficult to reconcile with, in the case of resignation, the requirement that a disposition of an equitable interest be in writing in accordance with s.53(i)(c) Law of Property Act 1925 and, in the case of death of a member, that property can only be effectively transferred by compliance with the Wills Act 1837 as amended (see sections 4.1 and 4.2). The gift will not fall foul of the beneficiary principle as it is a gift for the members; neither will it infringe any perpetuity principle unless there is something in the constitution of the association which prevents the members from dividing the property among themselves, or which renders the funds in some other way inalienable. For example, in *Re Grant's Will Trusts* (above) the trust was for a non-charitable purpose (i.e., the Chertsey Labour Party headquarters). The trust was held void for perpetuity as the members of the association did not control the property and were unable to change the rules of the association in order to gain control, because the rules were subject to the approval of, and only capable of alteration by, an outside body (the National Executive Committee). It was irrelevant that the restriction on disposing of the capital was not one imposed by the testator.

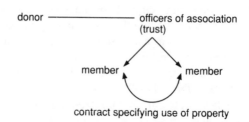

Figure 13.4

It is apparent from the decision in *Re Recher's Will Trust* [1972] Ch 526 that where assets are held for the members on a contractual basis the courts will do their utmost to find the gift valid under this fourth construction. Moreover, the decision made it clear that the construction is appropriate for 'inward' and 'outward looking' associations alike. Brightman J said:

> it is not essential that the members should only intend to secure direct personal advantages to themselves. The association may be one in which personal advantages to members are combined with the pursuit of some outside purpose, or the association may be one which offers no personal benefit at all to the members, the funds of the association being applied exclusively to the pursuit of some outside purpose.

It appears from the decision in *Re Lipinski* (above) that this fourth construction may still be appropriate where, although the gift is for the benefit of individuals, the donor specifies a particular purpose is to be carried out. It will be remembered that in *Re Lipinski* the fund was to be used solely in the work of constructing a new building for the association and/or improving existing buildings. Oliver J nevertheless held that the gift should be construed as an absolute one under the fourth construction. The specified purpose was a superadded direction which could be disregarded, as the prescribed purpose of constructing or improving the building was for the benefit of the members of the association and if the purpose was carried out, the members could vest the resulting property in themselves. This leaves the law on the construction of gifts to unincorporated associations in an unsatisfactory state (see further B. Green (1980) 43 MLR 460; J. Warburton [1985] Conv. 318); if a donor wishes to specify a particular purpose to which the property is to be applied, he or she will fall foul of the beneficiary principle if the court adopts the third construction or, if the court adopts the fourth construction, he or she cannot guarantee that the purpose specified will be carried out. As Green observes, 'For the donor, the price of validity is unenforceability.'

13.3 Surplus Funds on the Dissolution of an Unincorporated Association

The question to be considered here is: when an unincorporated association is dissolved leaving surplus funds, who is entitled to such funds? There are three possible destinations: (a) where the funds have been provided by donors outside the association, a resulting trust to the donors; (b) where the funds have been provided by members of the association, a distribution on a contractual basis amongst the members; or (c) whether the donor is a member of the association or not, *bona vacantia* to the Crown, as having no owner or person entitled to it.

At the outset a distinction must be drawn as to the original source of the funds which are now surplus. There are two possibilities: either the funds come from the members themselves by way of subscriptions, fines, etc., or they come from outsiders by way of donation. Each circumstance will be dealt with separately, but first it is necessary to decide at what point in time an unincorporated association may be said to be dissolved as it is at this point any funds left may be said to be surplus. There is no problem where the association has been wound up formally, but difficulties may be experienced in ascertaining the relevant date where no such steps are taken. In *Re GKN Bolts and Nuts Ltd (Automotive Division) Birmingham Works, Sports and Social Club* [1982] 1 WLR 774 a sportsground had been purchased by the trustees of a social club in 1946, but in 1975 membership cards ceased to be issued and the last annual general meeting was held. No further accounts were taken, stocks of drinks were sold and the steward dismissed. There was, however, a special meeting in December 1975 to deal with an offer to buy the land at which a resolution was passed to sell the land, although no sale in fact took place until 1978. It was held that mere inactivity was not normally sufficient for a club to cease to exist although it may be if it was prolonged, or in such circumstances that it was only reasonable to infer spontaneous dissolution. On the facts of the case the club ceased to exist on the date of the special meeting at which the resolution was passed to sell the land; the inactivity coupled with the positive steps to wind it up were sufficient to infer dissolution.

Funds derived from outsiders by way of donation

Funds derived from outsiders are funds which are given by persons who are not members of the association in question for the benefit of the members or for the benefit of the individuals or purpose(s) which the association exists to serve.

The leading case on the principles to be applied to funds derived from this source is *Re West Sussex Constabulary's Widows, Children and Benevolent (1930) Fund Trust* [1971] Ch 1. Here a fund had been established to provide benefits to widows and certain dependents of members who died. On the amalgamation of the West Sussex Constabulary with other police forces on 1 January 1968, the question arose as to the distribution of the funds. The funds from outsiders, as opposed to those from the members, came from three sources: (a) the proceeds of entertainments, jumble sales and other fund-raising activities; (b) anonymous donations through street collections; and (c) cheques and legacies. With regard to the first source Goff J concluded that the law of trusts had no bearing on the question. These funds arose out of a contract with the outsiders and as they had got what they bargained for there was no room for finding a resulting trust. He therefore held that the proceeds of the fund-raising activities went *bona vacantia*.

In deciding whether the remaining two sources of funds from outsiders should be given back to the donors Goff J asked a somewhat artificial, but nevertheless expedient, question: namely, whether the donors expected to get their money back if there were surplus funds. With regard to the anonymous donations he concluded that the donors would not have expected to get their money back as it was obvious that they could not be found. He therefore held that they had parted with their money out and out, and there was no resulting trust but instead the money went *bona vacantia*. Had a resulting trust been found these funds would have been paid into court, theoretically awaiting collection by the donors. However, it would have been impossible for anonymous donors to prove that they had made a donation to the fund, so the fund would have remained in court indefinitely. The decision therefore avoided the clearly undesirable result of finding a resulting trust with regard to anonymous donations in contrast to the earlier decision of Harman J in *Re Gillingham Bus Disaster Fund* [1958] Ch 300 where a resulting trust was found to arise. (This was not an unincorporated association case but concerned surplus funds resulting from a non-charitable disaster appeal.) Whilst Goff J in *Re West Sussex Constabulary* considered the resulting trust principles enunciated by Harman J in *Re Gillingham Bus Disaster Fund* to be relevant, he asked a slightly different question from Harman J which accounts for the different result. Instead of asking whether the donors expected to get their money back, Harman J had asked whether the donors intended to part with their money out and out or only to give it to the particular purpose specified. The only answer to this question was that they intended to give it to the particular purpose and consequently a resulting trust arose.

With regard to the cheques and legacies Goff J was able to reach a different conclusion from that of the destination of anonymous donations. In asking the question 'Did the donors expect to get their money back if there were surplus funds?', he was able to conclude that the donors would so have expected because they could be identified and found. However, even though *Re West Sussex Constabulary* leads to a better result than that of *Re Gillingham Bus Disaster Fund* in applying the principles of resulting trusts, it is questionable whether resulting trusts have any relevance at all in dealing with the distribution of surplus funds of a dissolved unincorporated association. It will be remembered (see section 13.2) that the validity of the initial gift to the association is today usually explained as being a gift to the members of the association subject to their contract. Consequently, to be consistent, any gift from an outsider should be regarded as an absolute one and surplus funds should be divided between the members of the association on a contractual basis.

Funds derived from the members themselves
Funds derived from the members of the association may take the form of subscriptions or fines.

The resulting trust approach
Early cases tended to favour a resulting trust approach in deciding who should be entitled to the surplus funds. For example, in *Re Hobourn Aero Components Air Raid Distress Fund* [1946] Ch 194 a fund was held for employees of a company who were on war service or who suffered loss in air raids during the Second World War. The funds had been accumulated by way of voluntary subscriptions, and surplus funds remained at the end of the war. It was held that each contributor present and past was entitled on a resulting trust basis in proportion to the amount of the contribution, but taking into account benefits received. However, more recent cases concerned with surplus funds of unincorporated associations have discredited the resulting trust approach. The view is now that the division of surplus funds from members' subscriptions should be determined purely as a question of contract. The explanation as to why principles of resulting trusts were thought to be relevant in earlier cases is that it was thought that the resulting trust followed naturally from the fact that the assets of the association were normally construed as being held on trust for the members. Thus if the trust failed, a resulting trust would arise. This is to confuse two issues. The division of surplus funds on dissolution of an unincorporated association is a question of the position of the members *inter se*, whereas the original holding of the assets on trust is looking at the holding of assets with regard to outsiders.

Having said that the resulting trust approach has been discredited in cases concerning surplus funds of unincorporated associations, the decision in *Davis* v. *Richards & Wallington Industries Ltd* [1990] 1 WLR 1511, which was concerned with surplus funds of a pension scheme, suggests that there may still be some life left in the resulting trust approach. Scott J was of the opinion that a pension scheme was 'a species of unincorporated association', and expressed the view that a resulting trust could arise out of a contractual relationship unless there was something express or implied in the terms of the contract which excluded a resulting trust. On the facts the surplus funds arose from three sources: (a) employee's contributions, (b) employer's contributions, and (c) funds transferred to the scheme in question from other pension schemes. With regard to the employee's contributions and the transferred funds, Scott J held that a resulting trust was impliedly excluded by the terms of the contract and the surrounding circumstances, with the result that these parts of the surplus funds went to the Crown as *bona vacantia*. In contrast, the employers could recover contributions on the basis of a resulting trust.

The contractual approach

The origins of the modern contractual approach are to be found in *Cunnack* v. *Edwards* [1896] 2 Ch 679. This concerned a society to provide funds for the widows of deceased members by means of subscriptions paid by the members. On the death of the last widow of a deceased member there were surplus funds. The personal representatives or the last surviving members of the association claimed the assets on a resulting trust basis. The court held that there was no resulting trust; each member had got what he contracted for (i.e., if he had left a widow, she had benefited). The subscription had thus been parted with out and out, subject only to receiving contractual benefits. The surplus funds were therefore ownerless property which passed to the Crown as *bona vacantia*. On the facts of the case the result does not seem to be unfair given that the members of the society were dead and as such incapable of benefiting from the surplus funds. However, the approach was followed in *Re West Sussex Constabulary* with regard to the subscriptions of the members. Goff J held that, unlike the position with funds from outsiders, principles of resulting trusts had no relevance. Members' subscriptions should be dealt with on a contractual basis and, as the members had received all they had contracted for, the property was ownerless and passed to the Crown as *bona vacantia*. Goff J's reasoning was influenced by the fact that the club existed to give benefit to third parties rather than being a club providing benefits for the members themselves, in which case a division of surplus funds amongst the members may have been acceptable. This view was criticised by Walton J in *Re Buckinghamshire Constabulary Widows and Orphans Fund Friendly Society (No 2)* [1979] 1 All ER 623, the facts of which arose out of the same re-organisation of the police force in 1968 as *Re West Sussex Constabulary*. Walton J expressed the opinion that it mattered not whether the society existed for the benefit of the members or to give benefits to third parties, as the assets were in either case controlled by the members and were their property from the beginning to end. Thus the assets should be divided amongst the members at the date of dissolution in either circumstance, and only if there were no members, or the members were so reduced that it was either impossible to continue the society or to dissolve it by instrument, should the assets pass to the Crown as ownerless property.

It should be noted, however, that statute law or the constitution of the society itself may affect the destination of surplus funds either directly or indirectly. For example, with regard to statutory provisions it may be prohibited to distribute assets of a registered Friendly Society to the members (see *Cunnack* v. *Edwards*) and consequently assets may only pass to the Crown. Alternatively, the constitution of an association may specifically lay down the destination of surplus funds on dissolution to a person or group of individuals other than the members. Nevertheless, assuming there is no expressed or statutory provision, the better view is that members' subscriptions will belong to the members at the date of dissolution in equal shares on the basis of an implied term to this effect in the contractual relationship between the members. Former members or their estates have no rights to surplus funds, these being extinguished on resignation (*Re Buckinghamshire Constabulary*).

How should the surplus funds be divided amongst the members?
The courts have provided a variety of views as to the way in which surplus funds should be divided amongst the members. In the early case of *Re Printers' and Transferrers' Amalgamated Trade Protection Society* [1988] 2 Ch 84, where a resulting trust approach to surplus funds was taken, the court decided that the members at the date of dissolution took in proportion to the amount contributed, and no account should be taken of benefits actually received by a member. In contrast, in *Re Hobourn* Aero Components Air Raid Distress Fund (above), also a resulting trust case, although the division was to be based on the amount contributed the court held that it should take into account benefits received and should, furthermore, be a distribution amongst present and past members, unless (in the case of past members) it was not possible to identify them.

In *Re Buckinghamshire Constabulary*, where the court took a contractual approach to surplus funds, it was said that the division of the funds should be in equal shares among the members at the date of dissolution, but the question has arisen as to whether this should necessarily be the case where the club or society has different classes of members. In the earlier case of *Re Sick and Funeral Society of St John's Sunday School Golcar* [1973] Ch 51, where a full subscription was paid by members over thirteen years of age but only half-subscription by those under thirteen years, the court held that those who were full members at the date of dissolution recovered on the basis of their full subscriptions whilst those who only paid half-share only got half. Nevertheless, the length of membership was irrelevant to the issue (rather like the Biblical story of the labourers in the vineyard who all got paid a day's wages despite the fact that some only worked for one hour before sunset!). Similarly, in *GKN Bolts and Nuts Sports and Social Club* [1982] 1 WLR 774 there were four categories of members: full, associate, temporary and honorary. Only the full members paid subscriptions. It was decided only the full members at the date of dissolution were entitled to receive a share of the surplus funds, and again the length of membership was irrelevant. Division was on an equal basis amongst all full members at the date of dissolution.

Summary

1 Validity of gifts to unincorporated associations

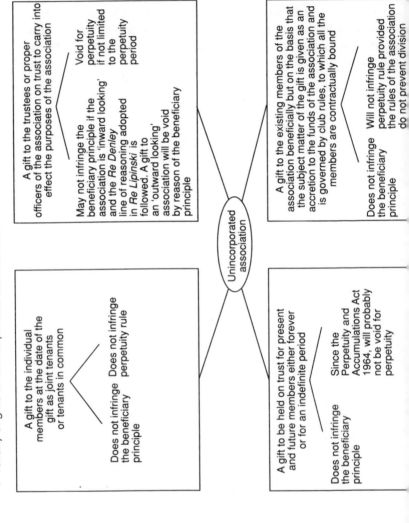

247

2 Destinations of surplus funds of an unincorporated association

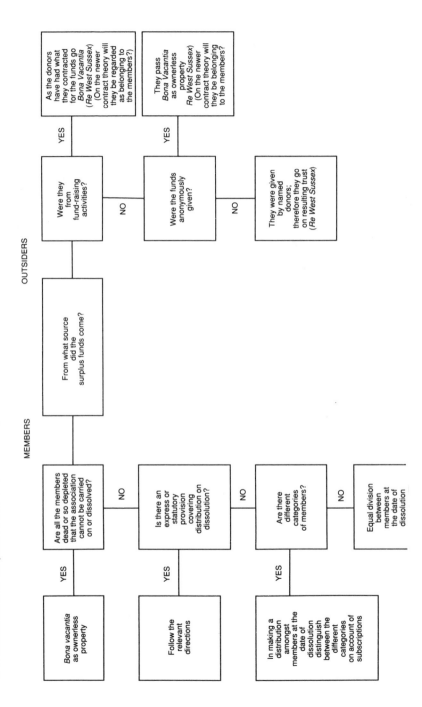

Exercises

1 Why is it possible that a gift to a non-charitable unincorporated association may be held to be invalid?

2 What difficulties arise for persons wishing to make a gift to an unincorporated association to be applied for a specific purpose?

3 Discuss the validity and effect of the following independent gifts to the Bolberry Beekeepers Association:

(a) '£200 to Bolberry Beekeepers Association';

(b) '£3000 to Bolberry Beekeepers Association to be used for the sole purpose of repairing and redecorating the club premises';

(c) '£500 to all present and future members of the Bolberry Beekeepers Association'.

4 In dealing with surplus funds of unincorporated associations, do the courts today favour the resulting trust or the contractual approach? Which is the better approach?

5 The Everest Climbers' Club was formed in 1946 to encourage attempts on Mount Everest and to provide annuities for widows of deceased members. Members paid an annual subscription of £25 and funds were also raised from raffles, jumble sales and the sale of Everest Club memorabilia, as well as from the annual ball for members.

The club has been inactive since 1975. There are six surviving members and the assets of the club are currently worth £12 000. How should the club's funds be distributed?

14 Charitable Trusts

14.1 Introduction

Where property is applied for a purpose which is charitable, this does not necessarily involve a trust. A gift to charity may be made to a charitable corporation (such as a hospital, or an educational establishment). In this case no trust arises; the corporation has full and beneficial ownership of the property which forms the subject-matter of the gift, but it must use the property for the exclusively charitable objects set down in its memorandum of association or its constitution. There may, however, be a resulting trust if the gift fails wholly or in part. In contrast, if the charity is an unincorporated association then it is likely that the gift will be construed as one for the purposes of the association to be held on trust. Gifts to charities are in fact usually made to charitable trustees.

The process of obtaining recognition as a charity is administrative and outside the direct control of the courts although ultimately it is for the courts to decide what activities fall within the definition of charity. The Charities Act 1960 requires (subject to exceptions) organisations seeking charitable status to apply for registration to the Charity Commissioners. The Act empowers the Charity Commissioners to grant or withhold registration according to their decision as to whether the purposes of the given organisation are, in law, charitable. Registration is then conclusive evidence of charitable status.

14.2 Charitable Trusts Compared with Private Trusts

The aim of a charitable trusts is to benefit the public at large, or at least a 'section of the public', whereas a private trust need only be for the benefit of a private individual or a group of such persons. It is necessary to differentiate between charitable and private trusts because of the various advantages that charitable trusts enjoy over private trusts. These may be categorised as (a) trust law advantages and (b) tax advantages. See Figure 14.1.

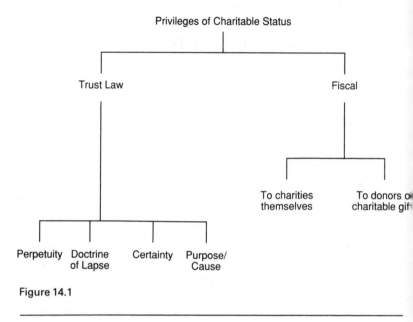

Figure 14.1

Trust law advantages

Certainty of objects
It has already been explained (see section 3.3) that private trusts have to satisfy what is now a fairly liberal test of certainty of objects as set down in *McPhail* v. *Doulton* [1971] AC 424. The test for charitable trusts is even less stringent, as it is in the public interest to give effect to a trust which must be of public benefit. Thus, provided a gift is made for exclusively charitable purposes (see section 14.8, below) it does not matter that the donor fails to specify the object precisely. It is possible simply to leave property to 'charity' or to 'charitable purposes'. This would not present a problem with regard to certainty of objects as what is charitable is defined by law, and the cy pres scheme (see section 14.9) would allow the Charity Commissioners or the Court to apply the property for a suitable purpose.

The doctrine of lapse
Generally if a non-charitable gift is made by will, the gift lapses if the individual(s) to be benefited predecease(s) the testator. This is not necessarily so if the gift is charitable and the charitable objects have ceased to exist at the testator's death. If certain conditions are satisfied (see section 14.8) the property may be applied to similar purposes to those which have failed, under the cy pres scheme.

Perpetuity
We have seen (see section 12.1, above) that, as a general rule gifts must vest in beneficiaries within the perpetuity period, and once vested must not be inalienable. Charitable gifts are not exempt from the rules relating to vesting but the subject-matter of the gift, once vested, may be inalienable. It should be noted with regard to vesting, however, the rule that a gift must vest within the perpetuity period does not apply where there is an immediate gift to a charitable purpose X followed by a gift over to another charitable purpose Y. For instance, in *Christ's Hospital* v. *Grainger* (1849) 1 Mac and G 460 there was a gift to the Corporation of Reading for the poor of Reading (charitable gift), with a proviso that if it was not applied for that purpose there should be a gift over to Christ's Hospital (also a charitable gift). It was held that the gift over to Christ's Hospital could take effect two centuries later, clearly outside the perpetuity period. The reason for this exception is that if one can have a gift to a charity which lasts indefinitely, as charities are not subject to the principle of inalienability, there seems to be no logical reason why one should not have a number of different charitable gifts together lasting in perpetuity.

Purposes/Causes
It has already been explained (see section 12.1) that, subject to exceptions, a private trust cannot be for a purpose or a cause rather than a person or persons. In contrast a charitable trust can clearly be for causes or purposes.

Tax concessions
The annual cost to the Inland Revenue of tax concessions to charities is about half a billion pounds which explains the number of cases involving the Inland Revenue in charity litigation. The concessions fall into two main categories: tax concessions to the charities, and tax concessions to the donors.

Tax concessions to the charities themselves
Charities established in the United Kingdom are exempt from income tax on income applied for charitable purposes and may, in some instances, recover from the Inland Revenue income tax paid (e.g., under 'four-year covenants'). They are also generally exempt from capital gains tax and, in the case of a charitable corporation, corporation tax. Charitable trusts are not subject to the 'periodic charge' levied as inheritance tax on capital held by trustees where there is no interest in possession. Charities are, of course, not subject to the community charge but may be liable to the business rate, although total or partial remission may be available in

many circumstances. Transfers, conveyances and leases to charities are exempt from stamp duty.

Concessions to the donors of charitable gifts

Concessions to the donors of charitable gifts are of indirect benefit to the charities themselves in that they encourage charitable giving. Neither inheritance tax nor capital gains tax is payable on gifts or bequests to a charity. Furthermore, where a donor makes an irrevocable voluntary covenant to pay money to charity for a period of at least four years, the payments are deductible by the donor in computing his or her income for higher rates of tax (as well as tax at the basic rate being recoverable by the charity). Where a corporation covenants to charity, provided certain conditions are satisfied the sum donated may be deducted from profits for the purposes of assessing corporation tax.

There is a growing opinion that the link between fiscal privileges and charitable status should be broken. There is evidence that the judiciary are affected by the extent of the fiscal privileges offered to charities in deciding what is charitable in borderline cases. Many causes may be worthy of the trust law privileges but not of the fiscal privileges.

14.3 Definition of Charity

There is no formal definition of charity, but in borderline cases the courts use as a starting point the preamble to the Charitable Uses Act 1601 and/or the 'Pemsel Classification'. The Charitable Uses Act 1601 sets out at list of purposes recognised as being charitable in 1601. The preamble cannot nowadays be followed to the letter as it was repealed by the Charities Act 1960. However, the House of Lords confirmed in *Scottish Burial Reform and Cremation Society* v. *Glasgow City Corporation* [1968] AC 138 HL that, although the words of the preamble are no longer authoritative, the case law following from it is. In *Incorporated Council of Law Reporting in England and Wales* v. *A-G* [1972] Ch 73 it was said that a gift must fall within the 'spirit and intendment' of the preamble. The Pemsel Classification is derived from the judgment of Lord MacNaughten in *Commissioners for Special Purposes of Income Tax* v. *Pemsel* [1891] AC 531. Without attempting to define charity, Lord MacNaughten set out four heads of charity:

(a) advancement of education;
(b) advancement of religion;
(c) relief of poverty;
(d) other purposes beneficial to the community.

According to Lord Greene MR in *National Anti-Vivisection Society* v. *IRC* [1948] AC 31, if a gift falls within one of the four heads it is prima facie charitable. It will nevertheless be necessary further to show that the gift satisfies the test of public benefit. Although the Pemsel Classification is a useful starting point it is not without problems. The fourth category, 'other purposes beneficial to the community', is merely a 'catch all' category and no satisfactory test has been devised to determine whether or not a particular purpose falls within it. Furthermore, the heads of the Pemsel Classification are not mutually exclusive: for example, a gift for choral singing in church may fall within the headings of both 'advancement of education' and 'advancement of religion'. This can be somewhat problematic as it will be shown that the test of public benefit varies in its application from one category to another. Despite its drawbacks it is nevertheless proposed to use the Pemsel Classification in order to examine the meaning of charity. Each head of the classification will be considered in turn to see what it involves, and at the same time the requirement of public benefit will be discussed.

14.4 Advancement of Education

The preamble to the Charitable Uses Act 1601 makes specific mention of 'schools of learning, free schools and scholars in universities . . . the education and preferment of orphans'. It is, however, clear that education extends much further than formal teaching, but how far is less clear. In *Re Shaw* [1957] 1 WLR 729 Harman J took a narrow view of education, expressing the opinion that a mere increase of public knowledge in one area was insufficient; there needed to be an element of teaching or education. The case concerned a gift in the will of George Bernard Shaw to carry out research, *inter alia*, into the advantages of developing a 40-letter British alphabet in the place of the present one, and to ascertain the time and labour wasted by the lack of at least fourteen unequivocal syllables, estimating the loss of income in both British and American currency! This was held not to amount to the advancement of education. In contrast, in *Re Hopkins* [1965] Ch 669 Wilberforce J took a wider view of education, holding that a trust for discovery and research into the Bacon–Shakespeare manuscripts was charitable both under the head of 'advancement of education' and the fourth category.

It is not possible to provide a test to delineate the boundaries of education; these can only be indicated by example. It is therefore proposed to consider the different areas which have been held to come within education, providing examples of each before going on to discuss the requirement of public benefit.

'Formation of taste and literary appreciation' (to adopt the words of Wilberforce J in *Re Hopkins*)
This aspect of the advancement of education was described by Lord Greene MR in the earlier case of *Royal Choral Society* v. *IRC* [1943] 2 All ER 101 as being 'one of the most important things in the development of a civilised human being'. Activities falling within this aspect of advancement of education have been held to include the advancement of:

- choral singing in London;
- the music of Delius;
- organists and organ music;
- Egyptology;
- English classical drama and the art of acting.

Gifts to professional bodies
Gifts to professional bodies are charitable if their object is the advancement of education, but not if the object or one of the objects is to promote the status of the profession and the welfare of its members. Thus in *Royal College of Surgeons* v. *National Provincial Bank Ltd* [1952] AC 631 a gift to the Royal College of Surgeons was held to be charitable as its primary object is the promotion and encouragement of the study and practice of the art and science of surgery.

Gifts which encourage or assist learning
An educational institution, whether it be a school, college or university, can be charitable provided that it is non-profit making. This is so even if it is a private institution, such as a private school. The following, however, would also qualify as charitable under the head of the advancement of education:

- gifts to learned institutions (e.g., Royal Geographical Society);
- the establishment of public museums and libraries;
- assistance in the publication of a book likely to be of educational value (e.g., a dictionary);
- the preparation and publication of law reports by a non-profit making body (e.g., the Incorporated Council of Law Reporting).

Research
In *Re Hopkins* (above) Wilberforce J said that in order for research to be charitable it must be (a) of educational value to the individual researcher, or (b) so directed as to lead to something which would pass into the store of educational material, or (c) be so directed as to improve the sum of communicable knowledge in an area which education might cover. It should be noted at this point that as a charitable gift must satisfy the

requirement of public benefit, it is clear that not any type of research will be charitable; there must be some sharing or teaching or dissemination, and the research must be of some value in the objective sense (see below).

Gifts for recreational purposes with an educational element
Some recreational purposes may fall within the fourth category, but as it appears that the application of the test of public benefit is less stringent under the heading of advancement of education (see section 14.7) it may be important to establish an educational element. The following have been held to be charitable within the head of advancement of education:

- a gift to the Boy Scout movement (the movement's charter states that it is for the instruction of 'boys of all classes in the principles of discipline, loyalty and good citizenship');
- a gift to provide an annual chess tournament for boys and young men in Portsmouth;
- the provision of an annual treat or field day for school children;
- the provision of a playground for children in a city.

In *London Hospital Medical College* v. *IRC* [1976] 1 WLR 613, a trust for the Students' Union of the London Hospital was held to be charitable. The objects of the Union were 'to promote the social, cultural and athletic activities amongst members and to add to the comfort and enjoyment of the students'. It was essential to this finding that the objects of the Union actually furthered the learning process of the college rather than merely being of private benefit to the students. This was held to be the case as physical, cultural and social outlets are all needed for students to be receptive to the teaching process. The court was also influenced by the geographical situation of the London Hospital in the deprived East End of London, which it described as a 'somewhat remote area of London'.

Sport with an educational link
It is clear that the promotion of a particular sport *per se* is not charitable under any head of the Pemsel Classification. In *Re Nottage* [1895] 2 Ch 649 CA a trust to provide a cup for the best yacht of the season to promote sailing was held not to be charitable, not being for the advancement of education or within the fourth category. In contrast, the provision of sports facilities within educational establishments will be charitable, being for the advancement of education. In *Re Mariette* [1915] 2 Ch 284 the provision of Eton Fives Courts at Aldenham School was held to be charitable, the reason being that good education involves giving attention not only to the mind of a child but also to his body. Eve J

also seemed concerned about boys in a boarding school 'quickly relapsing into something approaching barbarism' without channelled physical outlets. The House of Lords decision in *IRC* v. *McMullen* [1981] AC 1 now suggests a more incidental link with education may be sufficient for the promotion of a particular sport to come within the head of advancement of education. The case concerned the Football Association Youth Trust designed to improve facilities for playing Association Football for pupils at schools and universities in any part of the United Kingdom. Despite the fact that it was not linked to the geographical location of a particular school or university, it was held to be for the advancement of education on the ground that the objects of the trust were designed to improve the balance between the various elements which make up education, including the physical element. It should be noted that the House of Lords put limitations on the degree to which the courts would be prepared to find the necessary educational element in the promotion of sport. Lord Hailsham stated that the mere playing of games or competition was not *per se* charitable, and he implied that a trust for physical education needed to be associated with persons of school age 'or just above'.

The requirement of public benefit and the advancement of education

It is not sufficient purely to establish that the gift is for the advancement of education. A particular gift falling within any of the aforementioned must also satisfy the test of public benefit before it can be charitable. The requirement of public benefit is in theory the same for each head of the Pemsel Classification with the exception of relief of poverty, but in fact its application seems to have varied from one category to another. There is some judicial recognition of this. For example, in *Gilmour* v. *Coates* [1949] AC 426 (for facts see section 14.5), Lord Simonds stated that in applying the test of public benefit one cannot argue by analogy from one head of the Pemsel Classification to another.

It is clear that for a gift to show sufficient public benefit it is not necessary for everyone in the country to benefit, but only that a 'section of the public' benefits. Various tests have been formulated to explain the concept of a 'section of the public', the most widely adopted being the 'Compton test' derived from *Re Compton* [1945] Ch 123, which was approved by the House of Lords in *Oppenheim* v. *Tobacco Securities Trust Company Limited* [1951] 1 AC 297. For it to be said that a 'section of the public' has benefited two requirements must be satisfied: (a) the beneficiaries must not be numerically negligible; and (b) the quality which distinguishes them from other members of the public must not be a quality which depends upon their relationship to a particular individual; that is to say, there must be no *personal nexus*.

In *Re Compton* (above) a trust for the advancement of education of the descendants of three named persons failed to satisfy the test of public benefit on account of a personal nexus taking the form of a blood link. Similarly, a trust to provide education for the children of employees of a certain company failed on account of lack of public benefit in *Oppenheim* v. *Tobacco Securities Trust Company Limited*. As there were 110 000 existing employees, the beneficiaries were clearly not numerically negligible but there was a personal nexus, that of the relationship between employer and employee.

The concept of a personal nexus was criticised by Lord MacDermott in his dissenting judgment in the *Oppenheim* case and also received strong support from *obiter dicta* of Lord Cross in *Dingle* v. *Turner* [1972] AC 601. Lord MacDermott said he found difficulty in distinguishing between the qualities or attributes which may serve to bind human beings into two mutually exclusive groups, one involving individual status and being purely personal, the other disregarding such status and being impersonal. In the course of his judgment Lord Simonds had indicated that a trust for someone following a particular profession or calling (such as clergymen, lawyers, colliers or tobacco workers) would form a section of the public. Lord MacDermott asked why, if the bond between those employed by a particular railway is purely personal, should the bond between those who are employed as railwaymen be essentially different? Perhaps the explanation behind the decision in the *Oppenheim* case was that by awarding charitable status, tax concessions would be available to the company to give tax-free fringe benefits to employees. Lord Simonds indicated he was influenced by this in reaching his decision, and in *Dingle* v. *Turner* Lord Cross was of the view that this had been a relevant consideration. In *Dingle* v. *Turner*, Lord Cross thought that the class of people who were to be regarded as a section of the public should be a question of fact and degree, depending on the purpose of the trust. Such a formulation is not, it is submitted, any more helpful than the admittedly flawed 'personal nexus' test as it is too vague.

Preferred class cases

Attempts have been made to avoid the 'no personal nexus' requirement in trusts for the advancement of education by having a preferred class based on a personal nexus within a class with no personal nexus. For example, in *Re Koettgen's Will Trusts* [1954] Ch 252 a trust was established for the furtherance of commercial education among persons of either sex who were British-born subjects and who could not afford it at their own expense. This was clearly a section of the public, but the trust instrument went on to provide that preference should be given to the employees of a particular company or members of their families, but that not more than 75 per cent of the income in any one year should be applied to the preferred class. Taken alone the preferred class would not be a section of the public on account of the personal nexus of employer and employee. Nevertheless it was held that the beneficiaries were a section of the public as the court only had to consider the primary class (British-born subjects of either sex). It was important to this finding that the trustees were not obliged to apply any of the trust property for the preferred class. If there is an absolute right in favour of the preferred group then the trust will not be charitable. Thus in *Caffoor* v. *Income Tax Commissioner, Colombo* [1961] AC 584 where there was a trust for the education of 'deserving youths of the Islamic Faith' with a direction that the recipients were to be selected first from male descendants of the settlor and his collaterals, the Privy Council held that there was no public benefit.

It is questionable whether the decision in *Re Koettgen* is consistent with the Compton test of public benefit; it has in any case been doubted in a number of later decisions including *IRC* v. *Educational Grants Association* [1967] 2 Ch 993. In this case the Metal Box Company Limited provided funds under deed of covenant to the Educational Grants Association, which was claiming the repayment of tax due in respect of payment under the covenant. In the relevant tax years, between 76 per cent and 85 per cent of the income of the Educational Grants Association had in fact been paid towards the education of the children of persons connected with the Metal Box Company Limited. On these facts the Court of Appeal held that the tax paid under a covenant was not recoverable by the Educational Grants Association as the funds had not been applied for exclusively charitable purposes. It was necessary to see where the money was going to ascertain whether there was public benefit and, since most of it was going to the employees of the Metal Box Company Limited, it was given by virtue of a personal nexus.

Expert opinion and public benefit

A further factor to be borne in mind in relation to the requirement of public benefit as applied to the head of advancement of education is that the courts are prepared to evaluate the quality and usefulness of the purpose in order to determine whether it is really beneficial. This is illustrated by *Re Pinion* [1965] Ch 85 where the testator left his studio and its contents (which included paintings by himself and a quantity of not very special eighteenth and nineteenth century furniture and bric-a-brac) to enable it to be used as a museum. Expert opinion was unanimous that the collection had no artistic value. The Court of Appeal held that the trust was void and Harman LJ concluded that no useful purpose would be served by 'foisting upon the public this mass of junk'! In the course of his judgment he provided other examples of purposes which would be for the advancement of education but clearly lack public benefit, such as schools for prostitutes or training pickpockets and he referred to an earlier case where a school for training mediums was held not to be charitable (*Re Hummeltenburg* [1923] Ch 237).

Politics and public benefit

One final point which needs to be considered in ascertaining whether a gift satisfies the test of public benefit is whether the gift is in any way political. A gift falling under any of the heads of the Pemsel Classification will not be charitable if it is political (see section 14.7). The reason for this was explained by Lord Parker in *National Anti-vivisection Society* v. *IRC* [1948] AC 31: namely, that there is no means of judging whether a change in the law is of public benefit as the law cannot stultify itself by saying that a change in the law would be beneficial. For this reason the courts are very wary of political propaganda masquerading under the guise of advancement of education. For example, in *Re Hopkinson* [1949] 1 All ER 346 a trust for the advancement of education along the lines of a Labour Party Memorandum was held not to be charitable, as was a trust for the advancement and propagation of socialised medicine in *Re Bushnell* [1975] 1 All ER 721. However, the fact that political issues may be touched upon in the course of educational advancement will not render a trust too political to be charitable. Thus, in *Re Koeppler's Will Trust* [1985] 2 All ER 869, CA, which involved a series of conferences at which academics were invited to discuss international issues with the aim of promoting greater co-operation in Europe and the West generally, as well as contributing to the formation of an informed public opinion, the court held that the trust was valid as for the advancement of education because no one political standpoint was taken and the purposes did not propose any specific changes in the law or in government policy in any country. Similarly, in *A-G* v. *Ross* [1985] 3 All ER 334 where the constitution of the Students' Union of North East London Polytechnic provided, among many other things, that it existed to promote and develop political activities among students, this was held not to prevent the existence of a valid charitable trust as political activities were part of the educational process enabling the students to form political views. This decision should, however, be contrasted with *Webb* v. *O'Doherty, The Times*, 11 February 1991, where it was held that making payments out of student union funds for a *campaign* on a political issue (to stop war in the Gulf) was inconsistent with charitable status.

14.5 Advancement of Religion

The preamble to the Charitable Uses Act 1601 mentions repair of churches, but it is clear that the advancement of religion is now much wider. In *Neville Estates* v. *Madden* [1962] Ch 832 it was established that religion extends beyond the Christian religion. Cross J said, 'As between different religions the law stands neutral, but it assumes that any religion is at least likely to be better than none.' Despite this statement it is unclear whether all non-Christian religions will be regarded as charitable. In *Bowman* v. *Secular Society* [1917] AC 406 Lord Parker suggested that any form of monotheism will be recognised as a religion, with the implication that polytheism would not. The position was left open in relation to Buddhism in *Re South Place Ethical Society* [1980] 1 WLR 1565. The situation with regard to 'personality cults' is also unclear, but some have been registered as charities.

It is necessary to consider (a) what amounts to a religion; (b) what is involved in the advancement of religion; and (c) what needs to be established to satisfy the test of public benefit.

What is a religion?

The question arose in *United Grand Lodge of Ancient Free and Accepted Masons of England* v. *Holborn Borough Council* [1957] 3 All ER 281 as to whether Freemasonry is a religion. It was held that a religion requires a belief in a supreme being, and the taking of steps to increase belief by rituals, pastoral and missionary methods. As the Freemasons have no religious services or religious instruction they cannot be said to be a religion. This was so despite the fact that the Freemasons encourage high moral standards as a way of life and insist upon belief in a divine spirit, both tenets of religion, as these in themselves were not sufficient. The question of what precisely constitutes a religion arose again in *Re South Place Ethical Society* [1980] 1 WLR 1565. This concerned a society whose objects were the study and dissemination of ethical principles and the cultivation of a rational religious sentiment. Dillion J decided that this did not amount to religion. Religion is concerned with a person's relationship with God, whilst ethics is concerned with people's relationships with each other. Moreover religion is not the same as a philosophy, and the fact that the society may analyse what God is does not make its objects religious.

What is involved in the advancement of religion?

A further reason why the Freemasons were held not to be a charitable body for the advancement of religion was because they had no programme to encourage converts. For religion to be 'advanced' steps must be taken to promote the religion to people in general. Provided steps are in fact taken to advance the religion they need not be likely to succeed. All that is required is the possibility of acquiring converts. Thus in *Thornton* v. *Howe* [1862] 31 Beav 14, where a certain Joanna Southcott thought she was with child by the Holy Spirit and would give birth to the Second Messiah, even though she had very few followers and the court thought that her writings would be teaching largely to the converted, it was held the writings did amount to a trust for the advancement of religion. There was a similarity with the case in *Re Watson* [1973] 1 WLR 1472, where a trust was established for the propagation of truth as given in the Holy Bible in the form of pamphlets which gave 'the truth about life'. There were no followers of the author of the pamphlet outside his immediate family, and although expert opinion considered that the pamphlet was unlikely to obtain any converts, the trust was held to be for the advancement of religion.

It is now necessary to consider what type of activities done in the name of religion will amount to its advancement. Although not an exhaustive list, the following are the main categories:

(a) gifts to build, maintain, repair religious buildings or parts of buildings and graveyards (e.g., a trust to maintain a church or synagogue, to erect or maintain a window, a chancel, or a monument forming part of the fabric of the church or other religious building);

(b) gifts for religious observances, such as choral singing in church, bell ringing, preaching an annual sermon, provision of Sunday school prizes as well as the saying of masses for the dead (*Re Hetherington* [1989] 2 All ER 129, although they may lack the requirement of public benefit (see section 14.5) if not said in public);

(c) gifts to support ministers of religion (e.g., for payment of ministers, relief from their sickness, etc.).

It should be noted, however, that 'social work' or purely secular work done in the name of religion does not amount to the advancement of religion. Thus, in *Farley* v. *Westminster Bank* [1939] 3 All ER 491 where there was a gift to the vicar and church wardens of two named churches for 'parochial work', it was held that as this phrase involved more than strict religious activities it was not the advancement of religion in the legal charitable sense. It therefore follows that schools or hospitals run by religious groups will not amount to the advancement of religion although they may fall within another head of the Pemsel Classification, such as advancement of education or 'other purposes beneficial to the community'. Despite the fact that social work done in the name of religion does not amount to the advancement of religion generally, where a gift is made to a person holding a religious office (even though his or her work may involve more than the advancement of religion in the strict legal sense) it is construed as being given for the advancement of religion. Thus, in *Re Rumball* [1956] Ch 105 where a gift was made 'to the Bishop for the time being of the Windward Islands to be used as he thinks fit in his diocese', despite the fact that absolute discretion was given to the Bishop the gift was construed as being a gift donated for the charitable purposes inherent in his office.

Religion and the requirement of public benefit

As the law presumes that any religion is better than none, once it is established that the religion is being advanced, public benefit is presumed. It appears that the requirement of public benefit for religious charities is less stringently applied than in the context of advancement of education in the respect that the courts are far less willing to make an assessment of the value of religious belief. In *Thornton* v. *Howe* [1862] 31 Beav 14 Romilly MR commented that even if the court considered the opinions sought to be propagated to be 'foolish or even devoid of foundation' the gift would be charitable so long as it was not 'subversive of all morality'. This was followed in *Re Watson* [1973] 1 WLR 1472. It is arguable that the courts ought to be prepared nowadays to be more critical given the cost to the public purse in the form of tax concessions to such charitable bodies.

In what types of circumstance may a gift for the advancement of religion be regarded as 'subversive of all morality'? In *Re Hummeltenburg* [1923] 1 Ch 237 a college for the training of mediums lacked public benefit for this reason, and in *Yeap Cheah Neo* v. *Ong Cheng Neo* (1875) LR 6 PC 381 a trust to promote ancestral worship was held not to be charitable because it was subversive of all morality. Given the recognition of religions other than the Christian religion, the better view of this latter case today is that it lacked public benefit as it was not for a section of the public but only of family benefit. On the whole it appears that the courts and the Charity Commissioners are unwilling to condemn a religion as being subversive of all morality. There are some highly suspect groups (e.g., the Moonies, or the School of Economic Science) which still have charitable status. The Goodman Committee on Charity Law and Voluntary Organisations, which reported in 1976, recommended that religious organisations detrimental to the moral welfare of the community should not have charitable status (p.23).

A religion will not be of public benefit unless it is advanced in the way outlined above: that is to say, there is a possibility of obtaining converts. Thus in *Gilmour* v. *Coates* [1949] AC 426 a gift to a Carmelite Convent (a Roman Catholic cloistered community of nuns who devoted themselves to prayer and contemplation but had no communication with the outside world) was held not to be charitable. It was argued, among other things, that the public benefit they gave took the form of prayers for the outside world. However, the court decided that this was too vague to be susceptible of legal proof and in any case involved the courts in accepting the religion rather than merely tolerating it. As the law stands neutral between religions, this was inadmissible as evidence of public benefit.

Finally, on the question of public benefit and the advancement of religion, in *Dingle* v. *Turner* [1972] AC 601 Lord Cross suggested a trust to promote religion amongst the employees of a company might be charitable, despite the personal nexus, provided that the benefits were purely spiritual. It will be remembered that Lord Cross considered that what is to be regarded as a section of the public should depend upon the purpose of the trust. Even if the Compton test does apply, in *IRC* v. *Baddeley* [1955] AC 572 at 615 Lord Somervell thought that it was not necessarily true that what was regarded as a section of the public sufficient to support a valid trust in one category should, as a matter of law, be sufficient to support a trust in another category. He went on to say: 'There might well be a valid trust for the promotion of religion benefitting a small class.'

14.6 Relief of Poverty

It is here necessary to consider what is meant by relief of poverty and the extent to which public benefit must be shown.

The meaning of poverty

Poverty is a relative concept, so that it is quite clear that the objects of the gift do not have to be destitute. In *Re Coulthurst's Will Trusts* [1951] Ch 661 Evershed MR said, 'it is not unfairly paraphrased for present purposes as meaning persons who have to "go short" in the ordinary acception of that term, due regard being had to their status in life and so forth'.

This extract reveals, therefore, that poverty is not only relative to the society but also to the beneficiaries' position in society. A trust is for the relief of poverty if it is for the benefit of persons who have fallen upon 'evil days'. In this sense of poverty, gifts to 'decayed actors', 'distressed gentlefolk', 'ladies in reduced circumstances' and 'ladies of limited means' have all been validated as charitable trusts for the relief of poverty. In contrast, in *Re Sanders Will Trusts* [1954] Ch 265 a trust for the provision of housing for the 'working classes' failed as a charitable trust for the relief of poverty because the term 'working class' did not necessarily constitute poverty. It should be noted that the courts have in this area failed to consider the role of the state in the relief of poverty. If the beneficiaries do not qualify for state benefit by reason of their poverty, why should they indirectly benefit from the fiscal privileges afforded by charitable status? This illustrates the case for suggesting that fiscal privileges should be made separate from charitable status.

Two further points should be noted about trusts for the relief of poverty. First, the relief of poverty may be inferred from the circumstances of the gift. For instance, in *Re Lucas* [1922] Ch 52, income from a fund was to be given to the oldest respectable inhabitant of Gunville to the amount of five shillings a week. The very small amount offered showed that the aim of the gift was to help poor old people. The other point is that the trust must exclusively benefit poor people. It will fail if persons other than the poor can benefit. Thus in *Re Gwyon* [1930] 1 Ch 255 a trust was established to provide a foundation to provide knickers for boys of a certain age who were sons of residents in the district of Farnham. As rich boys could be supplied with knickers under the terms of the trust it was held not to be charitable.

Public benefit and relief of poverty
It is clear that the Compton test does not apply to trusts for the relief of poverty. This is not to say that there is no requirement of public benefit at all. In *Dingle* v. *Turner* [1972] AC 601, where a trust was established for the paying of pensions to poor employees of E. Dingle and Co., the House of Lords (reviewing earlier cases) decided that it did not matter that there was a personal nexus of employer and employee, and moreover went on to confirm that one could have a charitable trust for poor relations. The court approved the principles set down in *Re Scarisbrick* [1951] Ch 622 to distinguish between a charitable trust and a purely private trust in poor relation cases. In *Re Scarisbrick* it was said that it is a question of construction as to whether the trust is intended for particular individuals (where it would only be a private trust) as opposed to a particular description of poor people, in which case the trust would be charitable. Guidelines are given to help in deciding this question of construction. If the trust is perpetual, then this tends against the intention to set up a private trust, whereas if the capital and income from the trust are to be distributed immediately (although this is not conclusive of a private trust) it does indicate that the donor had particular individuals in mind.

Other classes of persons for whom a valid charitable trust for the relief of poverty has been upheld are poor club members and poor members of a society.

14.7 **Other Purposes Beneficial to the Community**

The fourth category of the Pemsel Classification is a catch-all head. No satisfactory test has been devised to determine whether or not any particular purpose or object falls within it. It is, however, clear that it is not sufficient only to show public benefit; the purpose must be beneficial in a way in which the law regards as charitable; it must be within the 'spirit and intendment' of the 1601 preamble or there must be sufficient analogy with some decided case. It is impossible to create an exhaustive list of categories of situations which fall within the fourth category, but it is posssible to look at common groupings. The Compton test (see section 14.4) applies with regard to public benefit, although in ascertaining a 'section of the public' we shall see that it has been more strictly applied. Under this head it is proposed to consider issues of public benefit as each individual grouping is discussed. However, a general point needs to be made at the outset. In considering trusts for the advancement of education it was noted that the courts are wary of political trusts (see section 14.4). This is true of any category of the Pemsel Classification, but it has particularly arisen in practice in relation to trusts potentially falling within the fourth category.

Political trusts

As legislation in the twentieth century covers so many aspects of life, the objects of many trusts can only be achieved by central or local government action. Supposing a group of people wishes to protect the countryside, or an endangered species of fauna or flora, or to try to secure better medical care in a particular locality, will the purpose be regarded as political? The following are guidelines. A trust will be too political to be charitable where, first, the trust is set up to press for a change in the law. In *National Anti-Vivisection Society* v. *IRC* [1948] AC 31 it was held that as the society has as its object the abolition of all vivisection, and this object can only be achieved by legislation, the trust was political and thus not charitable. As has already been explained, the courts feel unable to judge the question of public benefit for fear of prejudicing the judiciaries' reputation for political impartiality.

It will also be judged too political where the trust is established for the purpose of opposing a change in the law. Vaisey J explained in *Re Hopkinson* [1949] 1 All ER 346 that the court has no means of judging whether the absence of change in the law would or would not be of public benefit.

It should be noted, however, in relation to these two categories that the Charity Commissioners in their report in 1969 indicated that an activity would still be regarded as charitable if it involved opposing or giving support to private legislation and any other legislation regarded as being of a non-political nature.

Third, it will be too political if its object is to secure the alteration of the law of a foreign country. In *McGovern* v. *A-G* [1982] Ch 231 which concerned an Amnesty International trust fund, one of the reasons given for why such a trust would be regarded as too political was the court's inability to assess the extent of the risk that the trust, if enforced, would prejudice the relations of the United Kingdom with the foreign country concerned.

The fourth category concerns any trust whose object is to procure the reversal of government policy or a particular administrative decision in the United Kingdom or any other country (*McGovern* v. *A-G*). However, in their report of 1969, the Charity Commissioners indicated that a charity could properly give comments on proposed changes in the law if invited to either expressly or impliedly (e.g., through the publication of a Green or White Paper) by a government department, and it is also in order to present a government with a reasoned memorandum advocating changes in the law, provided the charity is acting in the furtherance of its purpose.

The fifth and last category concerns those trusts whose objects further the interests or principles propounded by a particular party. In *Re Bushnell* [1975] 1 All ER 721 a trust for the promotion of socialised medicine (set up before the establishment of the National Health Service) was held not to be charitable.

We will now consider individual groupings of trusts which fall in the fourth category, and how the test of public benefit has been applied to them.

Animals

A trust for a particular species of animal, or for animals generally as opposed to a specific animal(s) (e.g., a pet dog) may be and is normally charitable. The reason for this was explained in *Re Wedgewood* [1915] 1 Ch 113 as being because it benefits humankind by promoting 'feelings of humanity and morality' and curbing an 'inborn tendency to cruelty'. In *Re Grove-Grady* [1929] 1 Ch 557, a trust to provide a refuge for the preservation of all animals, birds or other creatures so that they would be safe from molestation and destruction by humans was held not to be charitable as on its facts it provided no advantages to humanity. It did not protect animals useful to humankind, and neither did it allow for observation or research or prevent cruelty to animals. Consequently there was no public benefit. The following types of trust involving animals have been held to be charitable:

- homes for lost or unwanted animals, such as dogs, cats;
- animal sanctuaries (e.g., for retired working horses);
- hospitals for sick animals;
- providing for the welfare of animals generally or for a particular species.

Trusts to campaign for the humane treatment of animals and to promote vegetarianism (*Re Slatter* (1905) 21 TLR 295) have been held to be charitable. However, one has to consider how such a campaign or promotion is to be effected; if it involves changes in the law the object of the trust may be regarded as political and thus not charitable.

Other trusts which encourage good citizenship or moral welfare
It has already been explained that animal trusts are regarded as charitable as they promote the moral welfare of humankind. Other trusts which are charitable for a similar reason include:

- a trust for the promotion of temperance;
- trusts to encourage ethical principles (e.g., *Re South Place Ethical Society*: see above);
- a trust to provide for a public memorial of a well-respected person.

Trusts for the sick
The preamble to the 1601 Charitable Uses Act refers to 'aged, impotent and poor'. The 'and' has been interpreted disjunctively so that it is unnecessary that the beneficiaries satisfy all three conditions. Nevertheless, as the purpose must be the *relief* of impotency, there must be a need arising out of the particular condition. Consequently if money payments were made to impotent millionaires it would not be charitable as such payments would not be needed to relieve their impotency; by definition a millionaire would have adequate financial resources of his or her own. Thus there will be a connection between 'poor' and 'impotent' in some cases, depending on the nature of the relief offered.

Relief of the 'impotent' includes those suffering as a result of a disability, sickness (mental or physical), injury or disease, and it also extends to the relief of stress. The relief may take the following forms:

- provision of non-profit making hospitals, hospices, rest homes or nursing homes;
- provision of specific amenities for patients (e.g., in one case accommodation for visiting relatives, and in another, flowers);
- training of doctors and nurses;
- furtherance of use of particular forms of treatment;
- research into treatments;

- aid for those suffering from a particular illness (e.g., blindness, drug addiction);
- provision of nurses' homes.

It should be noted that trusts benefiting a private non-profit making hospital may be charitable as well as trusts benefiting National Health Service hospitals. As with other areas of charitable relief, the courts have chosen to ignore political issues relating to the granting of charitable status. The political assumption is made, for example, in the Privy Council decision of *Re Resch's Will Trust* [1969] 1 AC 514, that a two-tier system of medical care is beneficial. The case concerned a private non-profit making hospital run by the Sisters of Charity. On the facts it was decided that the gift was charitable, first, because (provided that poor people were not excluded) it was not necessary for the beneficiaries to be impotent and poor. The poor were not excluded as they may have been able to afford the fees by being covered by medical insurance, or, on the facts, they may have qualified for exemptions or reduced fees. Second, public benefit was satisfied in part by the fact there were facilities of privacy and relaxation offered which were not available in the public sector (for those who could afford the fees!). Third, there was indirect benefit to those who could not afford to use the hospital as the existence of the private hospital took the strain of the public hospital. This last point is controversial as it could be argued that the existence of a private hospital simply diverts resources from a public hospital and that this is not, when viewed overall, of public benefit.

Trusts for the aged

It has already been explained that the words 'aged, impotent and poor' within the preamble to the 1601 Charitable Uses Act are read disjunctively. As with impotency, however, as the purpose of the trust has got to be the *relief* of the aged, financial relief exclusively for wealthy aged people would not be charitable. Trusts under this heading have taken the following forms:

- provision or maintenance of suitable accommodation for old people;
- financial aid;
- non-profit making nursing homes.

The case of *Joseph Rowntree Memorial Trust Housing Association Limited* v. *A-G* [1983] Ch 159 extends charitable relief in this area and is a further example of the courts' willingness to endorse indirect benefit as being sufficient to satisfy the requirement of public benefit. The case involved a non-profit making association which provided self-contained flats especially adapted for the elderly. The accommodation was provided at full cost but beneficiaries were means-tested in order to qualify as purchasers. Peter Gibson J held that the trust was charitable despite the fact that, having acquired a flat, the beneficiaries or their relatives could profit from the increase in value, as this was merely incidental to the purpose of the trust. The fact that a capital sum had to be paid to acquire a flat was also held to be irrelevant as one did not have to be 'poor and old'. Nevertheless, this case seems to go further than others in that, arguably, the poor are excluded as one had to be relatively well-off to find the capital sum to acquire the leasehold. The indirect benefit to the community as a whole arose from the possibility that the accommodation may prevent or at least defer the time when the beneficiaries needed state services.

Conservation of national heritage and maintenance of public works and buildings

Bodies such as the National Trust qualify under the heading of conservation of national heritage. The preamble to the Charitable Uses Act 1601 refers to 'repair of bridges, ports, havens, causeways . . . sea-brakes, and highways. This heading also includes such things as the provision or maintenance of a public library, museum, hall, park or cemetery.

Safeguarding human life

Safeguarding human life includes trusts for the emergency services (lifeboat, fire, ambulance or police).

'Education and preferment of orphans'

Funding a children's home is charitable.

Relief from disasters

Trusts for the relief of disaster are only charitable in two circumstances: first, if the relief is confined to relief of financial need occasioned by the disaster (i.e., relief of resulting poverty), or second, over and above poverty, a trust for the relief of a disaster may be charitable within the fourth category if the number of persons affected by the disaster is sufficiently large to form a section of the public for the purpose of the test of public benefit. On this basis, a number of cases concerned with colliery accidents in the first part of this century where there were in excess of 200 victims were held to be charitable, as was the disaster appeal which resulted from the Lynton and Lynmouth Floods in 1953, where again there was a large number of victims. There are other cases where public benefit was assumed, even though comparatively small numbers of victims were involved, but in *Re Gillingham Bus Disaster Fund* [1958] Ch 300 where there were only 24 victims, it was conceded that there was no public benefit as they did not form a section of the public for the purposes of the fourth category.

In the past disaster appeals have caused much anguish, largely due to poor drafting of the appeal and a lack of appreciation of the law as to when such an appeal will or will not be charitable. If the appeal is not charitable it may be subject to tax and members of the public who have dug deep into their pockets from resources already taxed in their hands resent the government filling its coffers again with further taxes collected from the trustees of the appeal. Furthermore, in the event of there being surplus funds, the destination of those funds will differ from that of surplus funds in a charitable appeal (see section 6.5 for the position of a non-charitable appeal and section 14.2 for a charitable appeal).

Trusts to increase the efficiency of the armed and police forces
Trusts to increase the efficiency of the armed forces include gifts to regiments, possibly for a specified purpose such as the training of officers or, as in one case, for the teaching of shooting. A trust to promote sport in a regiment may be charitable under this heading as it should make the regiment physically fit and thus more efficient (*Re Gray* [1925] Ch 362. This view was doubted, however, in *IRC* v. *City of Glasgow Police Athletic Association* [1953] AC 380 where a trust to encourage and promote all forms of athletic sport within a police force was held not to be charitable. On the facts it was found not to promote efficiency but purely to be of recreational value which did not provide for any public benefit.

Locality trusts
A trust for a particular village, town or city will be charitable even though no particular charitable purpose is specified. A scheme will be organised so that funds are applied for purely charitable purposes (see *Goodman* v. *Saltash Corp* (1882) 7 App Cas 633). An extension of this principle can be seen in *Re Smith* [1932] 1 Ch 153 where a gift 'To my country, England' was held to be charitable on the basis of the locality cases.

Sports and other recreational purposes
It has already been stated that a gift for the promotion of a particular sport *per se* is not charitable under any head of the Pemsel Classification, but that sport or other recreational activities expressly or impliedly linked with education may give rise to a charitable trust for the advancement of education (see section 14.4). Furthermore, a trust for the promotion of sport may possibly be charitable under the fourth

category if it increases the efficiency of the armed forces or the police force. In addition to this, in *Re Hadden* [1932] 1 Ch 133 land given generally for public recreation was held to be charitable within the fourth category. Outside these spheres sporting and recreational trusts are likely only to be charitable if they fall within the ambit of the Recreational Charities Act 1958. This Act was passed as a result of the House of Lords' decision in *IRC* v. *Baddeley* [1955] AC 572, which put in doubt the charitable status of many institutions such as Women's Institutes and village clubs. In *IRC* v. *Baddeley* the trust was to 'promote the moral, social and physical well-being of persons resident in West Ham and Leyton who were members or likely to become members of the Methodist Church' by the provision of recreational activities. The gift failed as a charitable trust for two reasons: first, the language used (with its reference to social purposes) was wider than the concept of charity and uncertain; and second, even if the trust's purpose had been limited to charitable purposes, the requirement of public benefit was not satisfied as the beneficiaries did not form a section of the public; they were 'a class within a class'. This suggests that the requirement of public benefit is more difficult to satisfy for the fourth category. Members of a church or other religious grouping (e.g., synagogue) are clearly a section of the public for the purpose of advancement of religion, as are the pupils of a school for the purpose of advancement of education.

The Recreational Charities Act 1958

The Recreational Charities Act 1958 was designed to give statutory recognition to trusts which had always been regarded as charitable in relation to recreational activities following the uncertainty introduced by the decision in *IRC* v. *Baddeley*, but it was not intended to enlarge the definition of charity. S.1 of the Act provides that the provision of facilities for 'recreation or other leisure time occupation' are charitable provided they are:

(a) in the interests of social welfare; and
(b) the trust is for public benefit.

Since s.1(1) states that 'nothing in this section shall be taken to derogate from the principle that a trust or institution to be charitable must be for the public benefit', it is arguable that even after the passing of the Act a gift such as that in *IRC* v. *Baddeley* would fail. The section suggests it may still be necessary to satisfy the test of public benefit set down in *IRC* v. *Baddeley* which, on the facts of the case was not satisfied.

The Recreational Charities Act defines social welfare (s.1(2)) as involving two elements:

(a)   the facilities must be provided with the object of improving the conditions of life of the persons for whom the facilities are primarily intended; *and*
(b)   the facilities must *either*:
       (i) be needed by those for whom they are primarily intended by reason of those persons' youth, age, infirmity or disablement, poverty or social and economic circumstances *or*
       (ii) be available to the members of the public (or female public) at large.

A restrictive interpretation was put on 'social welfare' in the Court of Appeal decision in *IRC* v. *McMullen* [1979] 1 WLR 1300. The majority said that the requirement of social welfare would not be satisfied unless the beneficiaries were in some way 'deprived', otherwise the facilities could not be said to be provided with the object of improving the conditions of life (s.1(2)). Bridge LJ took a more liberal approach, stating that 'Hyde Park improves the conditions of life for residents of Mayfair as much as for those in Pimlico or the Portobello Road'. The House of Lords left open the issue.

14.8 A Gift must be Exclusively for Charitable Purposes

It has been stated that the requirement of certainty is relaxed in relation to charitable trusts (see section 14.2). However, as a general rule a gift will fail if it is possible for the gift to be applied to non-charitable purposes without there being a breach of trust. Two main problems have been experienced in this area: first, words wider than the definition of charity have been used by persons believing that they are within the concept of charity or synonymous with the word 'charitable', such as 'public' or 'benevolent' purposes; second, a gift may be given for basically charitable purposes, but non-charitable objects may also be involved.

Use of words wider than the concept of charity
Words confused with the concept of charity, such as 'public' or 'benevolent' purposes, render a trust void for uncertainty. The Charitable Trusts (Validation) Act 1954 was passed to try and overcome the misapprehension people were under concerning such terms, and to validate trusts until people corrected their ways. The Act therefore only operates retrospectively and now only affects gifts which were made before 16 December 1952 but which take effect after 30 July 1954. In this event, if words wider than the concept of what is charitable are used, they are deemed to be for a charitable purpose and the trustees must apply them

exclusively to charitable objects to prevent a breach of trust. The Act may be relevant, for example, if property was given in the will of X who died in 1951 to 'A for life, with remainder for purposes X (charitable) and Y (non-charitable)'. A died in 1990, thus the gift in remainder takes effect. The trust is deemed to be for purposes X and must be exclusively so applied. The trustees would be in breach of trust if they applied the property for purposes Y.

Quite apart from the Charitable Trusts (Validation) Act it may be possible to establish that a trust is exclusively charitable where words wider than charity are used in two other situations: first, where the word charitable is followed by the word 'and' and a word potentially wider than the definition of charity (see Figure 14.2). As the word 'and' is normally construed conjunctively, the term wider than charity must be limited to what is charitable. For example, in *Blair* v. *Duncan* [1902] AC 37 property was given for 'charitable and public' purposes. The court held that the public purposes selected had to be charitable.

Prima facie the word 'and' is construed conjunctively, but it is a question of construction of the testator's intention as to whether this should be the case. There are decisions where 'and' has been construed disjunctively, causing a gift to fail for uncertainty.

It should be noted, in contrast, that where the word charitable is followed by the word 'or', and a word wider than the definition of charity, as a general rule 'or' is construed disjunctively and consequently allows the trustees to apply the gift for a non-charitable purpose, causing it to fail (see Figure 14.3). Thus in *Houston* v. *Burns* [1918] AC 337 where property was given for 'such public, benevolent or charitable purposes', the gift failed.

Second, where a gift is made to different organisations or purposes within a specified locality it may be possible to interpret words wider than the concept of charity to be intended to be limited to exclusively charitable purposes. For instance, in *Re Allen* [1905] 2 Ch 400 property

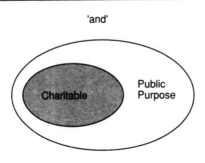

Figure 14.2

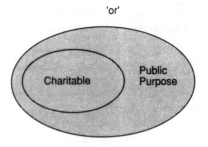

Figure 14.3

---

was given 'for such charitable, educational or other institutions in the town of Kendal and also for such other general purposes for the benefit of Kendal'. Specific examples of institutions to be benefited were provided (e.g., the Memorial Hospital, the grammar school and the library). As these were all charitable objects the court found there was an intention to give exclusively to charity.

Gifts to charitable purposes where non-charitable objects are involved
Where there is a gift to a charitable purpose and a non-charitable object is involved, the non-charitable purpose may be purely incidental to the work of the trust or it may be subsidiary to the purpose of the trust. Alternatively, the non-charitable purpose may be the means through which the primary charitable purpose is carried out. Each of these situations requires separate consideration.

Purely incidental non-charitable purposes
Provided the non-charitable purpose is merely incidental to the work of the particular association, it will not invalidate an otherwise charitable gift. This was seen in the *Joseph Rowntree Memorial Trust* case (see section 14.7). In *Incorporated Council of Law Reporting for England and Wales* v. *Attorney-General* [1972] Ch 73, the fact that the law reports produced by the Incorporated Council benefit legal practitioners who earn fees by using law reports was held to be irrelevant 'as it was incidental to the main aim of providing material for the academic study of case law'.

Non-charitable purpose subsidiary to work of the trust
If the non-charitable purpose subsidiary to work of the trust is a subsidiary part of the work of the trust, the whole gift will fail as a charity. In *Oxford Group* v. *IRC* [1949] 2 All ER 537 the gift failed to qualify as a charitable trust because the non-charitable objects were not

merely incidental but subsidiary. The objects of the Oxford Group were threefold: (a) advancement of religion (clearly charitable); (b) to maintain and develop the Oxford Group; and (c) to establish 'charitable and benevolent' associations. As benevolent was a concept wider than charity and not construed conjunctively, it was held that the non-charitable purposes were not merely incidental but a subsidiary part of the movement's work, and as they were wider than what is charitable the gift failed.

Non-charitable purpose through which the primary charitable purpose is carried out

Where a donor gives property to a primary charitable purpose and there is a non-charitable purpose through which the primary charitable purpose is carried out, the gift will not fail. In *Re Coxen* [1948] Ch 747 £200 000 was given to the Court of Aldermen of the City of London on trust (a) to apply an annual sum of not more than £100 for a dinner for the Aldermen to meet and discuss the business of the trust and (b) to pay one guinea to each Alderman for attending, and (c) to apply the balance for orthopaedic hospitals. As purposes (a) and (b), which were non-charitable, were designed to promote the good administration of the main aim of the gift, namely the hospitals, which were charitable, the gift was held to be exclusively charitable.

14.9 Cy Pres

Where a private trust fails, the beneficial interest normally results to the settlor or testator (see Chapter 6). This is so whether the trust fails from the outset (e.g., due to the doctrine of lapse) or subsequently (e.g., where there are surplus funds (see section 6.5)). Where a charitable gift fails the beneficial interest may also result to the settlor or testator, but often such gifts are saved by the operation of the doctrine of cy pres. Where the cy pres doctrine applies the Charity Commissioners or the court will apply the trust property for other charitable purposes which resemble as near as possible (cy pres) the original purposes. The trustees themselves generally have no power to apply trust property cy pres. This may only be done after an application to and direction by the court or the Charity Commissioners, although trustees do have limited power under the Charities Act 1985 to, in effect, determine their own cy pres application with the concurrence of the Charity Commissioners. The Charities Act 1985 only operates within a narrow sphere (namely, local charities for the relief of poverty), although it also covers some other very small charities (where the capital is less than £25 and the gross income is £5 or less (s.4 Charities Act 1985)). It is important to note that where the circumstances indicate a need to apply property cy pres, s.13(5) Charities Act 1960 imposes a duty on the trustees to make the necessary application for the property to be applied cy pres.

In order to decide whether a gift may be applied cy pres the questions indicated in Figure 14.4 need to be considered. The various elements which make up that decision-making process will now be discussed.

Impossibility

Before the Charities Act 1960 there were only limited circumstances in which property could be applied cy pres, namely where it was impossible

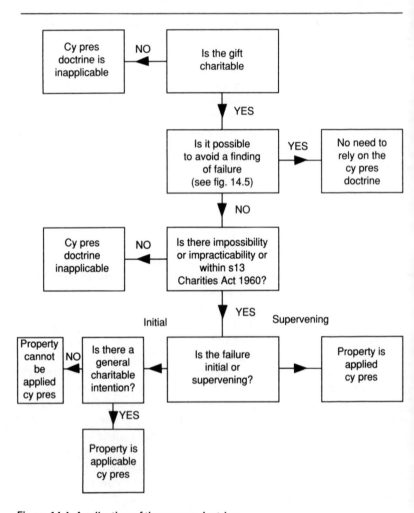

Figure 14.4 Application of the cy pres doctrine

to carry out the trust or where it had become impractical to do so. A trust would be impossible to carry out within the meaning of the common law where, for instance, no suitable land could be found to build an institution intended by the donor, where the money donated was insufficient to carry out the purpose specified; where a particular institution to which the property was donated has closed down prior to the date of the gift; or where there are surplus funds due to the fact that there were no longer eligible beneficiaries. However, if for some reason it was merely inexpedient (i.e., the money could be better applied elsewhere) to carry out the trust because the performance of it was uneconomic, inconvenient or served no useful purpose, the property could not be applied cy pres at common law. Judges attempted to circumvent the limitations of the common law by putting a very wide construction on the terms 'impossible' and 'impractical': for instance, it was fortunately regarded as impractical by the late eighteenth century to apply money for the advancement and propagation of the Christian religion among the infidels in Virginia (*Attorney-General* v. *City of London* (1710) 3 Bro CC 121), and in 1947 it was considered impossible to operate what was effectively a 'colour bar' at a students' hostel; the terms on which the charity provided the hostel in Bloomsbury was with a restriction to students of European origin (*Re Dominion Students Hall Trust* [1947] Ch 183). Despite such flexibility the courts still had to give effect to charities which were essentially undesirable.

The circumstances in which property may be applied cy pres have now been extended by s.13(1) Charities Act 1960. The section in part restates the common-law position before the Act, but also extends the circumstances in which property may be applied cy pres. S.13(1) provides that, subject to any other necessary conditions being fulfilled, property may be applied cy pres in any of the following circumstances:

(a) where the original purposes, in whole or in part:
     (i) have been carried as far as may be fulfilled; or
     (ii) cannot be carried out, or not according to the directions given and to the spirit of the gift; or
(b) where the original purposes provide a use for part only of the property available by virtue of the gift; or
(c) where the property available by virtue of the gift and other property applicable for similar purposes can be more effectively used in conjunction, and to that end can suitably, regard being had to the spirit of the gift, be made applicable to common purposes; or
(d) where the original purposes were laid down by reference to an area which then was but has since ceased to be a unit for some other purpose, or by reference to a class of persons, or to an area which

has for some reason ceased to be suitable, regard being had to the spirit of the gift, or to be practical in administering the gift; or
(e)   where the original purposes in whole or in part, have, since they were laid down:
(i) been adequately provided for by other means; or
(ii) ceased, as being useless or harmful to the community or for other reasons, to be in law charitable; or
(iii) ceased in any other way to provide a suitable and effective method of using property available by virtue of the gift, regard being had to the spirit of the gift.

It should be noted that the section does not supersede the pre-1960 case law, and thus such cases are relevant as a guide to the circumstances in which jurisdiction exists for a cy pres order to be made.

Initial and supervening impossibility
Once it has been established that there is impossibility within the meaning of the common law or s.13 Charities Act 1960, it is next necessary to decide whether the impossibility is initial or supervening (the latter is sometimes known as subsequent failure). If it is initial then a second condition will have to be satisfied before the property can be applied cy pres, namely proof of general charitable intention (see next section). Impossibility is initial where the gift fails at the date of the trust. It is said to be supervening where the trust becomes impossible at some point in time after it has come into operation. In this event no general charitable intention need be shown; once impossibility within the common law or s.13 Charities Act 1960 has been established, the property may be automatically applied cy pres. Two points should be noted about the meaning of initial impossibility: first, where the trust arises by will the relevant date is the date of the testator's death as this is when the gift comes into being; second, initial impossibility is still determined from the date when the gift is made even though the gift does not fall into possession until some future date. For example, in *Re Wright* [1954] Ch 347 the relevant date for determining whether a gift by will to maintain a convalescent home failed for impossibility was the date of the testator's death. This was so even though the gift took effect subject to a life interest and only became impossible to carry out due to insufficient funds by the death of the life tenant. As the gift could have been carried out at the testator's death this was a case of supervening impossibility.

Has there been a failure?
As general charitable intention is necessary before property can be applied cy pres where there is an initial failure, the courts have by various

HAS THE CHARITABLE GIFT FAILED?

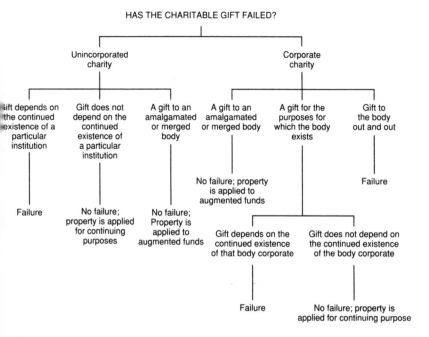

Figure 14.5

principles of construction tried to avoid a finding of failure in order to
make it unnecessary to rely on the cy pres doctrine. The various
constructions which may be put on gifts will now be considered in order
to establish the circumstances in which a court may find that there has
been no impossibility and accordingly the cy pres doctrine is irrelevant
(see Figure 14.5). It is necessary to distinguish at the outset between gifts
to unincorporated charities and gifts to corporate charities, as the rules of
construction differ. Although the differing rules of construction as
between unincorporated and corporate charities would appear to be
logical in themselves, as Goff J admitted in *Re Finger's Will Trusts* [1972]
1 Ch 286, they could lead to anomalies.

Gifts to unincorporated charities

As an unincorporated association is defined as a group of people who
come together for a common purpose, according to *Re Vernon's Will
Trusts* [1972] Ch 300 a gift to an unincorporated charity must be
construed as a gift for a purpose. This may or may not avoid a finding of
failure. First, if the gift is for the purposes of the specific institution only
(in the sense that it is only intended for the persons benefited from time

to time by that institution), then if the institution does not exist at the date of the gift it will be a case of initial impossibility. In *Re Spence* [1979] Ch 483 money was left *inter alia* to the Old Folks' Home at Hillworth Lodge, Keighley, 'for the benefit of the patients'. The home was no longer in existence at the testatrix's death. Megarry v-c held that it was not a gift to the old people of the area generally, but depended on the existence of that particular old folks' home and accordingly failed.

Second, on the other hand, the gift can be construed as a gift for the charitable purpose(s) for which the institution exists, and the existence of the particular institution is not material, provided that the purpose is still continuing there will be no failure and no necessity to apply cy pres. For example, in *Re Finger's Will Trusts* [1972] Ch 286 a gift was made to an unincorporated charity, the National Radium Commission. The charity had ceased to exist at the testator's death but the purposes it carried out were still continuing. The court held the gift did not fail for impossibility as it was a trust for the work of the commission which did not depend upon the continued existence of that named charitable organisation. The finding of such a construction was certainly made easier by the fact that it was a national body where the identity of the particular institution would therefore seem to be less important.

Gifts to corporate charities
According to *Re Vernon's Will Trusts* (above) a gift to a corporate body is capable of two main constructions: first, the gift is intended as a gift to the corporate body out and out as part of its general funds. This is the more usual construction. If it is applied, the gift lapses if the institution does not exist at the date of the gift unless a general charitable intention can be shown. This construction was adopted in *Re Finger's Will Trusts* (above) for the testator's gift to the National Council for Maternity and Child Welfare, a corporate charity. The second construction concerns whether the gift is for the purpose(s) for which the charitable corporation exists. There will need to be special indications in the wording or terms of the gift for this construction to be adopted (i.e., words indicating that the gift is on trust for work of the body) and it will not necessarily prevent a finding of failure. Within this construction, it is necessary further to ask whether the gift is for the purposes of the specific corporation (in which case the gift will fail if the corporation is not in existence at the date of the gift) or whether it is for the purposes of the specific corporation in circumstances where the continuance of that corporation is not vital to the intention of the donor. In this latter case, there will be no failure.

Gifts to bodies which have merged or amalgamated
Where a charity ceases to exist under a particular name, this does not

necessarily mean that the charity itself has ceased to exist. Two or more charities may be amalgamated under the name of one of them or under a new name, and the objects of the original charities may be incorporated or substantially incorporated into the amalgamated charity. In such circumstances the objects of the original charity do not fail for impossibility, merely because of the change in name and/or alteration in the constitution or objects. It seems that a gift may be construed as one to a merged or amalgamated charity whether the body is corporate or unincorporated. However, as applied to an unincorporated charity it should be noted it is inconsistent with the view expressed in *Re Vernon* and *Re Finger's* that such a gift should be construed as a gift for the purposes for which the charity exists, as the approach assumes that the gift is to the charity itself. An example of the approach is seen in *Re Faraker* [1912] 2 Ch 488, where a gift was made to 'Mrs Bayley's Charity Rotherhithe'. This was a charity founded in 1765 for poor widows of Rotherhithe. In 1905 the Charity Commissioners had consolidated the endowments to a number of charities with the general purpose of relief of the poor of Rotherhithe. The Court of Appeal held that the Bayley Charity had not been destroyed by the scheme and consequently the consolidated charities were entitled to the legacy. It should be noted that the charity in this case was a perpetual charity which no one had power to terminate. If a charitable institution can be terminated and its constitution provides for the disposal of funds elsewhere, then the charity will cease to exist and there will be a failure on the grounds of impossibility (*Re Stemson's Will Trusts* [1970] Ch 16).

General charitable intention

As mentioned above, if a charitable gift is impossible from the outset, general charitable intention must be established. A general charitable intention can be said to exist where the donor's main interest is to see that a particular charitable purpose is carried out, and it is not material to him or her which particular body carries it out. In contrast, if the donor only wants to give to a particular charitable institution carrying on a specified charitable function, there is no general charitable intention. It is a question of construction in every case as to whether the donor has a general charitable intention, but the following guidelines have been used by the courts.

First of all, it is easier to establish general charitable intention where the gift is expressed as being for a purpose as opposed to being made to a named institution, as purposes generally continue indefinitely, even though the institutions which carry them out alter. In *Biscoe* v. *Jackson* (1887) 35 Ch D 460 a gift was to be applied towards the establishment of a soup kitchen in Shoreditch, and also a cottage hospital. It was impossible to carry out the gift from the outset as there was no land available. The Court of Appeal found there was an underlying general charitable intention to benefit the poor of Shoreditch generally and thus the property could be applied cy pres. If, however, the mode of giving effect to the purpose is expressed in specific terms this will detract from a finding of general charitable intention. In *Re Good* [1950] 2 All ER 653 the testator sought to provide rest homes in Hull. As he set out detailed plans as to the type of homes to be provided, the persons to be allowed to benefit and the management powers of the trustees, the court decided that the detailed instructions were inconsistent with a finding of general charitable intention.

The willingness of the courts to find a general charitable intention when a gift is expressed as being for a purpose is illustrated by the somewhat dubious decision of *Re Lysaght* [1966] 1 Ch 191. Here a testatrix gave a fund to the Royal College of Surgeons for the establishment of medical studentships. There was a provision in the terms of the gift to the effect that Jews and Roman Catholics should be excluded from benefiting. As the college refused to accept the gift on these terms there was an initial failure on the ground of inpracticability. It was therefore necessary to establish general charitable intention before the property could be applied cy pres. Buckley J held that the provision excluding Jews and Roman Catholics was not an essential part of the testatrix's intention; her paramount intention was to ensure that the college was trustee of the fund and to benefit medical education, and this paramount intention would not be permitted to be defeated by her minor requirement that Jews and Roman Catholics could not benefit. A scheme was therefore ordered in which the discriminatory provision was deleted. It is suggested if a donor is disposed to include a specific discriminatory provision, it indicates that they feel (rightly or wrongly) strongly about the persons who should be excluded from benefit and thus it is difficult to see how something so specific can give rise to a general charitable intention. The decision has, despite criticism, been followed in *Re Woodhams* [1981] 1 WLR 493.

Second, where a gift is made to a specific institution but an institution with that name has never existed, provided that it is clear that the institution, if it had existed, would have been charitable, then a general charitable intention is inferred. For example, in *Re Harwood* [1936] Ch 285 a gift was made to the 'Peace Society of Belfast'. Such a society had never existed. There were other gifts in the will to peace societies which did exist and in these circumstances the court held that the testator had a general charitable intention to promote peace, particularly in the Belfast area.

Third, where a gift is made to an unincorporated charity which has ceased to exist at the date of the gift and it is construed as being a gift to the objects or persons from time to time benefited by that institution (see p.279) it will be possible but difficult to establish general charitable intention (*Re Spence* [1979] Ch 483).

Finally, where a gift is made to a corporate charity no longer in existence at the date of the gift, it will be difficult but not impossible to prove general charitable intention (*Re Stemson's Will Trusts* [1970] Ch 16).

Anonymous donations

The requirement of proving a general charitable intention in cases of initial impossibility poses a problem where the donors are anonymous. For example, if a charitable appeal is launched and funds are raised from such sources as street collecting boxes and raffles, no general charitable intention could be proved, and as the donors could not be found there would be a resulting trust and the funds would be paid into court. S.14 Charities Act 1960 now provides a solution by allowing property to be applied cy pres where there is an initial failure in the absence of general charitable intention if either of the two grounds listed are satisfied.

(a) The property is given for a specific charitable purpose which fails and the donor cannot, after reasonable advertisement or enquiries, be identified or found. S.14(2) goes on to provide that where property has been given by means of cash collecting boxes or other means by which it is not possible to distinguish one gift from another, or the funds are the proceeds of lotteries, competition, entertainment, sale or similar money-raising activities, it is conclusively presumed to be given by unidentifiable donors. This makes it unnecessary to advertise for claimants.

(b) The donor has given a written disclaimer. S.14(3) further provides that where the sum donated is so small that it would be unreasonable to incur expense with a view to retaining the property or it would be unreasonable having regard to the nature, circumstances and amount of the gifts and to the lapse of time since the gifts were made for the donors to expect the property to be returned, then no disclaimer is necessary as the property is treated as belonging to a donor who cannot be found.

Effects of a disclaimer by the donee of a charitable gift

If the donee of a gift is a charitable institution and it refuses to accept the gift, the gift fails and there is no cy pres application.

If, on the other hand, the donee is merely a trustee for some charitable purpose then equity will not allow the trust to fail for want of a trustee and some cy pres arrangement will be made. However, this will not, it seems, be the case where the refusal of the donee wholly frustrates the purpose of the trust; in this event the trust will fail. In *Harris* v. *Sharp* (unreported) (1988) Conv. 288 Sharp, a trustee on the board of trustees of a certain charity, was convicted for misappropriating trust monies. Subsequently he instructed his solicitors to use a draft for £50 000 to provide a fellowship at Liverpool hospital. Liverpool Health Authority initially refused the gift as Sharp would not guarantee that the money had not been derived from his fraud, but later changed its mind and tried to claim the money from Sharp who by this time wanted it back. Mervyn Davies J held that this was a case of subsequent failure and the draft could be applied cy pres.

Summary

1 A charitable trust is one for the benefit of the public or a 'section of the public', and because of this charitable trusts enjoy certain trust law privileges and tax advantages not available to private trusts.

2 There is no formal definition of what is charitable. In borderline cases the courts have regard to the preamble of the Charitable Uses Act 1601 and/or the Pemsel Classification. The Pemsel Classification sets down four heads of charity: advancement of education, advancement of religion, relief of poverty and other purposes beneficial to the community.

3 If a gift falls within one of the four heads of the Pemsel Classification, the gift is prima facie charitable but is still necessary to establish that the gift is of public benefit. The test of public benefit varies in its application between one category of the Pemsel Classification and another.

4 The most widely adopted test of public benefit is the Compton (Oppenheim test). This provides that the beneficiaries must not be numerically negligible *and* that there must be no personal nexus. It is clear that the Compton test does not apply to charitable gifts for the relief of poverty.

5 If a gift is political it will not satisfy the test of public benefit whichever category of the Pemsel Classification the gift falls into.

6 Where a charitable trust fails, the gift may be saved in some circumstances by the cy pres doctrine, under which the subject-matter of the gift is applied for a similar purpose.

7 In applying the cy pres doctrine it is necessary to distinguish between initial and subsequent (supervening) failure of a gift. Whereas in the case of a subsequent failure the property may automatically be applied cy pres, it is necessary to establish general charitable intention before property can be applied cy pres where the failure is initial.

8 In order to facilitate the application of property for charitable purposes the courts have attempted to place certain constructions on gifts to avoid a finding of failure in order to circumvent the difficulty of establishing general charitable intention (see Figure 14.5).

Exercises

1 Why might it be desirable to establish that a particular trust is charitable rather than being a private trust?

2 Put the case for the separation of the fiscal privileges granted to charitable trusts from the trust law privileges.

3 In what way(s) is the Pemsel Classification of charitable gifts unhelpful?

4 Discuss critically the Compton (Oppenheim) test of public benefit. Can you improve upon the test?

5 Selina Floyd-Evritt, a successful British professional tennis player, approaches you with draft clauses for her will. One clause provides 'I give £100 000 to promote the game of tennis in such ways as my trustees in their absolute discretion think fit.' Selina tells you she wishes the gift to be charitable and that she has in mind that the money be spent on such things as tennis trophies and coaching for potentially talented players. Advise Selina as to whether the clause as it stands would give rise to a charitable trust, and if not suggest ways in which the clause may be drafted to ensure the gift is in terms which the law regards as charitable.

6 Read *Re Koettgen's Will Trusts* [1954] Ch 252, *IRC* v. *Educational Grants Association* [1967] Ch 993 and *Caffoor* v. *IT Colombo* [1961] AC 584 and consider the extent to which a preferred class may be incorporated into a charitable trust in order to avoid the 'no personal nexus' requirement of the Compton test of public benefit.

7 Would the following gifts give rise to valid charitable trusts?
(a) 'I give £200 000 to my trustees to apply as they in their absolute discretion think fit to charitable or benevolent purposes for the benefit of the inhabitants of Great Snoring, particularly having regard to the needs of the village school and the church.'
(b) 'I give £40 000 to establish a campaign to remove religious instruction from the National Curriculum.'
(c) 'I give £4000 to be shared amongst my relations who have fallen on hard times.'

8 Why have the courts tried to avoid a finding that there has been an initial failure of a charitable gift? How satisfactory is the approach they have adopted in so doing?

9 (In applying the cy pres doctrine) distinguish between 'general charitable intention' and a 'specific charitable intention'.

10 How does the question of whether the donor of a charitable gift has a general charitable intention in making the gift to a charitable unincorporated association which has ceased to exist at the date of the gift differ from the question of whether there has been 'a failure of the gift' to an unincorporated charity at the outset?

11 Daniel Flare, who died recently, left £6000 by his will to 'St Luke's Hospice for the Dying, Heavenly Close, Hellston, Cornwall'. The home, run by an unincorporated charity, closed down prior to Daniel Flare's death. His will contained a gift to another hospice in Cornwall (St Francis) which is still in existence, as well as a number of gifts to unrelated charitable purposes in Cornwall to which effect can also be given.

Advise the executors of Daniel Flare's will as to what should be done with the £6000 for St Luke's Hospice.

Part V

Trusts and the Family Home

15 Trusts and the Family Home

15.1 Introduction

Commonly today, the family home is held in co-ownership. Co-ownership arises where two or more persons hold the same estate in land (e.g., a grant of land to A and B in fee simple). Usually, in relation to the family home the co-owners are husband and wife or co-habitees, but sometimes other family members may be involved, such as parents or brothers and sisters. In many cases the parties are expressly co-owners of the legal title, and indeed this is the safest and simplest way of holding property in co-ownership. However, there may be circumstances where the legal title is vested in one or more persons and the beneficial interest of another or others is not declared. Here, prima facie, the equitable title follows the legal title, but where the intention or expectation is that someone else should have an interest in equity, the law relating to resulting and constructive trusts comes into play. It will be remembered that resulting and constructive trusts do not require any form of writing; therefore, if a party who is not named as a legal owner wishes to establish a co-ownership interest in land in equity, and there is no express declaration of trust manifested and proved in writing in accordance with s.53(1)(b) Law of Property Act 1925 (see section 4.1), reliance will have to be placed on resulting or constructive trust principles.

This chapter is chiefly concerned with how the law of trusts may be used to establish an interest in the family home. However, if a party is unable to establish an interest in the family home by use of trust principles, he or she may be able to rely on the doctrine of proprietary estoppel, and thus in section 15.7 consideration is given to this important equitable doctrine.

15.2 The Structure of Co-ownership of Land

In order to put in context the trust principles to be discussed it is useful to provide a brief introduction to the structure on co-ownership of land.

Since 1925, whenever land is held by co-owners it must be held on a trust. The trust is normally a trust for sale but it is possible for co-ownership to arise under a strict settlement. The main feature of a

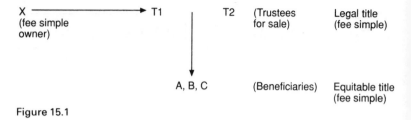

Figure 15.1

Figure 15.2 Effect of a conveyance of land to A, B, C in fee simple

---

trust for sale is that the trustees have a duty to sell the land and merely a power to postpone sale. A trust for sale in relation to co-ownership may arise expressly, or impliedly under the provisions of s.34–6 Law of Property Act 1925. An express trust for sale arises where land is conveyed to trustees who are under a duty to sell land and hold the proceeds of sale for specified beneficiaries (see Figure 15.1).

If there is no express trust for sale but in fact two or more persons are to be co-owners of land, s.34–6 Law of Property Act 1925 automatically imposes a trust for sale (see Figure 15.2).

It has already been explained (see section 15.1) that in relation to the family home the existence of co-ownership is not always obvious, and it may appear that the fee simple is held by one person alone. This is because another or others may only be able to establish a beneficial interest in the property on a resulting or constructive basis. It was established in *Bull* v. *Bull* [1955] 1 QB 234 that where co-ownership arises under the doctrine of a resulting or constructive trust, this still gives rise to a trust for sale under s.35 Law of Property Act 1925. This was clearly not a situation envisaged by the 1925 legislators. In *Bull* v. *Bull* a mother and son had contributed in unequal shares to the purchase price of a house conveyed into the son's name alone. The court found that the mother had not intended to make a gift or a loan to the son, and accordingly she had an interest in the property on the basis of a resulting trust. When an argument occurred between the son's wife and his mother he tried to claim she had merely a licence to occupy and that he had revoked the licence. The Court of Appeal held that, as the mother had an interest on a resulting trust basis, and as (since 1925) co-ownership can only exist behind a trust, the son held the legal estate as trustee on trust for himself and his mother as tenants in common in equity (see Figure 15.3).

Whether the trust for sale arises expressly or impliedly, s.2(1)(ii) Law of Property Act 1925 provides that, if the purchase money is paid to two trustees, the interests of the beneficiaries are overreached (i.e., on sale the interests of the beneficiaries thereafter attach to the proceeds of sale). In the context of the family home it is especially important to appreciate that the imposition of a trust for sale is purely a conveyancing device. The aim of the 1925 property legislation was to facilitate the alienation of land.

The imposition of a trust for sale enables the land to be dealt with commercially. By taking the beneficial interest off the title through the concept of overreaching, the purchaser is only concerned with the legal estate to which there is only one title as the trustees hold as joint tenants. The interests of the beneficiaries are also protected as they are ensured an interest in the proceeds of sale and that the legal title to the property is dealt with in accordance with the strict duties of trusteeship. Additional protection for the beneficiaries arises under s.26(3) (in the case of a statutory trust for sale), which provides that the trustees shall consult the beneficiaries of full age and, in so far as is consistent with the general purpose of the trust, give effect to the wishes of such persons or, in the case of a dispute, the wishes of the majority. Furthermore, under s.30 Law of Property Act 1925, if the trustees refuse to exercise any of their powers or refuse to sell the property the beneficiaries may apply to the court and the court may order a sale.

Since 1925, although there is a duty to sell under a trust for sale, s.25(1) provides that a power to postpone sale shall be implied in every case. Thus the net effect is that the trust for sale in relation to the family home is a land-holding device to facilitate conveyancing, directed at the retention of land rather than sale. In *Re Evers T* [1980] 1 WLR 1327 at 1330, Ormrod LJ said: 'The trust for sale has become a very convenient and much used conveyancing technique. Combined with the statutory power of the trustees to postpone sale it can be used to meet a variety of

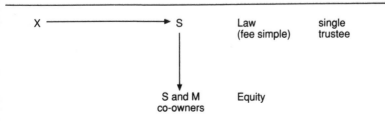

Figure 15.3

situations in some of which the actual sale is far from the intentions of the parties at the time when trust for sale comes into existence.'

15.3 Express Trusts

An express trust of the family home may arise in two basic ways: first, by a conveyance of the legal title into the joint names of two or more persons on trust for themselves as joint tenants or tenants in common, in equal or unequal shares (see Figure 15.4). Joint tenancy and tenancy in common refer to the two forms of co-ownership. It is necessary to distinguish between them as, in the case of a joint tenancy, the co-owners do not have a distinct share in the property; their position is dependent on the doctrine of survivorship. Under the doctrine of survivorship, if a joint tenant dies his or her interest in the property passes to the survivor(s). In contrast, where co-owners are tenants in common, they have a distinct trust undivided share in the property which may be an equal or unequal share. The shares are undivided as the co-owners are all entitled to physical possession of any part of the property.

The second way in which an express trust of the family home may arise is if one or more persons declare themselves to be trustees of the legal title for the co-owners in equity (see Figure 15.5).

In this event the declaration of trust must be evidenced in writing in accordance with s.53(1)(b) in order to be enforceable.

However the express trust comes into existence, once constituted, it remains fixed. Thus if, for example, the terms of the trust state that X and Y are tenants in common in equal shares, it is irrelevant that they contributed to the purchase money in unequal proportions. It follows, from what has been said about the nature of a joint tenancy, that the co-owners do not have a fixed share; their position depends on survivorship. A joint tenancy may, however, be 'severed' during the lifetime of a joint tenant so as to create a tenancy in common. In this event it was said in *Goodman* v. *Gallant* [1986] Fam 106 that the co-owners will take in equal shares irrespective of the contributions made to the purchase

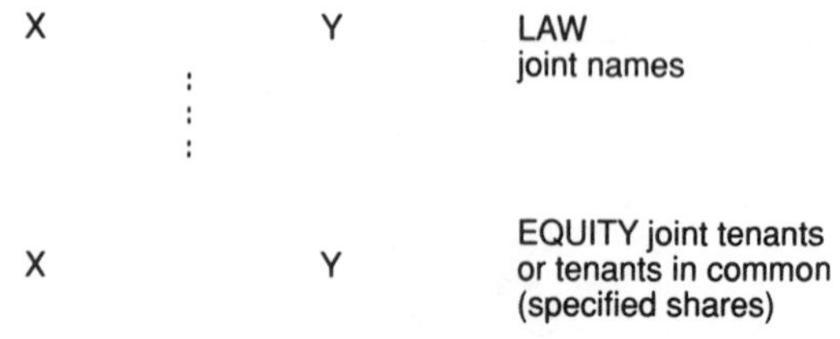

| X | Y | LAW
joint names |
| X | Y | EQUITY joint tenants
or tenants in common
(specified shares) |

Figure 15.4

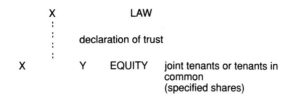

Figure 15.5

---

moneys. It should be noted, *obiter dicta*, the court expressed the view that this would not necessarily be so in the case of a statutory trust for sale arising under s.34–6 Law of Property Act 1925 (see section 15.2 above). The reason given for this is that the imposition of a trust in these sections is to simplify the mechanics of conveyancing. The statute has no effect on the nature and extent of the beneficial interests in the proceeds of sale and therefore the shares should be determined by resulting and constructive trust principles.

There are two very limited exceptions to the rule that an express declaration of trust is conclusive in its effects: first, where there is a fraud or mistake at the time the trust is created; and, second, where the remedy of rectification operates to give effect to the intention the parties clearly had at the time the trust was created, but which was not given effect to in the terms of the written declaration (*Wilson* v. *Wilson* [1969] 3 All ER 445).

Equitable accounting

Where the family home is acquired by means of an instalment mortgage and the relationship between the co-owners breaks down so that one remains paying the mortgage to which both had previously contributed, the principle that an express declaration of trust is conclusive and cannot be adjusted by the courts would seem to operate unfairly. Thus in *Leake* v. *Bruzzi* [1974] 1 WLR 1528 the Court of Appeal held that the court would give credit to the party who continued to make the loan repayments. On the facts of the case the house was held by a husband on an express trust for himself and his wife as joint tenants. Both contributed to the mortgage repayments until the wife left the matrimonial home. The husband carried on paying the mortgage instalments and the court decided that, on sale, the wife's half-share in the proceeds of sale (arising out of the severance of the joint tenancy) should be reduced by half of that part of the mortgage repayments made in respect of the capital. The court was in effect treating the repayment as to one-half (which, before the marriage broke down, was paid by the wife for herself) as having been paid on behalf of the wife who had left. It should be noted that no

nce was made for interest payments as it was necessary to take
nt of the fact that the husband had the house solely for his own use;
nterest payments were in effect an 'occupation rent' to the wife.

15.4 Establishing an Interest in the Family Home by means of a Resulting Trust

If no express trust of the family home can be established, a party will
have to establish a resulting trust or rely upon the doctrine of constructive trusts. Let us first consider resulting trusts. (For general principles
see section 2.2.) The leading cases of *Pettit* v. *Pettitt* [1970] AC 777 and
Gissing v. *Gissing* [1970] 2 All ER 780 provide that, in order to establish
an interest in the family home on a resulting trust basis, it is necessary to
show that the parties had a common intention that the beneficial interest
was to be shared. Both *Pettitt* v. *Pettitt* and *Gissing* v. *Gissing* were
concerned with married couples, but it is now clear that the same
principles apply as between unmarried couples, although in *Bernard* v.
Josephs [1982] Ch 391 Griffiths LJ pointed out that with regard to
unmarried couples the nature of the relationship needs to be closely
scrutinised as it may have a bearing on the ascertainment of the parties'
common intention. If the relationship involved a lesser degree of
permanance than marriage, different inferences may be drawn about
their intentions in relation to property. In *Pettitt* v. *Pettitt* a house was
vested in the name of a wife and purchased out of her own money. Her
husband alleged that he had done work by way of improvement to the
property which gave him an interest in it. The improvements he relied
upon to establish this were redecorating, making a garden and building a
wall and patio. The House of Lords held that this was not sufficient to
show a common intention that he should have an interest in the property.
It was work of an ephemeral nature and basically the type of 'do it
yourself' jobs which any husband would be expected to take on during
his leisure hours. Similarly, in *Gissing* v. *Gissing*, the House of Lords
found that the contribution made by a wife was insufficient to infer the
necessary common intention in order to establish a resulting trust. There
the legal title to the matrimonial home was vested in the name of the
husband who had provided the deposit and paid the mortgage, but the
wife claimed an interest on the basis that she had worked throughout the
marriage and had been instrumental in getting her husband a job. In
addition, she had paid for some of the fittings in the house and had also
paid for her own and her son's clothing. The reasons given by the House
of Lords in rejecting the claim of the wife differed from one judgment to
another. Lord Diplock seemed to suggest that no common intention
could be inferred as the wife had made no direct contribution to the

acquisition, whilst Viscount Dilhorne indicated that there was no resulting trust as the wife's contribution was too insignificant to allow the inference of a common intention. An alternative view, on which there was no agreement, was that the contribution to the household expenses, although relieving the husband's expenditure, was not sufficiently referable to the acquisition of the property in order to infer a common intention that the wife should have an interest in the property.

Pettitt v. *Pettitt* and *Gissing* v. *Gissing* left the law in a state of uncertainty as to precisely how an interest in the family home could be established by means of a resulting trust. Two issues were particularly ambiguous. First, what type of contribution would be sufficient for a court to infer a common intention that a party should have an interest in the property? Second, it was left unclear whether a resulting trust could be established by evidence of intention alone, irrespective of a contribution. It is therefore proposed to look at what light subsequent cases have shed on these issues. However, the issue of whether evidence of intention alone will suffice to establish an interest on a resulting trust basis will be deferred until after the examination of constructive trusts and the family home (see section 15.5).

What contribution will be sufficient for the courts to infer a common intention?

For the purpose of inferring a common intention, contributions may be divided into direct contributions and indirect contributions.

Direct contributions

A direct contribution is one made to the purchase price either by way of deposit or outright purchase (where there is no mortgage), or a contribution to or payment of the legal expenses. Contributions made to the mortgage instalments have also, in most cases, been regarded as direct contributions to the purchase price. On the basis of the general equitable presumptions outlined in section 2.2 above, where one party purchases property which is then conveyed into the name of another, it is presumed (unless there is evidence to the contrary) that the transferor did not intend a gift and that the transferee therefore holds on resulting trust. Thus, in the absence of evidence to the contrary, this would be sufficient to infer the common intention that the party providing the purchase price or part thereof for the family home is to have an interest in it. Whether this is necessarily so with regard to a contribution to the mortgage instalments is not absolutely clear. In *Cowcher* v. *Cowcher* [1972] 1 All ER 943 a house was in the sole name of a husband who had sole responsibility for payment of the mortgage. However, his wife had in fact made some repayments on the mortgage. Bagnell j took the view that one could only infer a common intention that the party contributing to a mortgage should have an interest in the property where the parties were jointly responsible for the repayments. This seems to be an unduly harsh view. If regular contributions are made to the mortgage instalments it would seem unnecessary for the payer to have a joint responsibility for payment. Clearly, however, it may be more difficult to infer a common intention that the party was to have an interest in the property where there were irregular contributions to the mortgage (e.g., to help out where the mortgagor was in temporary financial difficulty), as this could be construed as a gift or a loan.

Indirect contributions

In most of the reported cases it has been a woman who has tried to establish an interest on a resulting trust basis by means of an indirect contribution. The indirect contribution alleged to be sufficient to infer a common intention that the party should have an interest in the property has commonly arisen in three ways.

(a) The woman has not worked but has stayed at home and cared for the family (i.e., looked after the husband and children). Here the argument has been that a 'cash value' can be placed on her contribution to the care of the family. If she had gone out to work she would have been able to have contributed directly to the acquisition of the property, but because she had stayed at home this had obviated the necessity of paying for domestic help and a nanny.

(b) The woman has been in paid employment full-time or part-time. The man has in fact paid the mortgage instalments, but would not have been able to do so without the woman contributing to the day-to-day living expenses, such as food and clothing.

(c) The woman has been in paid employment full-time or part-time, and has in fact contributed to the family budget. The man has paid all the mortgage instalments and would also have been able to pay for all the household expenses if this had been required of him.

Performance of ordinary domestic tasks

It is quite clear from the decision in *Gissing* v. *Gissing* that caring for the family is not a sufficient contribution to infer a common intention that the party is to have an interest in the property. The contribution is not sufficiently referable to the acquisition of the property. *Gissing* v. *Gissing* concerned a married couple, but this view was confirmed by the Court of Appeal in relation to an unmarried couple in *Burns* v. *Burns* [1984] 1 All ER 244. The court held it could not impute a common intention that the woman in the case was to have a beneficial interest in the property merely because she had lived with the man for nineteen years and had looked after the family. It is worth noting at this point that this view is unfortunate when one considers the implications for an unmarried partner. Usually the dispute as to whether the party has an interest in the family home arises on the breakdown of a relationship. If the parties are married the divorce court has very wide powers to transcend all legal and equitable rights and exercise discretion as to how the property should be divided between the spouses. One of the factors taken into account in making a division is the parties' contribution to the welfare of the family (i.e., care for husband and children). There is no such jurisdiction to ensure a fair division of property taking into account such factors when the parties are unmarried.

Contribution to household expenses

Where the woman goes out to work and makes a contribution to the household expenses enabling the man to pay the mortgage, although there were suggestions in *Gissing* v. *Gissing* that this would not be sufficiently referable to the acquisition of the property to infer a common intention, it has subsequently been held to be adequate. In *Falconer* v. *Falconer* [1970] 1 WLR 1333, Lord Denning said that where there was a *substantial* financial contribution towards the family expenses this would be sufficient to infer the existence of a common intention, and the Court of Appeal in *Burns* v. *Burns* confirmed this view, pointing out that it was quite consistent with the House of Lords decision in *Gissing* v. *Gissing* as the contribution was indirectly referable. However, in *Kowalczuk* v. *Kowalczuk* [1973] 1 WLR 930 it was observed that it would be more difficult to establish a common intention from this type of contribution where the legal title holder had bought the house before the relationship had begun.

With regard to the woman who contributes to the household expenses in circumstances where the man could afford to pay the mortgage and all the household expenses if called upon to do so, despite a number of earlier authorities to the contrary, *Burns* v. *Burns* now suggests that such payments would not be sufficient referable to the acquisition of the property to allow inference of a common intention for the purpose of a resulting trust.

Improvements

In *Pettitt* v. *Pettitt* Lord Upjohn expressed the view that contributions to repairs/improvements to property were of quite a different quality from contributions to the acquisition of the property, with the consequence that neither resulting or constructive trust principles were relevant. He thought estoppel principles might, however, be relevant (see section 15.7).

S.37 Matrimonial Proceedings and Property Act 1970 now allows for the finding that an interest or an increased share has been acquired in the property as a result of carrying out, or paying for, improvements to property, but it only applies as between husband and wife. In order for the provision to operate (a) the contribution must be of a substantial nature, (b) there must be no express or implied agreement to the effect that no such interest should be acquired, and (c) arguably the nature of the work carried out must be an improvement as opposed to a repair. However, given that the contribution must be substantial, any repair work of a substantial nature is likely to be regarded as an improvement.

The position of unmarried parties as regards to improvements is unclear. Despite the statement of Lord Upjohn in *Pettitt* v. *Pettitt*, there are cases which support the view that improvements may be regarded as an indirect contribution sufficient to establish a common intention that the beneficial interest is to be shared. For example, in *Hussey* v. *Palmer* [1972] 1 WLR 1286 where a mother-in-law paid for an extension on to a house belonging to her son-in-law, the Court of Appeal held she had an interest in the property although Lord Denning MR considered the trust to be 'more in the nature of a constructive trust'.

Construction work

In *Smith* v. *Baker* [1970] 1 WLR 1160 CA, help in building a bungalow was considered to be sufficient indirect contribution to infer a common intention that the party should have an interest in the property.

Quantification of the interest

Before *Gissing* v. *Gissing* the maxim 'equality is equity' was readily applied once an interest had been established on a resulting trust footing. However, in *Gissing* v. *Gissing* both Lord Diplock and Lord Reid said that, in the absence of any agreement to the contrary, the proceeds of sale should be divided according to the contributions made and only when it was not possible to ascertain the contributions 'an equitable knife must be used to sever the Gordian Knot' (i.e., an equal division made). In *Stokes* v. *Anderson*, *The Independent*, 10 January 1991, the Court of Appeal said, as regards quantification, the starting point was the common intention of the parties expressed or inferred, and that all payments made and acts done by a party were to be treated as illuminating the common intention as to the extent of the party's beneficial interest. Difficulties arise where the parties make contributions to the acquisition of the property over a long period of time, particularly indirect contributions. In *Bernard* v. *Josephs* [1982] Ch 391 Griffith LJ expressed the view that the court must do its best to determine the contributions of each party to the 'family' finances, and he added that this was not a 'strict mathematical exercise'; contributions had to be considered broadly. The court also shed light on the relevant time for ascertaining the shares in the property. The orthodox view is that the intentions at the time of acquisition of the property are crucial, but all the judges agreed that acts and events up to the date of a separation of the parties, and sometimes even after this, were relevant to ascertaining the common intention to be inferred.

A separate issue is the date at which the shares in the property are to be valued. This is, of course, important if the property increases or decreases in value before it is actually sold. The Court of Appeal in *Hall* v. *Hall* [1982] 3 FLR 379 suggested that the appropriate date for valuation is the date of separation of the parties but, given that there may be significant delays before the property is sold, this potentially enables a trustee to profit from his trust. The better view therefore is that of the Court of Appeal in *Turton* v. *Turton* [1987] 3 WLR 622: namely, that the valuation can only be made at the point when the trust is terminated which is on sale to a third party or when one co-owner buys the other out.

15.5 Establishing an Interest in the Family Home by means of a Constructive Trust

Traditionally, the constructive trust would only have operated in the sphere of establishing an interest in property where a conveyance or other transfer was obtained by fraud, such as in *Bannister* v. *Bannister* [1948] 2 All ER 133 (see section 2.4). However, the vagueness of the boundaries of the constructive trust have enabled it to be developed, and one area of particular development has been in establishing an interest in the family home.

The 'new model' constructive trust

In the 1970s the courts, and particularly Lord Denning, widened the concept of the constructive trust largely to give protection to unmarried partners on the breakdown of a long relationship who have no equivalent of the divorce court jurisdiction under the Matrimonial Causes Act 1973 to enable the courts to do justice between the parties. In order to enlarge the scope of the constructive trust, and in particular to gloss over the strict property law principle that requires a common intention for the acquisition of an interest in property (except in the residual category of fraud), Lord Denning sought to say there was no distinction between a resulting and constructive trust. For example, in *Hussey* v. *Palmer* [1972] 1 WLR 1286 he stated: 'Whether a trust is a resulting or constructive trust is more a matter of words than anything else. The two run together and are imposed when justice and good conscience require it.'

He was able to reach this conclusion by taking out of context a passage from the judgment of Lord Diplock in *Gissing* v. *Gissing* which, in relation to the question of acquisition of an interest in the family home said: 'A resulting, implied or constructive trust – and it is unnecessary for present purposes to distinguish between these three classes of trust . . .' It is quite clear from a reading of Lord Diplock's judgment, as a whole, that he did envisage a distinction between the role of resulting and constructive trusts in the sphere of acquisition of an interest in the family home. Exactly what the distinction might be will be discussed in section 15.7.

The effect of Lord Denning's approach was to enable him to impose a constructive trusts irrespective of intention 'wherever justice and good conscience require it'. He referred to his approach as involving a 'constructive trust of a new model'. An example of it is seen in *Eves* v. *Eves* [1975] 3 All ER 768. Here a woman formed an association with a married man. He bought a house and promised to put the title to it in their joint names but, as an excuse, told her he could not do so yet as she was not aged 21. She had two children by him and looked after the house and garden. He later deserted. Lord Denning held that she had a one-quarter share in the property on a constructive trust basis as 'it would be inequitable for him to deny her a share in the house'. The law, he said, would 'impute or impose a constructive trust'. It should be noted that the majority of the court reached the same conclusion as Lord Denning by use of traditional reasoning. They considered that there was an enforceable agreement between the parties that the woman should contribute her labour towards repair and improvement of the house on the understanding she was to have a beneficial interest. This view is consistent with the requirement of a common intention in order to establish an interest in property.

The requirement of a common intention

The Court of Appeal in both *Burns* v. *Burns* [1984] 1 All ER 244 and *Grant* v. *Edwards* [1986] 2 All ER 426, and the House of Lords in *Lloyds Bank* v. *Rosset* [1990] 2 WLR 867 have now decisively rejected Lord Denning's broader approach and reaffirmed that whether the doctrine of resulting or constructive trusts is relied upon in order to establish an interest in the family home, a common intention that the party should have a beneficial interest in the property must be shown.

In *Grant* v. *Edwards* (above) the Court of Appeal laid down that, in order to establish a constructive trust, it was necessary to prove (a) a common intention and (b) that the party had acted to their detriment *on the basis of the common intention* (i.e., there must be a causal link). This approach was expressly approved by Lord Bridge in the House of Lords in *Lloyds Bank* v. *Rosset*. *Grant* v. *Edwards* appears to take a very strict line by demanding compliance with these requirements, but two factors indicate a slightly more liberal approach than some earlier cases. First, the court showed a willingness to find 'a common intention' by holding that such an intention could be implied by conduct. The facts of the case concerned an unmarried couple who had been locked in a stable relationship for some eighteen years, during which time the plaintiff had a child by the defendant. The plaintiff made no direct contribution to the purchase price but the defendant told the plaintiff at the time of purchase that her name would not appear in the title deeds as this would prejudice her divorce proceedings against her husband. The court was of the view that this implied that she was to have an interest in the property as there was no other reason for the defendant's excuse. The second factor, which shows a fairly liberal approach to the finding of a constructive trust, is the opinion of Browne-Wilkinson vc that, once a common intention has been established, there is at least a presumption that any act done by the claimant to her detriment and relating to the joint lives was done in reliance on the belief that she was to take an interest in the property. On the facts the plaintiff made a substantial contribution towards the household expenses and maintenance of the children, which enabled the defendant to pay the mortgage. This was held to be a sufficient causal link between the common intention and the acts to detriment relied upon.

Lloyds Bank v. *Rosset*, whilst agreeing with the law as stated in *Grant* v. *Edwards*, may make it more difficult for a party to establish a common intention to have an interest in the family home. Lord Bridge stated that buying a house as a 'joint venture' was not the same as an agreement to share the beneficial interest. The Rossets had purchased a semi-derelict farmhouse. Most of the purchase price came from a Swiss Trust fund of Mr Rosset, and on the insistence of the trustee of the fund the farmhouse was put in Mr Rosset's name. A mortgage was also needed. Mrs Rosset claimed to have an interest in the home under a constructive trust. Lord Bridge, however, drew a distinction between an agreement that a party should have an interest in the family home on the one hand, and buying the house as a joint venture on the other. The Rossets had agreed that the house should be bought as a joint venture but this was not the same thing as agreeing that Mrs Rosset should have an interest in the home. This seems to be both an artificial and fine distinction to draw and, if applied to the facts of the other cases, could narrow the circumstances in which a party can establish a constructive trust.

15.6 The Relationship between Resulting and Constructive Trusts in the Sphere of Acquisition of an Interest in the Family Home

Sometimes the courts do not make it very clear whether they are applying resulting or constructive trust principles when they are dealing with the acquisition of an interest in the family home. Some judges seem hesitant as to where the boundaries of each principle lie. For example, in *Burns* v. *Burns* Fox LJ said of indirect contributions to the purchase price that the term resulting trust was 'probably not inappropriate'. The importance of distinguishing between the two concepts in this sphere is clearly reduced by the fact that both are exempt from the requirement of writing and for both a common intention must now be shown. However, it is important, it seems, to distinguish between resulting and constructive trusts in this sphere for two reasons. The first reason came to light in *Re Densham* [1975] 1 WLR 1519. Here a wife had paid for one-ninth of the family home which was vested in her husband's sole name. The husband was later declared bankrupt and the question before the court was whether his wife had an interest in the home enforceable against the trustee in bankruptcy. The court accepted that the husband had agreed that she should have a half-share in the home. As she had acted to her detriment this gave her a half-share under a constructive trust. However, such a gratuitous disposition in her favour was void under s.42 Bankruptcy Act 1914 (now replaced by s.339–342 Insolvency Act 1986). In contrast, her contribution of one-ninth to the purchase price gave her an interest under a resulting trust which, as a purchaser, bound her husband's trustee in bankruptcy. Thus it is important to distinguish between resulting and constructive trusts in bankruptcy cases as a claimant under a constructive trust may be (but is not necessarily so) a volunteer. The second reason why it is necessary to distinguish between a resulting and constructive trust is also apparent from the decision in *Re Densham*. In the case of a resulting trust the quantum of the share is determined by the value of the contribution made, whereas in the case of a constructive trust it is determined by what the parties agreed upon. Thus, with a constructive trust, once it has been established that there is a 'common intention' that the party should have, say, a half-share in the property and the party has acted to his or her detriment by reason of the common intention, it matters not that the financial value of the detrimental reliance does not equal a half-share.

What, then, is the distinction between resulting and constructive trusts in the sphere of acquisition of an interest in property? It is submitted that a resulting trust does not involve an actual agreement, but the common intention that the claimant is to have an interest in property is drawn from the contribution they have made to its acquisition. This contribution may be direct or indirect (although Lord Bridge in *Lloyds Bank v. Rosset* suggested indirect contributions are not sufficient, and Fox LJ in *Burns v. Burns* was hesitant about this), or possibly by way of improvement to the property. In contrast, in order to establish an interest on the basis of a constructive trust, there needs to be actual agreement (express or tacit) or an express representation that the beneficial interest is to be shared and then, by reason of the agreement or representation, the claimant has acted to their detriment.

15.7 **Proprietary Estoppel**

If there is no express trust by which a party may establish a beneficial interest in the family home, and the party is also unable to rely upon principles of resulting or constructive trusts, a final possibility may be to rely on the doctrine of proprietary estoppel. A classic statement of the doctrine is to be found in the judgment of Lord Kingsdown in *Ramdsen v. Dyson* (1866) LR 1 HL 129:

> If a man, under a verbal agreement with a landlord for a certain interest in land, or, what amounts to the same thing, under an expectation created or encouraged by the landlord, that he shall have a certain interest, takes possession of such land with the consent of the landlord and upon the faith of such promise or expectation, with the knowledge of the landlord and without objection by him, lays out money upon the land, a court of equity will compel the landlord to give effect to such promise or expectation.

The elements of the doctrine were elaborated upon by Fry J in *Wilmott v. Barber* (1880) 15 Ch D 96, in which he set down the following requirements which have become known as the 'five probanda':

(i)   the plaintiff must have been mistaken as to his legal rights; and

(ii) the plaintiff must have expended some money or must have done some act (not necessarily upon the defendant's land) on the faith of the mistaken belief; and

(iii) the defendant, the possessor of the legal right, must know of the existence of his own right which is inconsistent with the right claimed by the plaintiff; and

(iv) the defendant the possessor of the legal right, must know of the plaintiff's mistaken belief of his rights; and

(v)   the defendant, the possessor of the legal right, must have encouraged the plaintiff in his expenditure of money or in the other acts which he has done either directly, or by abstaining from asserting his legal right.

Although the five probanda have been strictly applied in some modern cases (for an example, see *Coombes* v. *Smith* [1986] 1 WLR 808), in recent times the courts, on the whole, have taken a much broader approach to proprietary estoppel in wich the five probanda are no longer rigid criteria to be satisfied, but are regarded as guidelines to assist the court in deciding whether proprietary estoppel is made out. An example of the broader approach taken to proprietary estoppel can be seen in the judgment of Scarman LJ in *Crabb* v. *Arun DC* [1976] Ch 179, where he says of proprietary estoppel: 'The court having analysed and assessed the conduct and relationship of the parties has to answer three questions. First, is there an equity established? Secondly, what is the extent of the equity, if one is established? And, thirdly, what is the relief appropriate to satisfy the equity?'

It is proposed to take these three questions to analyse the elements of proprietary estoppel more closely, and then to consider briefly the functions of proprietary estoppel and the nature of the rights arising under the doctrine.

Is there an equity established?

In order for the doctrine of proprietary estoppel to operate it is not sufficient that a party seeking to rely on the doctrine has been led to believe he or she is to have an interest in the property; it must also be shown that he or she has relied upon the belief and acted to his or her detriment. *Ramsden* v. *Dyson* suggests that the detrimental reliance will involve expenditure of money on the land, but as the application of the doctrine has become more flexible other forms of detrimental reliance have been accepted. For example, in *Greasley* v. *Cooke* [1980] 1 WLR 1306 the defendant successfully relied upon the doctrine of proprietary estoppel without spending any money on the land. The defendant had entered into occupation of a house as a maid to the then owner but later she co-habited there with one of the owner's sons, Kenneth. Upon his father's death Kenneth and one of his brothers, Howard, inherited the house in equal shares. The defendant continued to look after the household generally, and in particular a handicapped sister, but she received no payment for her work and neither did she ask for payment. She was, however, encouraged by both Kenneth and Howard to believe she could regard the house as her home for the rest of her life. When Kenneth died, his share in the house passed to another brother, Hedley. Howard also died intestate. As the defendant was, by this time, alone in occupation of the property, Hedley and the beneficiaries of Howard's share on intestacy served notice on the defendant requiring possession. The defendant counterclaimed that they were estopped from evicting her and that she was entitled to occupy rent-free for the rest of her life. The Court of Appeal upheld this claim.

Greasley v. *Cooke* is also a significant decision in that the Court of Appeal held that once the defendant had shown that she had relied upon the assurances made to her by Howard and Kenneth, the onus of proving that she had not acted to her detriment lay on the plaintiffs. Lord Denning MR went even further than his fellow judges, suggesting that once reliance upon the assurances had been established it was not necessary for a claimant to show an element of detriment. This view has not been followed in later cases.

It has already been said that the five probanda set down in *Willmott* v. *Barber* are no longer regarded as rigid criteria to be satisfied. A further illustration of the broader approach taken to establishing an equity may be seen from the decision in *Griffith* v. *Williams* (1977) 248 EG 947. This case involved an action for possession of a house by executors. Under her will, the testatrix had left the house in question to her granddaughter but her daughter had lived there with her for most of her life and had been assured by the testatrix that the house was her home for life. In this belief the daughter spent all her savings (£2000) on improvements or outgoings on the house. On these facts the Court of Appeal held that the doctrine of proprietary estoppel operated. It had been argued that the daughter's claim must fail because at the time she carried out the improvements, the testatrix did not know of the daughter's mistake as to her position. The condition of *Wilmott* v. *Barber* were therefore not satisfied. However, Goff LJ said that this was not necessary and, in so far as it was necessary to show a mistake, the daughter had made a sufficient mistake in believing she would be allowed to stay in the house for her whole life. The case is also significant as being the first case in which there had been no encouragement for the daughter to expend money on taking up occupation of the house; she had lived in the house and then subsequently, believing she could remain for life, spent money on it.

What is the extent of the equity?

The idea behind the doctrine of proprietary estoppel is to give effect to the expectation of the party who has relied on an assurance and acted to his or her detriment. The extent of the equity is therefore linked to the expectation. On this point it is instructive to compare *Inwards* v. *Baker* [1965] 2 QB 29 with *Pascoe* v. *Turner* [1979] 1 WLR 431.

In *Inwards* v. *Baker*, at his father's suggestion, and with the father's encouragement, a son built a bungalow on land belonging to his father. The bungalow was largely built by the son's own labour at a cost of £300, of which the father contributed approximately half. The son went into occupation of the bungalow in the expectation he would be allowed to remain there for his lifetime or for so long as he wished. However, under the father's will the land was vested in trustees for the benefit of persons other than the son. When the trustees of the will brought proceedings for possession, the son successfully claimed to have a right to remain for life. In contrast, in *Pascoe* v. *Turner*, the defendant acquired the fee simple by placing reliance on the doctrine of proprietary estoppel. The defendant had moved into the plaintiff's house and had a relationship with him. Eventually the relationship broke down and the plaintiff went to live elsewhere. The plaintiff had told the defendant not to worry about her security as the house and its contents were hers. The defendant, to the plaintiff's knowledge, spent £230 (representing about a quarter of her capital investment) on improving and repairing the property. The Court of Appeal ordered that the equity be satisfied by conveyance of the fee simple to the defendant as the plaintiff had been led to believe that the house and its contents were hers.

What relief is appropriate?

Unlike other estoppels, proprietary estoppel may in some circumstances act positively, resulting in the transfer of a proprietary right to the claimant, as in *Pascoe* v. *Turner*. In other cases, it operates negatively. In *Inwards* v. *Baker* the son merely had an equitable right to remain in the bungalow for life or for as long as he wished, and similarly, in *Greasley* v. *Cooke*. The flexibility of the doctrine of proprietary estoppel has allowed for a wide variety of reliefs which are made appropriate to the circumstances surrounding the case. For example, in *Re Sharpe* [1980] 1 WLR 219 the court declared an equitable lien over the property for expenditure incurred, and in *Dodsworth* v. *Dodsworth* (1973) 228 EG 115 where a sharing arrangement had failed to work out, but the plaintiff had died before the action, the defendants were entitled to remain in occupation of the house in question until the money they had expended on it had been reimbursed. In *Griffith* v. *Williams* (above) the daughter was granted a long lease at a nominal rent, determinable upon her death, rather than a life interest. This was in order to avoid the undesirable creation of a strict settlement.

It is apparent from the decision in *Pascoe* v. *Turner* that the relief appropriate is not purely governed by the expectation created. There were other reasons given in the case as to why the defendant was granted the fee simple as opposed to a lesser interest: first, because she had so little capital (if improvements or repairs became necessary on the property, she would be unable to obtain a mortgage to finance them unless she had the fee simple); second the court feared that if the plaintiff (who was described as being 'ruthless') retained an interest in the property he might make excuses to enter it and thereby be a nuisance to the defendant.

The nature of rights arising and of the doctrine of proprietary estoppel

The question to be considered here is whether rights arising out of proprietary estoppel in some, or in all, circumstances give rise to an 'interest in land'. It has already been noted that in some situations proprietary estoppel only acts negatively, giving the claimant, for example, merely an equitable right to remain supported by an injunction, whilst in other circumstances it acts positively, leading to the grant of some established proprietary interest, such as fee simple. Where the doctrine has operated negatively it has not always given rise to an established proprietary interest. For example, in *Greasley* v. *Cooke*, where the former housekeeper had an equitable right to remain in occupation, it is quite clear that this right was only personal to her and did not allow her to participate in the 'investment' or 'capital' value of the land. It was simply a licence to occupy irrevocable by reason of the doctrine of proprietary estoppel.

However, whether the estoppel gives rise to an established proprietary interest or not, it seems that such rights are capable of binding a third party. In *Inwards* v. *Baker* an equitable right to remain was held to be binding on the personal representatives of the licensor's estate, and in later cases it has been consistently assumed that rights arising out of the doctrine of proprietary estoppel bind personal representatives of the legal owner. In *Ives (ER) Investments Ltd* v. *High* [1967] 2 QB 379 a right arising out of the doctrine of proprietary estoppel was held to be binding on a purchaser who bought with express notice of the right, and subsequent decisions have, once again, consistently assumed this to be the case. As yet there is no decision in which a right arising by reason of proprietary estoppel has been held to bind a party with merely constructive notice of such a right, but there are *obiter dicta* to the effect that this would be the case (see *Ives (ER) Investments* v. *High*; *Re Sharpe*).

In conclusion, it seems that even if the application of the doctrine of proprietary estoppel does not give rise to an established proprietary interest, the rights do have some of the characteristics of an 'interest in land' in that they are capable of binding third parties.

The functions of proprietary estoppel

Moriarty (1984) 100 LQR 376 says that the function of the doctrine of proprietary estoppel is to enable the informal creation of interests in land. In other words, where a party has failed to satisfy the written formalities necessary for the creation of a legal or equitable interest in land, but there has been an element of 'detrimental reliance', the doctrine of proprietary estoppel overcomes the need for formalities in order to make the rights enforceable. This view is borne out in many cases, a notable example being *Pascoe* v. *Turner*. Sam Pascoe had assured Mrs Turner that the house was hers, but had not granted a conveyance of the fee simple. As Cummings-Bruce LJ observed: 'If it had not been for S.53 Law of Property Act 1925 the gift of the house would have been a perfect gift.' However, it needs to be noted that overcoming a lack of formalities is not the sole function of proprietary estoppel. It has already been shown that the doctrine sometimes leads to recognition of a right which falls short of an established proprietary interest (see p.307) and, furthermore, even in cases where the function is to overcome a lack of formalities there are often other factors at play. For instance, in *Pascoe* v. *Turner* the order to conveyance the fee simple was also influenced by factors related to the circumstances of the parties (see p.306).

15.8 **Proprietary Estoppel and Constructive Trusts**

The distinction between the doctrine of proprietary estoppel and a constructive trust is a difficult issue as it has not been explored very much by the courts.

In *Re Basham* (*deceased*) [1986] 1 WLR 1498 Edward Nugee QC seems to view the role of the constructive trust, in some cases, as being complimentary to the doctrine of proprietary estoppel. He said that where in a case of proprietary estoppel the expectation related to a right to be given in the future 'it is properly to be regarded as giving rise to a species of constructive trust'. It is submitted that use of the concept of a constructive trust to assist in establishing proprietary estoppel is both confusing and unnecessary. Proprietary estoppel is a sufficiently flexible doctrine in itself (see [1987] Conv. 211 (J Martin) and (1987) 46 CLJ 215 (D Hayton)).

In *Grant* v. *Edwards*, Sir Nicholas Browne-Wilkinson V-C expressed the view that the concept of a constructive trust and that of proprietary estoppel rest on the same foundation, and it is simply that they 'have been developed separately and without cross-fertilisation between them'. This would appear to be a more correct summary of the situation. The concepts would seem to overlap: both constructive trusts and proprietary estoppel involve claimants showing that they have acted to their detriment. The 'common intention' that the claimant should have an interest in the property, necessary for a constructive trust, may arise out of an 'expectation created or encouraged' (as per Lord Kingsdown in *Ramsden* v. *Dyson* (1866) LR 1 HL 129, 170, in laying down the requirements of proprietary estoppel). But proprietary estoppel would appear to be a more flexible and wider concept than the constructive trust in that proprietary estoppel is used to give effect to agreements or the representations other than those giving rise to an interest in property as a co-owner (e.g., it may require a conveyance of the fee simple to the claimant, as in *Pascoe* v. *Turner* [1979] 1 WLR 431) and the requirement of detriment is less stringent. (Proprietary estoppel has been successfully claimed in some cases where the financial detriment has been minimal, e.g., *Pascoe* v. *Turner, Ungurian* v. *Lesnoff* [1989] 3 WLR 840.) Probably the truth of the matter is that the doctrine of constructive trusts in the sphere of acquisition of an interest in the family home is a narrow application or sub-set of the broader principle of proprietary estoppel.

Summary

1 Trusts of the family home arise very commonly. Since 1925, whenever land is held in co-ownership it must be held on trust. This is so even where the co-ownership interest is not expressly stated but arises by means of a resulting or constructive trust.

2 In order to establish an interest in the family home by means of a resulting trust, it is necessary to show a common intention that the claimant is to have an interest in the property. The inference of a common intention is drawn from the contribution of the claimant to the acquisition of the property. The contribution may be direct or indirect (provided it is sufficiently referable to the acquisition of the property), and possibly by way of improvement. There is a specific statutory provision in s.37 Matrimonial Proceedings and Property Act 1970 which provides in the case of *husband and wife*, any improvement to property may give rise to a share or an increased share in the property. The courts determine the size of a claimant's share in accordance with the actual contributions made although, in the case of indirect contributions which may be difficult to ascertain, a strict mathematical approach is not required. Where it is impossible to ascertain the extent of the contributions, the maxim 'equality is equity' may be applied. The share in the property is to be valued at the date when the property is sold.

3 An interest in the family home can also only be established by means of a constructive trust where there is a common intention that the claimant is to have an interest in the property except in the residual category of fraud. For such a common intention to be established there needs to be an express or tacit agreement or representation that the claimant is to have a beneficial interest in the property. In addition it is necessary for the claimant to show that, by reason of the agreement or representation, he or she has acted to their detriment.

4 If a party is unable to establish an interest in the family home on the basis of an express trust, or a resulting or constructive trust, he or she may still be able to rely on the doctrine of proprietary estoppel. This operates where one party acts to his or her detriment by reason of the encouragement or acquiescence of another. The aim of the doctrine is to give effect to the expectations of the party who has acted to his or her detriment, and may, but not necessarily, involve the granting of an interest in the family home. In some cases a lesser right, such as a licence to remain, has arisen under the doctrine.

Exercises

1 Explain the distinction between a resulting trust and a constructive trust in the sphere of establishing an interest in the family home.

2 Explain the distinction between the doctrine of a constructive trust and that of proprietary estoppel in establishing an interest in the family home.

3 Do you consider the test of 'common intention' to be a satisfactory basis for the finding of a resulting or constructive trust in relation to the family home?

4 In 1980 Maurice and Felicity (an interior designer) bought a house. The deposit of £5000 was provided by Maurice's mother. The house, subject to a mortgage, was conveyed into Maurice's name alone as Maurice intimated to Felicity that this was necessary to avoid potential claims of creditors should her business collapse. Maurice paid the mortgage, but Felicity contributed to the household expenses even though Maurice was able to afford to pay for all of these in addition to the mortgage. Felicity applied her expertise as an interior designer to improve the property but the work was carried out by Maurice and Felicity jointly. Maurice and Felicity have now separated and Felicity claims a half-share in the house.
  Advise Maurice.

5 In 1975, Joan (now aged 50) formed a relationship with Dick and moved into 'Wit's End', of which Dick was the fee simple owner. In 1989 the relationship broke down and Dick went to live with his mother. When he left, he told Joan he would always ensure she had a roof over her head. In 1990 Joan, to the knowledge of Dick, spent £2000 on repairs to the roof of 'Wit's End'. Dick is now claiming possession of 'Wit's End' from Joan.
  Advise Joan.

Bibliography and Further Reading

General

Hanbury and Maudsley, *Modern Equity*, 13th edn (Stevens)

Hayton, *The Law of Trusts* (Sweet & Maxwell)

Hayton and Marshall, *Cases and Commentary on the Law of Trusts*, 8th edn (Sweet & Maxwell)

Maudsley and Burn, *Trusts and Trustees (Cases and Materials)*, 3rd edn (Butterworth)

Moffat and Chesterman, *Trusts Law, Text and Materials* (Weidenfeld & Nicolson, 1988)

Parker and Mellows, *The Modern Law of Trusts*, 5th edn (Sweet & Maxwell)

Pettit, *Equity and the Law of Trusts*, 6th edn (Butterworth)

Sheridan and Keeton, *Law of Trusts*, 11th edn (Barry Rose)

Underhill and Hayton, *Law Relating to Trusts and Trustees*, 14th edn (Butterworth)

Chapter 1   Nature of Trusts

Hanbury (1929) 45 LQR 198

Hart (1899) 15 LQR 294

Latham (1954) 32 Can BR

Maitland, *Equity*, 2nd edn

Pollock and Maitland, *History of English Law*

Scott (1955) 71 LQR 39

Waters (1967) 45 Can BR 219

Chapter 2   Implied Trusts

Birks, *An Introduction to the Law of Restitution* (Clarendon Press)

Jones (1968) LQR 472

Mitchell (1951) 4 MLR 136

Sullivan (1979) 42 MLR 711

Chapter 3   Certainty

Crane (1970) 34 Conv. NS 287
Emery (1982) 98 LQR 551
Grbich (1974) 37 MLR 643
Hopkins (1965) 32 CLJ 36
McKay (1974) 38 Conv. 269
Martin (1984) Conv. 304
Matthews (1983) NLJ 913
Matthews (1984) Conv. 22

Chapter 4   Evidential Requirements

Battersby (1979) Conv. 17
Green (1984) 47 MLR 385
Holdsworth (1937) 53 LQR 501
Jones (1966) 24 CLJ 19
Perrins (1972) 88 LQR 225
Sheridan (1951) 67 LQR 814
Youdan (1984) 43 CLJ 306

Chapter 5   Constitution of Trusts

Elliot (1960) 76 LQR 100
Feltham (1982) 98 LQR 17
Garner (1964) 28 Conv. 298
Hornby (1962) 78 LQR 228
Jones (1965) CLJ 46
Lee (1969) 85 LQR 213
McKay (1976) Conv. 139
Marshall (1950) CPL 43
Meagher and Lehane (1976) 92 LQR 427
Walker (1964) LQR 328

Chapter 6   Consequences of Failure to Satisfy Requirements of Trust

Battersby (1979) Conv. 17
Green (1984) 47 MLR 385

Chapter 7 Private Trusts

George and George (1946) 10 Conv. 125
Law Reform Committee, 23rd Report (Cmnd 8733, 1982)
Tiley, *Revenue Law* (1981)
Whitehouse and Stuart Buttle, *Revenue Law*

Chapter 8 Variation of Trusts

Cottorrill (1971) 34 MLR 93
Harris, *Variation of Trusts* (Sweet & Maxwell)

Chapter 9 Management of Trusts

Goodhart (1980) Conv. 333
Hayton (1990) 106 LQR 87
Law Reform Committee, 23rd Report (Cmnd 8733, 1982)
Matthews (1989) Conv. 42
Paling (1973) 37 Conv. 50
Paling (1975) 39 Conv. 318
Samuels (1965) 28 MLR 220

Chapter 10 Breach of Trust

Jones (1931) 47 LQR 330
Jones (1959) 22 MLR 381
Law Reform Committee, 23rd Report (Cmnd 8733, 1982)
Maugham (1898) 14 LQR 159
Stannard (1979) Conv. 345

Chapter 11 Personal and Proprietary Remedies

Birks, *An Introduction to the Law of Restitution* (Clarendon Press)
Goff and Jones, *The Law of Restitution*, 3rd edn (1986)
Goode (1976) 92 LQR 360
Goode (1983) 103 LQR 433
Jones (1968) LQR 472
Khurshid and Matthews (1979) 95 LQR 78
Matthews (1979) 95 LQR 78
Millett (1991) 107 LQR 71
Pearce (1976) Conv. 277
Scott (1966) 7 WALR 463

Chapter 12   Private Purpose Trusts

Cohen (1971) CLP 153
Everton (1983) Conv. 121–5
Gravells (1977) 40 MLR 397
Lovell (1970) 34 Conv. 71

Chapter 13   Unincorporated Associations

Green (1980) 43 MLR 460
Warburton (1985) Conv. 318

Chapter 14   Charitable Trusts

Luxton (1983) Conv. 107   ell)
Picarda (1981) 131 NLJ 436
Picarda, *The Law and Practice Relating to Charities* (Butterworth)
Plowright (1975) 39 Conv. 184
Tudor on Charities, 7th edn (Sweet & Maxwell)

Chapter 15   Trusts and the Family Home

Hayton (1987) 46 CLJ 215
Hayton (1988) Conv. 259
Martin (1987) Conv. 209
Moriarty (1984) 100 LQR 376

Index